GENEALOGY

GENEALOGY

Essential Research Methods

Helen Osborn

ROBERT HALE · LONDON

© Helen Osborn 2012
First published in Great Britain 2012

ISBN 978-0-7090-9197-4

Robert Hale Limited
Clerkenwell House
Clerkenwell Green
London EC1R 0HT

www.halebooks.com

A catalogue record for this book is available from the British Library

2 4 6 8 10 9 7 5 3

Typeset by e-type, Liverpool
Printed in the UK by Berforts Information Press Ltd

Contents

Acknowledgements 7

Foreword 9

Preface 11

1 The Challenges of Genealogy 14

2 Effective Searching – Technique and Belief 35

3 The Records Framework 59

4 Find What You Need 76

5 Has It Been Done Before? 105

6 Analysing and Working with Documents 122

7 Planning and Problem-solving 149

8 Recording Information and Citing Sources 174

9 Organize, Store and Pass On 202

10 Prove Your Research and Meet Your Challenges 238

Recommended Short Reading List 256

Bibliography 257

Other Sources 262

Index 267

Acknowledgements

I would particularly like to thank Sarah McAlpine and Jacky Meigh who have allowed parts of their family history to be reproduced here, and Darryl Lundy for permission to use an image from www.thepeerage.com. I am indebted also to Sherry Irvine and Tom Osborn for reading and commenting on the drafts, and to Guy Grannum. Thanks also go to the many others who have inspired me and acted as my genealogy role models. Finally, a thank you to my mother for always being interested in whatever information I uncover in my research.

Foreword

Sources, and the skills to understand them, are the key tools we need to unearth our family history. Now, with the flourishing of the internet, online catalogues and search tools make it ever-easier to discover sources, both online and in archives, that are of potential use to us as family historians. In turn, the wealth of historical sources that are accessible on the web, both national collections and more local or specialized ones, grows week by week, leaving us in the luxurious position of having ready access to millions of records in which we can search for our ancestors at any time of the day or night that we choose. However, as anyone who has begun researching their family history will know, it's not always (in fact, rarely) as straightforward in practice.

So, we have some sources, but how do we use them to best effect, to thoroughly and accurately trace the generations before us, and how can we tackle the infamous 'brick walls' that may seem to blockade our route back to the past? This is where Helen Osborn's 'essential research methods' come into their own, as she explains how to gain and improve the skills we all need to trace our family history successfully. Family historians often, quite rightly, see themselves as detectives, investigating the evidence from the past to glean information, and a methodical and organized approach to research is essential to ensure that you have identified your ancestors correctly.

Combining case studies and genealogical insights born from years of experience from both her professional research and personal family history, Helen gives practical advice and guidance on how to become a more skilled genealogist. Fluid and authoritative, the chapters take you through each of the stages: from actually understanding the record collections in which you are searching to thinking logically so that you can dispel preconceptions and misinformation and get to the facts; from how to cite your sources to ways in which to organize your notes to make your research intelligible and easy to use and refer to; from creating a pedigree to collaborating online.

The internet continues to make family history an ever more popular hobby, enabling people to track down and search through records that would have been far harder to come by even a decade ago. But rather than simply creating family trees quickly, let's put the resources that the web has made so readily accessible to the best use possible, to create better family histories with full and accurate family trees. Tracing your family history truly is a voyage back to the past, and learning the essential research methods will help to ensure that you have the skills needed for a productive, problem-solving and enjoyable genealogy journey.

Helen Tovey
Editor, *Family* Tree

Preface

Family-history beginners get plenty of useful advice about record sources – what is available and where to find it, and a great deal of encouragement from the media to get out and 'have a go'. By the time most people have got the census and civil registration under their belt, and been bitten by the genealogy bug, it can seem a little late to start questioning the methods used and the extra skills that should be acquired. Researching using mainly the internet has made the tendency to dive in without proper preparation even more prevalent than it was. Only when the cliché of the brick wall frustrates our research are we forced to stop and take stock. It is then that we slowly come to discover how the need for some trusty and half-forgotten old tools of the genealogy trade has never actually gone away. Don't think that because you have been researching for years, you are immune to some common research mistakes. We can probably all hold our hands up to some basic errors at one time or another. Sadly, it is often those who have been happily and steadily working their way backwards over many years who may be the most reluctant to examine the way they go about things, yet there is always room for improvement. For my own part, writing this book has brought it home to me how I really must redouble my own efforts to practise what I preach, if only because it saves time in the long run. This book is therefore intended as a source of help for all those who are researching their family tree online or offline, and are now in need of extra techniques and inspiration in order to help them get over a problem, or to understand how to move on to the next stage in their research. It is not about record sources and what they contain because there are already many excellent books that concentrate on this. What it *is* about is record contexts, methods, documentation and problem-solving.

The book takes English records and English genealogy as its main theme, although I firmly believe that all genealogists will find passages of general use, regardless of where their ancestors came from. The internet means that more and more we are able to research further and further afield, and perhaps eventually develop international standards in the most effective ways of doing research – those effective ways of course include searching online as well as offline. There is plenty of commonality between research under-taken in all the parts of the world where British and Irish peoples have ended up, as well as back in the 'mother countries'.

It is impossible to subtract the practice of genealogy from the legal, historical and geographic framework that surrounds it, and the more I thought about general methods and good standards in genealogy research for this book, the less this framework seemed to go away. We cannot start out with a search in Lithuanian records without knowledge about Lithuania; to do so would be just fool-hardy, yet many British genealogists assume they know about the records framework of Britain simply by virtue of being British. I recently came across a comment made by someone on Rootschat who said that a genealogy course required too much work because it was written about stuff 'before the databases'. He just didn't 'get it'. Good genealogy methods have not been fundamentally changed by everything that has recently come online. It does not require a different set of knowledge. You still need to know about all the stuff that occurred 'before the databases'. I hope this book will help to fill that gap by pointing out the common challenges that we all face, and show you how fundamental an understanding of historical 'stuff' can be.

I have thought long and hard about why there is no good up-to-date book on genealogical methods published in the UK and I have come to the conclusion that the sheer weight of record resources has simply made it much easier for writers to concentrate on describing the records, stating who created them, where they are held and what they contain, rather than wrestle with advanced information about how to do genealogy research. In order to gain the knowledge that work on many, many different family trees provides, one has to have been a professional genealogist. This book, then, tells you what the successful professionals do. Over ten chapters I examine separate themes that have a bearing on the success or failure of all genealogy research.

Chapter 1 provides an overview of the common challenges we all encounter; Chapter 2 explores the search process and examines what an effective search actually consists of; Chapters 3 and 4 look at how you can go about finding the right sources and start to understand their context; Chapter 5 asks you to consider whether someone else has already solved your problem for you, and where you can look to find out; Chapter 6 shows you how to analyse a document to make sure you really are making the most of your sources once you find them; Chapter 7 looks at problem-solving using analysis and a research plan; Chapter 8 is about recording your information correctly; Chapter 9 is all about organization and presenting your results; and Chapter 10 discusses the important question of how to prove family connections by using good proof standards in your research.

If you have ever been in the unhappy and frustrating situation of your research becoming stuck and just cannot see how to solve a problem or find the correct record or entry, you will certainly want to read on.

1

The Challenges of Genealogy

The current enthusiasm for and interest in family history, fed by the media and rapidly accelerated through the internet, actually has its origins more than forty years ago. Many would suggest that the 1970s TV series *Roots* is the place where it all began, although actually there had been a groundswell of interest earlier than this – certainly my own family had always been quite keen on discussing family history at all family gatherings, or so it seemed to me at the time. Wherever it began, a turning point for all hobby genealogists, at least in England, was the arrival in 1984 of the very first magazine catering to their interests, *Family Tree*. By comparison, the current market place is crowded with information, yet very little space is devoted to research problems in a systematic way. By contrast, in the past there was plenty of advice about both problems and pitfalls in genealogy. The writer and genealogist Pauline Litton wrote a whole series of very readable articles in *Family Tree* on this topic.[1] And the budding genealogist who read the magazine, and perhaps took an evening class or two and served an apprenticeship among documents at the old Somerset House or St Catherine's House, very soon had acquired a good part of the skills needed to progress, although they might have taken several years to build a family tree back to 1837. Now with so much online, it does not take half as much skill or effort to build a tree of some sort in a couple of afternoons.

It is true that some problems, such as those specific to searching the census on microfilm, have been solved by internet sites hosting

---

1 Recently reissued as a book: Pauline Litton, *Pitfalls and Possibilities in Family History Research* (Swansong Publications, 2010).

indexes and original images, but by no means all of them. In addition, like a many-headed hydra, the internet cuts out one problem only to bring us more to take its place. The internet age has seen many long-standing genealogical puzzles solved, simply by the power of making millions of bits of data available online, but as fast as these are solved, more arrive. No doubt in the future some current problems will be solved, but yet more new ones created. There are now problems with websites and online indexes, and the very way that databases return results from search queries, to add to the already well-known problems with records and documents and, dare I whisper it, the researcher's own shortcomings.

Yet it seems as though each generation of genealogists is doomed to repeat some of the errors of the past. Genealogy is not easy. In fact, it is deceptively complex, and can be very challenging, but the complexity is hidden from the beginner by a veneer of button-pushing speed brought to us by the internet. It is really important to remember that any one search does not result in an ancestor; it finds a record. Only the careful piecing together of records and analysis of results in the round brings us information about our ancestors.

Each family is unique and, in that sense, each problem or challenge you will face is also unique. Likewise, all researchers are unique in bringing their own experience (or lack of it), their preconceptions and their habits to the research process. But there are areas of commonalty.

I have identified seven common genealogical and research challenges, which I outline here and go on to explore in greater depth throughout the rest of the book. Those challenges are ones of: historical interpretation, naming, geography, indexing, belief, technique and record survival. The first six are all concerned with genealogical method, or lack of it. These can be overcome. The seventh is one we personally can do nothing about: the survival of the record we need in the first place, although there are some techniques for getting round gaps in records.

The great genealogist Anthony Wagner, Garter King of Arms and professional genealogist, stated in his book *English Ancestry*[2] that

---

2 Anthony Wagner, *English Ancestry* (Oxford University Press, 1961), pp. 8ff.

he believed the four things vital to success in any search were: status, record, name and continuity. The first, he explained, was easily understandable. Everybody knows that the ancestry of the elite sectors of society, whether the aristocracy or the comfortable professional middle class, is easier to trace than the working man who may hardly have come into contact with the record-keepers in any meaningful way. The second and third are also self-explanatory. For the genealogist to discover anything, there has to be a record of it. No record, no tracing backwards. The type of name plays a significant part as well. John Smith is a difficult person to identify against a background of a lot of other John Smiths; Humphrey Clinker, however, gives the researcher a fighting chance. Wagner's final point is more subtle. By continuity he means that you may have agricultural labourers with common names, but if they lived in the same parish for many generations and good records survive, then chances of success are high. Likewise, if a particular piece of property is handed down father to son, then the chances of success are higher. On the other hand, you might be pleased to discover your ancestor is called Humphrey Clinker, but if Humphrey has moved around the country, and particularly if he has moved from the country into a big town, the trail could end prematurely. What Wagner does not mention are any techniques for searching effectively, and most other genealogy books also gloss over this as though all that was required was the right name on the right record, job done, and we can all go home and put our feet up. I believe genealogy success is actually far more subtle and complex a process.

(1) The challenge of interpreting the past

Perhaps the first easy mistake that can be made is the expectation that the past is somehow just the same as the present, only in olden-day clothing and without electrical appliances. They may be 'our' ancestors, but they lived in a different world. For example, don't assume that because it is easy to get divorced today, that it was just as easy or common in the past. Don't assume that because adoptions are now subject to formal proceedings, that the same formality existed in the past. Don't assume that a case brought before a civil court today would have been heard in a civil court in the past. Don't even assume that the New Year started on the same day as now. The law in Britain has been constantly changing and evolving since Saxon times; this has affected the records made and kept, the people recorded in those records, and the interpretation we need to put on them. The very best professional genealogists are usually well versed in the legal and administrative system of the period they are investigating and you will need to be as well.

To be a successful genealogist you must assume nothing and be prepared to clear your mind of all preconceptions, while at the same time, and perhaps paradoxically, informing yourself of the historical legal system, the geography of the area, and the historical context. It is hard work, but ultimately worth it because your research will proceed much more smoothly with less stopping and starting, puzzling over problems. And you will become so much better informed about the lives your ancestors led.

If it were not for the archivists, librarians and other keepers of the records of the past, it would be impossible to do any meaningful research. Even more fundamentally, it is only because our society has needed to create a written record in the first place that we have any documentation of the past at all. Thankfully, modern governments and local administrations in the Western world evolved from early times into record-creating and record-keeping ones. Very often this was due to the need for a legal process surrounding the passing of land and possessions from one person to another. Where you attract lawyers, you create records. Where you create records, you create information about people and their activities, and the records that get kept and passed from generation to generation are often the ones that were originally created due to some kind of legal or administrative framework or requirement. There are more surviving records from tax collection or the justice system in the Medieval period than private letters. The cost of creating a record has also played a part in record survival. Parchment documents tend to have a higher survival rate than paper ones as they are not as fragile. Britain is blessed with one of the most complete sets of historical records of any country. In fact, we have an abundance of documentation about the past. This is due no doubt to our mainly stable administration since 1066. The main exception is the period of the Civil War in the seventeenth century, which is notable for creating many problems and gaps for genealogists.

Running alongside this continuous seam of documentation and record-keeping is an ever-evolving legal and governmental system. The law is in a continuing process of flux as new laws are enacted by each administration, old ones repealed, and all the time revisions and precedents are set by the courts. This process of law-making and revision is of great importance to historians and genealogists because it creates the framework within which we need to interpret the records made about our ancestors. Not only might the quirky laws of the past provide us with extra information about our ancestors, but having found, or not found, our ancestor in the records created as a direct result of those laws, we need to know the reasons why they are included or excluded. For example, the hearth tax of the late seventeenth century was an early attempt at a general tax that would include as many people as possible, being a tax on all domestic hearths. You may be able to use it on a simple level just to check whether your ancestors are listed. But on a deeper, more analytical level, when dealing with complex problems and interpreting the records for any given area, you will need to understand both the general exemptions and the local situation. Confusing instructions to the collectors of the tax led to many inconsistencies, and that was before the regulations were changed and local taxpayers challenged interpretations. The lists of people who paid the tax are used very frequently by genealogists, yet the lists cannot simply be removed from the whole background of regulation, local interpretation, exemptions, challenge and reinterpretation, if they are to be used and interpreted correctly. The legal system surrounding the making and granting of wills is another prime example whereby the genealogist needs to be aware of the full historical and legal background before coming to conclusions about his or her family's circumstances based only on the seeming evidence of just the written document. Other records notorious for their ability to spread confusion and misinterpretation are title deeds to property in all periods from the thirteenth to nineteenth centuries.

There is thus a whole hinterland of historical information that lies hidden behind any particular record or document that we may use to build our family tree, and we ignore that hinterland at our peril.

When you are stuck, good questions to ask yourself are these:

- What is the historical period?
- Where am I searching?
- What are the relevant laws for that place at that time?
- What is the status of the people I am looking for?
- Where can I find out more about this place at this time?

When interpreting the past, even individual words can provide problems or lead us into wrong assumptions. An example of this would be the word 'gentleman', perhaps as found on a Victorian census. What exact interpretation is the genealogist to put on this when found in the column under occupation? Was this something that had a precise meaning? How often did people exaggerate themselves in this way? How might a misinterpretation of its meaning put a block in the way of research? In this case, it is knowledge of what is normal for that society at that particular time that we need. Under an older system, the term 'gentleman' did have a more precise meaning. In the Medieval period it meant 'noble', but then came to mean a man of a status between that of a yeoman and a baron. Attempts were made to restrict it to people who could prove they had a right to bear arms, but they failed, and popular use has always been to mean those who did not work with their hands. When found on a census it can mean someone who is of higher status and who has never worked: the old landed gentry. Or it might be used by a professional man who has retired on a small private income, or it might be used by the originally more humble man who has made a bit of money and come up in the world and is now retired. I have found it describing a retired 'Licensed Victualler' as one among many other examples. When found on a marriage certificate it often indicates a snobbish urge by the bride or groom to aggrandize their parents' circumstances.

Thus in interpreting the past, the challenge we face is to both know about and take into account not only a strict definition of the law or societal rules, but also what was the popular usage and actual and accepted practice, because there can often be a difference between legal use and popular use of a term or interpretation of a law.

(2) The challenge of names and identifications

The biggest clue in the whole detective puzzle can also turn out to be the biggest red herring and lead the researcher seriously astray. I am talking, of course, about the surname. The name being researched is one of Wagner's four factors influencing genealogical success in England,[3] and it will be a factor in success in many other countries as well. It can also be a huge challenge.

The good genealogist takes care to read and understand a little about the history of surnames, how they have evolved and changed over time, and how variations of spelling arise. This is as true for any English surname as it is for European surnames, or Jewish surnames. Recent work on surnames and their history has turned up some surprising results and the work of both David Hey and George Redmonds should be sought out, particularly if you have ancestors from Yorkshire and Lancashire. Their recent book on the subject was published by Oxford University Press in 2011 as *Surnames, DNA, and Family History*.[4] The Guild of One-Name Studies has members working on a large number of more rare surnames and their register of members' interests can be checked to see if your own names are among those being researched. Even more recently, work combining surname studies and DNA analysis is also producing some very interesting results. It is a beginner's mistake to think that there could be no genetic connection between people of similar but differently spelled surnames.

A lot of emphasis in genealogy writing is put on making sure you check spelling variations. Most genealogists beyond the basics will

---

3 Wagner, *English Ancestry*, p. 8.
4 George Redmonds, Turi King, and David Hey, *Surnames, DNA and Family History* (Oxford University Press, 2011).

have come across their surname spelled slightly differently (or maybe very differently) both in an index and in an original record. Some of these differences are obvious and easy to spot in a written index: Gardener, Gardiner, Gardner, for example. Others are much more difficult. Surnames that begin with a vowel sound – for example, Izzard – are awkward to look up when they could also start with a Y or an E. The 'zz' sound is often written as 's' or 'ss'.

Names can be mis-indexed and mis-transcribed so that they become almost impossible to find. This happens most frequently when a rare surname is misunderstood to be a common name. For a long time I searched for Maria Julia Rigby, until finally I found the missing information that told me the surname was actually written as Righy, at least for a couple of generations; it may turn out to be something quite else if I manage to trace the family back further – Riggi is now looking like a distinct possibility in fact. Finally, I was able to find her marriage and break down this particular brick wall.

People do, and did, sometimes change their names. This was not very common, but it did happen. I have most commonly found changes of name in the context of people of Jewish or foreign ancestry in London anglicizing a name, or perhaps changing to a completely different name in order to become more British. In these cases it is the fitting together of lots of pieces of the genealogical puzzle that prove that the family were using two names. It is not often understood that, at least under English law, anybody can call themselves anything they want. As long as they don't assume someone else's identity, or use a false name with intent to deceive, they are not breaking a law. I have only come across one case of deliberate assumption of another person's identity in a genealogy case, although a few clients have mistakenly believed that this has occurred in their family. People often assume when they cannot find an ancestor that he/she must have changed his/her name, but all other avenues should be explored first, because it is actually not the most likely thing to have happened.

Probably the biggest challenge to research is a very common name. There are no particularly special techniques that will help and the main method is to research in the same way that you would with uncommon names, but be even more methodical, write everything down, try to concentrate on one problem at a time, and do not make leaps and assumptions about relationships without careful consideration. When you have more than one candidate, you will have to 'kill off' one or more of them, so follow them all up. Who did they marry, what happened to them?

Ironically, for the unsuspecting researcher, uncommon names can lead you into greater misinterpretation and difficulties than common names. It is too easy to jump to conclusions that there must be relationships. I had an example of this recently with a client who had a name that was rare in almost every part of the British Isles, except for two places, and in one of those – which happened to be Cheshire – it was not uncommon at all. His assumption, because he did not himself live in Cheshire and had never or rarely come across anyone with his name, was that his family must be closely related to another family of the same name that had ended up in London. He had even spent a lot of time and money researching the line into Australia, but unfortunately I could find no documentary evidence that any relationship did in fact exist, other than a coincidence of surname. Perhaps he has since managed to get a group of people together with the surname and got their DNA tested as this would be one way to prove conclusively if there was in fact a relationship.

A final challenge of names and identity that is more common than you might think is the propensity of men to take two wives who share the same first name. Possibly a gap between children might alert you; it can be very difficult to spot the two women named Mary Smith and Mary Jones who both married Daniel Johnson, unless you use all of the techniques that will be discussed later in the book.

It is far too easy to jump to conclusions about identity and relationships based solely on coincidence of names, and the challenge for all of us is to make sure this does not happen in our own research.

(3) The challenge of place

All events happen somewhere. Every birth, marriage and death is associated with a place. People live and study in places. It is therefore very important that the genealogy researcher has a good understanding of the geographic area within which these events happened and how that may have differed in the past. As far as the legal framework is concerned, place will also equate to jurisdiction. When searching for a will, for example, you may need to know the ecclesiastical jurisdiction and where exactly the boundaries were, before you can find out where the records are now kept. If your ancestor died in Sussex before 1858, for example, you will need to know whether the parish fell into the Archdeaconry of Chichester or the Archdeaconry of Lewes, or whether it was outside both those jurisdictions and came under the Deanery of Battle or South Malling or Pagham and Tarring or the diocese of Rochester. Each county has a similarly complicated pattern of places where probate might have been proved in the years prior to 1858 when a national probate calendar first came into being. The best published guide to these is still Gibson's and Churchill's *Probate Jurisdictions.*[5] Andrew Millard is building an online supplement to *Probate Jurisdictions* hosted by Durham University at www.dur.ac.uk/a.r.millard/genealogy/probate.php. Both resources should be used together. There is no better example of a very complex geographical picture than in the records created for the purposes of probate.

Place names also change, and places can even come and go completely. Anybody researching in Eastern Europe will know how invasion, conquest and capture changed places, their names, and even the country they were in. But places alter in Britain too, albeit on a lesser scale. A local place name may be used in a document that does not appear in a gazetteer, and place names change in subtle ways over time. You may come across particular problems with Welsh place names. In the past they were anglicized, then they reverted to a Welsh form, so that modern maps show Welsh place names, and now even places that always had English names are being converted to Welsh for the purposes of road signs and maps. Just as place names change over time, so too do industries, employ-

---

5 Jeremy Gibson and Else Churchill, *Probate Jurisdictions: Where to Look for Wills* (Federation of Family History Societies, 5th edn 2002).

ment opportunities, agricultural practices, and of course transport.

Other problems and challenges with place can arise in relation to the continuity of our ancestors in any one location. Some areas suffered constant migrations and it may be necessary for you to find out whether a parish was welcoming to newcomers or contained waste ground that could be moved on to, or whether a parish was closed to incomers with one large landowner controlling the parish administration. Big towns suck in migrants, and travel routes into and out of places may have to be studied. The movement of people between two places may be because a special relationship existed between two towns in the past – for example, they both carried on the same trades, and when work was scarce in one town it was sought in another. People may have migrated for a number of economic reasons. You may be doing research because you know where your ancestors ended up, but not where they came from. The opposite kind of research may be done because you know they disappeared, but where did they go?

I can summarize the hidden importance of place in two ways, because it is not just about finding the name of the village or parish and locating it on a modern map. First, it is important to know about topography. This is the lie of the land, the geographical features that may determine not only how they lived, but where they came from and where they went. Second, it is important to know about jurisdiction. Genealogists need to know who ruled over this place. What area did they rule over, where were the courts held, and where are the records held now?

(4) Understanding and working with indexes

A good name and place index is most definitely the researcher's friend, and even a not very good index can still be helpful. Using an index is more than likely the way we find ourselves looking at the records in the first place. Almost all the genealogy websites you use regularly will include or be based around an index or indexes, and of course every single time you use a search engine to find something on the internet you are also using a complex indexing system, which is designed to find and retrieve words from the billions of words found on the millions of existing websites. If you have an uncommon surname, no doubt you look in every index you can find to see if the name appears. I spent a very happy day or so extracting all my Beachcroft entries from all the printed parish register volumes of the Harleian Society[6] and in the Phillimore parish series when I started out, managing to construct some rudimentary trees and add substantially to my knowledge of the family. But sitting in a library going through the indexes in printed volumes is now an old-fashioned method because so many of our indexes are online.

Apart from those publications that are made by the genealogy community, such as the Harleian Society, the printed index at the back of a book should never be relied upon to be a good index of all the names that may possibly appear in that volume. Often I have been frustrated with an index because it only partly indexes the people in the book; the most common problem being that only the people of higher status are indexed and this is particularly frequent in older volumes.

Commercial online indexes

Indexes are great when they produce the results you need, and frustrating and baffling when they don't. But even a positive result can mask a problem with the index, and when you draw a blank you need to know why. No web-based index is going to draw attention to its shortcomings on the first page. And even if it did, most people wouldn't read it. They want to find people, not bother with detail. Good researchers, on the other hand, learn to work out where the gaps lie. The major problem with any index, whether it is printed at the back of a book, or part of a database such as those that bring us the census returns online, is that there are always mistakes in the indexing process. *Always.* Indexes for major series of records that are rushed online are particularly

---

6 The Harleian Society exists to transcribe, print and publish the heraldic visitations of counties, parish registers or any manuscripts relating to genealogy, family history and heraldry.

suspect. Some of the data websites in the past have been very quick to publish only partly correctly indexed material, and slow to rectify problems. They thereby add an extra layer of complexity for the unwary researcher. The big data websites, and even government archive-backed projects, get the indexing done by hand by the cheapest bidder, who may be in India or the Prison Service.

Indexes by volunteers

The biggest and best-known series of genealogical indexes are held by the Church of Jesus Christ of Latter-day Saints, also known as the Mormons. Their project to index parish registers and other vital records on a worldwide basis became known as the International Genealogical Index (the IGI). Originally available on microfiche, and then on CD, since 2001 the IGI has been online and is free to use. Part of a very ambitious project to make record sources available from all over the world in one place, the IGI also exemplifies many of the problems caused by using indexes to do genealogy research. Because the IGI has been available for a relatively long time, most genealogists are well aware of its pitfalls, but the main trap has to be that it is a very incomplete index. Not only does it not index all the parishes in England and Wales, but within each parish it does not index all the possible available records. The reasons for this are historical and varied, but there are methods for getting round the deficiencies of the IGI (as there are for any incomplete index), including going to the original un-indexed record and reading through it all. The IGI has recently been combined with other indexes held by the Church of Jesus Christ of Latter-day Saints to form a seamless set of searchable indexes all at the Family Search website (www.familysearch.org).

An obvious example is where a partial index leads you astray and an uncommon name gives you unwarranted confidence. If you are searching for a baptism of a Joseph BEACHCROFT in Derbyshire in the 1700s, you might feel confident that with an age range of only one or two years, there would not be too many of them. But what if there are two Joseph BEACHCROFTS of the right age, but only one of them is uncovered by an IGI search? The other candidate is hidden to you in a parish not covered by the IGI.

If the name was more common you would never jump to the conclusion that you had found the correct one, but with uncommon names the likelihood is that you would feel it safe to assume you had found the right person.

Other volunteer-led indexing projects, such as those organized and run through the many Family History Societies, will also suffer from similar problems, albeit on a much smaller scale. Generally, Family History Society members should be reliable as indexers because they will know the local area, but ultimately human error will always come into play and entries may be missed, garbled or otherwise obscured.

The moral of the story is to be very careful when working with both partial indexes as well as indexes that appear to be complete. You may have heard some off-putting stories about the IGI, so much so that you do not trust it at all. But that would be a common mistake of *application*. When faced with an index, the first bit of research needs to be on the index itself, not the people. The careful and effective researcher will ask: Who compiled it? For what purpose? What does it index? How complete is it? Allied to this is knowledge about the version of the index. Many indexes worked on by volunteers appear in different versions. For example, you might make a search in the National Burial Index (available as a set of CDs from the Federation of Family History Societies), but was that search in version 1 or version 3 of the index? Version 3 is more recent and more complete.

(5) Overcoming belief – the sceptical enquirer

Family stories have a whole lot to answer for. Sometimes they contain a germ of truth, slightly changed by each person they have passed through, like a game of Chinese whispers. Many of my clients originally came to me because they wished to prove or disprove a family story. The stories range from the plain snobbish, to the downright mysterious.

Migration stories are widespread, so much so that social anthropologists have studied and found common themes in migration stories that occur worldwide. In other words, your firmly held belief that your ancestor left his homeland under a cloud, in disgrace, due to marrying the wrong girl (tick the one applicable to you), suffered terribly on the journey (actually probably true), and arrived only to have all his belongings stolen, but then was helped by a kind stranger and other variations on this theme, may not actually be true in all its detail, but be a construct later put on the truth. Genealogists starting with family stories that include the migration of one original ancestor should be prepared to take the whole story, or at least parts of the story, with a pinch of salt – in other words, leave aside their belief and turn into a sceptical enquirer. On the other hand, some persistent oral traditions shared by an extended family over a long period often do turn out to be essentially true, although the detail has been lost.

There are a few common genealogy myths that are fairly easily disproved, such as that someone has direct ancestry from a famous person not known to have had any children; or that some unclaimed fortune survives lying in Chancery. Illegitimate descent from royalty is less easy to disprove without the help of DNA testing, but it too is a surprisingly common belief. Even more common is the theme of the pregnant servant girl with the offspring of aristocracy. Perhaps more likely is the pregnant servant with the offspring of the second footman, but of course that is a much less romantic story. Many stories and family beliefs have been fuelled by a stiff upper lip attitude to family. Many people today take the failure of Mum or Granny to speak about the past as a sign that something 'dark' or mysterious must have happened, when in fact the truth is that previous generations did not speak about family matters and certainly not in front of the children. For them, family matters were ordinary, but private. This may or may not put certain barriers in front of your research, but it pays to remember that things that we now discuss quite openly, like marital breakdown or illegitimacy, were taboo subjects in the past.

Another and very interesting aspect of this is that memory is a very slippery thing and can play you false in many ways. This can range from completely forgetting or falsely remembering the year a parent or grandparent died, thus creating a false trail for others to follow when writing up a family tree or making notes on the family history for posterity, to actually inventing something. I have an example of this 'inventing' which I did myself; and if I had not turned into a researcher keen to find out the truth, then this invented story might well have survived to be passed down the generations. The invention started with the adults in my own family talking about family history, being half listened to by my adolescent self. The conversation was about the surname Eden, which is in the family. Was there a connection with Anthony Eden? How common was the name? By the time I had became interested in the story from a research point of view, I had extrapolated the vague memory of this overheard conversation into a memory that my grandmother had said there was a *definite* connection with Sir Anthony Eden. I started out my research into the Eden family with this belief. Of course, it is not true. Our Eden line does not appear to link up in any way with the line of the former Prime Minister.

Belief can also exist in the 'truth' of the written or printed word, and also in the words of our ancestors as recorded on the census or on a certificate. These beliefs can be equally limiting to your research and the only way is to go forwards, trusting nothing and no one until verified with several independent bits of evidence. American genealogists who are tracing lines from early emigrants such as the Mayflower Pilgrims have a great many examples of false belief in the printed word. There are many thousands of words written about some of these early emigrants by genealogists who have not been very concerned with accuracy. They have been published in many types of book and have been picked up and repeated into other books and pedigree charts. Many of these false pedigrees are all over the internet. Suffice it to say that you would do well to disbelieve most printed pedigrees until you can check them against original sources, or unless the author has provided a comprehensive set of citations to *original* sources, and not just secondary works.

(6) The challenge of technique

Problems of technique are nearly always overcome to some extent by constant practice. There are, however, many bad habits that are difficult to shake off. I still sometimes suffer from forgetting to write down all the details of a search, or taking the skimpiest of notes, telling myself that I will remember the detail later – and of course I don't. In so many ways it is 'less haste, more speed'.

In the good old days, when genealogists spent hours sitting at a microfilm reader, the slow pace of turning the handle to read everything page by page meant that it was far easier to remember to stop and write something down. Whereas the speed with which you can jump from result to result using a computer means you have to force yourself to slow the pace down enough to take note of what you are doing. Of course it no longer always means that if you miss something, you might miss it for ever because you may never get that particular microfilm out of its box again and spend the two or three hours needed to go through it. It is more likely that an internet search will be repeated at some point because it is much easier to do it again. However, it is still wasting your time if you do not force yourself to make notes of what you find and where you find it. This is a habit that is hard to come by, but becomes easier as you practise. I discuss why we should all be taking notes in Chapter 8 on documenting your research.

Other problems of technique and habit are easier to overcome. Most beginners to new websites want to search right away and not bother with reading any extra information. But those who are wiser know that it is vital to check what information is being offered, find out the quirks of the search facility, and read all the instructions first. This can save you hours of frustration and turn a negative search into a positive one.

Another problem with rushing to find something is that you probably will not search for all the surname variants you need to try. When you scan a whole page of text, or a printed index in a book, it is usually fairly obvious when a surname variant presents itself. When using an online index it is very easy to forget to search using a number of different variants, or to try some and not others.

Other very common problems of technique include not keeping track of exactly which records you have searched for each ancestor, and not keeping your records in order so that you can easily find them again. It is useful to know when it might be necessary to make a full extract of all occurrences of your surname from a document, and when you can skip this. However, the most common failing is to forget to document your sources as you actually do the research. The importance of correct documentation is discussed further in Chapters 8 and 9.

Most people begin their genealogy journey using the internet and there is no reason not to do so. But you do need to recognize the particular challenges that are inherent in internet searching. The speed with which one can find results means that proper recording of searches and sources can fall by the wayside. Second, there are wide differences in the way website databases return results – and this is not always obvious; and, third, there is also variation in the way online catalogues work. The speed with which some aspects of research can now be accomplished means that many newcomers are taught to have high expectations. Eventually, this will lead to the other side of the same coin: a propensity to give up a search too readily.

I do believe that successful genealogists have a certain type of personality. They tend to be methodical, analytical, painstaking, organized and tidy, and perhaps stubborn in their searches. If your character type is the opposite to this, then your own personal challenge will be to recognize this fact and work hard to remember to write things down, not get distracted, keep your records in order, and do all those other things that do not come naturally to you.

Finally, another important technique is the ability to find out exactly what survives that will be relevant to your research and where to access it. We look further at this in Chapter 4.

(7) The challenge of record survival

There is no doubt about it, the records you need in order to take all your ancestral lines back to the next generation, and the one beyond that, and so on and so on, do not survive.

Great Britain is blessed with some of the most record-rich archives in the world. We should be very grateful to past record-keepers who stored the records away in the first place and didn't just use them to light a fire. We are also lucky with our climate which, although damp, at least is not hot and steamy with a subsequent rapid rate of decay. Once in an official archive or repository, the standard of care has usually been good, but records suffer from many problems before they get to the state of being accorded the status and protection of archives. While they are in day-to-day use by the people who created them, they of course are subject to all the normal wear and tear and to being torn, having ink spilled over them, suffering poor storage conditions in the various cellars in which they are almost automatically allocated, and so on. Just one or two stories from the record-keeping past will show you how precarious a journey most of our records have had.

Parish registers are acknowledged as being among the most useful and important sources for genealogists, and as they were brought into being in 1538, they can enable us to trace families right back to the mid-sixteenth century. However, many parish registers have been lost entirely due to being kept in their original parish chests from the date of their creation, and left to the vagaries of mice, rats, flood and civil unrest, let alone the actions of the parish priest who might decide to have a good clear-out and burn the whole lot. A survey undertaken as far back as 1831 showed the then state of the situation, with many older registers gone for ever. In the late nineteenth century an attempt was made by several campaigners to organize the centralization of parish registers, and if this had been successful many subsequent losses would not have occurred. The pace of destruction and loss did not slow down until well on into the twentieth century when historic parish registers began to be deposited with the County Record Offices on a large scale. In the 1960s and 1970s it was still common to have to physically visit the parish of one's ancestor to see the registers still in their original location; and some parish priests even today have refused to give up custody. The very fact that, despite all the problems inherent in their handling and care over many centuries, so many of them do survive is probably testament both to the sturdiness of the parish chest and a general feeling that many incumbents have had for the history and records of their parish.

Government records have certainly not been immune from

damage and loss either; well-known examples include part of the census returns, some of which were stored in less than ideal conditions in an attic in the Houses of Parliament. The whole parish of Paddington, and part of Kensington, as well as other places in Middlesex and large parts of North Wales, is missing from the 1841 census. The 1851 returns for Manchester and the surrounding area suffered extensive water damage and many parishes in Essex and some parishes from Cambridge, Suffolk and Dorset are completely missing for 1851. Many gaps also occur in the 1861 returns.[7]

Well-known examples of records lost during bombing in the Second World War include about two-thirds of soldiers' documents from the First World War and the very sad loss in 1942 of all probate records for the diocese of Exeter, including most of the pre-1858 wills and administrations for the counties of Devon and Somerset. While the loss of the soldiers' documents is very sad, for most people it does not put an absolute block in the way of further research backwards, but the loss of the Devon probate material is a much more serious gap for all of us with Devon ancestry and can be a serious problem in your research.

If it is lost, it is lost. Maybe other methods, or simply looking for other records that hold similar information, can help you get round the absence of a record. But where whole sections or series of records are lost, such as happened in what are known as the 'burnt counties' of some American states, then there can be serious problems and the research stops. Through persistent and assiduous work, people with ancestry in those burnt counties have devised some excellent ways of making sure they get over the known gaps. These techniques are useful to all genealogists wherever they are researching and we will look further at how to get round the problem of missing records in the coming chapters.

These, then, are my seven genealogical challenges, the seven gauntlets that I throw down for you to take up and reflect on how they

---

7 You can find out exactly what is missing from the census returns on the website findmypast at www.findmypast.co.uk/helpadvice/knowledge-base/census/index.jsp.

may relate to your own research: your interpretation of the past, the names you research, the places where your ancestors lived, the indexes you use, your beliefs, your techniques and, finally, the actual survival of records.

2

Effective Searching – Technique and Belief

I n the previous chapter, I said that the genealogist Anthony Wagner had given us four elements that need to be present for a successful search: name, status, continuity and record. What Wagner did not mention, or assumed perhaps, was that you also need the ability to make effective searches.

Dealing with 'brick walls'

T he term 'brick wall' is peppered throughout genealogy articles as if we all know its precise definition. The genealogical community needs to reconsider exactly what this cliché means and to whom, because your brick wall might not be my brick wall. Brick walls are problems in genealogy research that bring the researcher to a sudden dead end. They block the path backwards or prevent any further research being done. Brick walls are only met when you have truly exhausted *all* the available options. Most people have what they term brick walls in their research, but they simply have not searched widely enough or they lack the knowledge of extra sources and methods they could use. In those cases, the walls are not really made of bricks, but straw.

Over and over again, I meet people who have built walls in their minds. They refuse to search more widely because 'that could not have happened', or a family story is perhaps persuading them only to search in one place or within a certain time period. What they need to do is simply to forget what they *think* they know and only start from what they really do know. A related problem is where the research has been blocked because of deficiencies in the researcher's own search techniques, particularly common using the census without checking against civil registration records. They then wish to engage a professional researcher to look at obscure or difficult sources, believing they themselves have done the obvious things, when they have not. Many times I have had to persuade a client that a proper search among the familiar sources would be a better idea. But this advice is hard to take, because it involves recognizing that your technique is lacking, and nobody wants to pay for work that they think they have already done.

I generally find that when people write to me with their problems, they fall into four categories; sometimes all four are present:

1 A lack of knowledge of sources.
2 Self-imposed limits on thinking – either being wedded to a family story or suffering from a lack of imagination.
3 Not searching in an effective manner.
4 Record sources are missing and there may be a genuine dead end.

Amanda Bevan acknowledges this when she says, 'A successful search looks in the right place in the right way: you may not find what you want (not everything survives) but you won't miss it by error. Sometimes a negative answer is the best you can get – but it is far better than missing what was there all the time simply because you were looking in the wrong way.'[8]

Genuine brick walls, those made with sturdy bricks, should only be met in research when the record sources are seriously deficient. Or, and this is going to be rare, there has been a deliberate attempt by the subject or family themselves to change names and identities. Every other kind of brick wall is a deficiency in the search. It is true that there are some other kinds of brick walls,

---

8 Amanda Bevan, *Tracing Your Ancestors in The National Archives, The Website and Beyond* (The National Archives, 7th edn 2006), p. 2.

where you have a candidate for an ancestor, but just can't work out if he or she truly does belong in your tree. Or, you may have too many candidates and cannot find the evidence you need for positive identification. This may be the case if you have common first names in a parish that has many people of the same surname. There are some techniques for dealing with these particular cases that we will look at later on.

To make sure you don't fall into the first two problem categories above you need to educate yourself about likely sources, where they are held, what they consist of, and how they were made. This is a continuing process and takes effort. We look more at finding sources in the next two chapters and in the chapter on problem-solving. To get over the hurdle of self-imposed limits, I have some suggestions that should help in this chapter and we look at problem-solving using planning in Chapter 7.

I start with a very simple example of self-imposed limits on thinking that had to be broken down before an effective search could take place. This example demonstrates how confidence and knowledge enable effective searching by looking in detail at the search for one death registration. At each stage, the thought processes involved are examined.

Sarah was looking for the death of her grandfather, Edward Price. She knew that her grandmother had died in 1967, and since she had heard very little about her grandfather and had never met him, the assumption was that he must have died a long time before her grandmother. His marriage to her grandmother was located in 1911; her mother's birth was found a few years later. She had no idea what had happened to her grandfather, although divorce from her grandmother was a possibility. His own birth certificate showed that he had been born in 1882 and his family lived in one of the poorer parts of Kensington, London.

Sarah's research thinking then went like this: 'Let's get death certificates for Edward Prices who have died in the Kensington area.' A number were purchased from the period 1919–30. None was correct. The GRO indexes were re-examined for the period 1930–45; a few people matched in age, but not location. Those certificates were sent for – again, not right. At this point, a full extract of *all*

Edward Price deaths was not being made, just those in Kensington or the North London districts.

The research became stymied, and Sarah turned to family rumour. There was a family story about him perhaps being in Belgium. So the Overseas GRO indexes were searched. Nothing. Could the divorce indexes held by The National Archives at Kew help? They could not. There were no Edward Prices in the indexes with a wife of the correct name.

The thinking continued to be, 'Well, he must have died in the period 1920–45 because my mother never spoke of him and didn't see him at all after she was a teenager.'

A re-examination of the GRO indexes took place. This time a better extract was made, matching all the ages at death and looking at all the areas in England and Wales. This process took some time and the certificate costs were mounting up. Sarah was becoming increasingly frustrated. I asked her to consider widening the GRO death index search beyond 1950. She was very reluctant; there were a lot of Edward Prices, and anyway how could he have been alive after she, herself, was born? Surely her mother would have known?

Finally, somewhat in desperation, she did a much lengthier search, and with relief found his death registration in 1962. The death was registered by a 'brother in law' – an unknown person. A search for a marriage ensued. This was found in 1925, and it transpired that for nearly forty years her grandfather had lived with a second 'wife' only 10 or 15 miles from his first wife, his daughter, and his granddaughter Sarah, whom he had never met. Astonishment from Sarah, and a really good example of a genealogy problem solved with the use of something that was obvious.

I have chosen Sarah's story because it neatly exemplifies many of the problems that are found in genealogy, but that are almost always overcome with an *effective* search. Common names throw up a high number of candidates who need to be eliminated one by one. The expense of sending away for death certificates (and the inevitable wait while they are sent to you) means that a mental block about costs and time starts to play on the mind. The researcher looks for short cuts. In this case, divorce records, overseas records. The length of the search, when contrasted with the ease of other similar searches in the civil registration indexes, also became off-putting. It used to take a lot of time to make extracts from the GRO indexes before there were any online indexes, so each quarter had to be searched, entries written down, and so on. A sixty-year death search in the original GRO death index books held at St Catherine's House, and then the Family Record Centre, could take an inexperienced searcher perhaps half a day, and was also very boring. This put up a huge barrier to effective searching. Even with online indexes, too many possible candidates can put you off-track looking for quicker ways to get at the information.

The effective researcher is used to being disciplined in his or her approach. No matter how wearisome, if you need to do a very long search, you need to do it. Just get on with it. The five hours you spend on a task now may save you so much other work in the long run.

Another aspect arises from the story. Sarah's trust in the indexes was being shaken and she began to wonder how reliable they were. It is quite true that there are registrations missing from the national indexes, most notably discovered and commented upon at length by Michael Whitfield Foster in his 1998 book, *A Comedy of Errors*.[9] There are certainly deaths that I have been quite unable to find. In this instance, it seemed very unlikely that Edward Price would be wrongly indexed by name, because the more ordinary and common the name, usually the more readable it is – even with bad handwriting. And the possibility that he had been missed from the GRO index and yet would appear in the local registrar's indexes was also only slight. The researcher must learn to trust any index up to the point where the whole index has been searched effectively. In this case, it had not. Abandoning an incomplete search for a one in a hundred chance that the right entry is missing or mis-indexed is bad practice, and can lead to far more work than is necessary.

The amateur approach results in a reluctance to expand a search

---

9 Michael Whitfield Foster, *A Comedy of Errors or The Marriage Records of England and Wales 1837–1899* (published privately, 1998; ISBN: 0-473-05581-3).

into a different time period, due to self-imposed limits. The professional research approach would have been to do a death search for Edward Price up to the age of 100, making a complete extract of all people who fitted the name and age within one or two years for the whole country. Once this was done, it would then have been more obvious which registration was the correct one, since it most clearly matched everything known about Edward Price, including name, age and location. It is a very good idea always to expand a search, even if this is a wearisome task.

I have another illustration of this block to thinking arising from the search for a long-lost friend of my mother. She had wanted to find this friend, someone who had been at school in London with her. But the problem was, 'She married an Australian and went to Australia, so it will be impossible.' I kept hearing the refrain, 'How I wish I could find my friend who went to Australia.' Finally, I decided to do something about it.

As this friend had a fairly unusual first and second name, I thought it possible I could track her down. The starting point was the friend's marriage certificate which gave me her married name. I decided to forget that the friend was said to have gone to Australia, so I searched for the birth of children to this couple in the UK. Two daughters were relatively easily located; both were born in London in the 1960s. I surmised that the friend had not in fact gone to Australia after all. I looked for the daughters' marriages, and found them in the 1980s. The whole family was obviously in London all the time. Finally, and this time with a stroke of luck, I used Google to track down a business that involved the friend, in London, where she was still working despite being over the official retirement age. My mother and her friend were absolutely delighted to be put back in touch with each other, and their friendship continues. All the time they were just 30 miles apart.

This story is a very clear example of *supposed* knowledge that turns out not to be true. Every good professional genealogist will tell you never to trust what people say. The only way to get at the truth is via the records.

Thus an *effective* search must start by clearing the mind of any of these impediments to clear thinking.

What exactly is an effective search?

The main theme of this chapter is effective searching. We have looked at two examples where self-imposed limits prevented a search from being effective, or from getting started in the first place. Can we go on to define what an effective search consists of?

An effective search is systematic; it does not break off halfway through and it covers all the bases. An effective search is also properly documented so that the researcher knows exactly what has been covered and what has not. An effective search recognizes that there will be negatives. People are not always found where you expect them to be. The effective researcher learns to use those negatives – in fact, to *trust* that the negative search will eventually lead to the right information. A lack of trust in the research process inevitably means that searches are repeated, thought processes go round in circles, and brick walls are built up. An effective search is objective, even forensic; it does not rely on hearsay evidence. How we go about building that trust into the research process is a theme we return to in the chapters on documentation and proof later in the book.

The cry of a 'brick-wall researcher' is always 'Where else can I look?' Hardly ever does someone ask, 'What could I be doing better?' Sometimes the answer as to where else to look is actually 'at your *methods*' and back where you have *already* looked, hard though that message is to hear.

Effective searching *always* includes some of the following, and occasionally has to include *all* of the following:

- Starting from what is absolutely certain.
- Analysis of the problem.
- Examination of original records.
- Reading and understanding records properly.
- Recording accurately where information has come from.
- Knowledge about indexes and their gaps and problems.
- Searching for all possible spellings and misspellings of the names.
- Width and length (across time, geographic space and record series).

- Not allowing family stories or preconceived ideas to override doing the obvious.
- Expanding a search sideways into collateral lines.
- Combining sources together.
- Using techniques to narrow down a search.
- Checking other people's un-cited research.
- Understanding the historical and legal context.
- Method.
- Persistence.
- Rationality.
- Deduction and logical thinking.

Finally, an effective researcher is always balancing probability against possibility. What is probable and what is most likely are the routes to be taken first. It was probable that Edward Price had died in England, yet it was possible he had died abroad. It was possible that the index was faulty, but this was not as likely as him actually just living longer than believed.

Let's go back and examine the problem of Edward Price's death, and take some of the stages from the above list. Starting the search with what is absolutely certain gives us two pieces of information. First, he was last found in documentary evidence in 1915, being named on his daughter's birth certificate; second, family members still alive had never met him and did not know what had happened to him. He was born in 1882, was last known to be alive in 1915, and could have survived – albeit unlikely – until the 1980s.

This was certain and these facts were the starting point.

Some theories about him had rushed into this information vacuum; these had included divorce and disappearance abroad. The good researcher has to think about which sources to use to find out what happened to people who seem to disappear from the records – in this case, where and when he died. At the time when the original searches were taking place, the GRO death indexes were online, but only quarter by quarter, although some relevant years were available at FreeBMD (www.freebmd.org. uk). The researcher always needs to ask, 'Am I looking at original records, or am I looking at indexes or copies?' In this case, the search was going to be partly on original indexes (although filmed and made available online) and partly in an online index. A good understanding of the gaps and drawbacks in the online index was required. A quarter by quarter search was required to cover those gaps.

Where could a search have been made quickly for his death using online indexes allowing us to search by name? Two immediate answers come to mind: the free indexes at FreeBMD and the First World War indexes and records hosted by Ancestry.co.uk and findmypast, as there must have been at least a possibility that he was called up in 1916 and died in the First World War.

Two problems could immediately occur if he had not been found in either of these sources; the first is that he died during the First World War, but his record had not survived, and that was perfectly possible since only about 30 per cent of soldiers' records do survive. The second is that he died outside of the war period, but the free online indexes did not cover the correct time period.

However, the name Edward Price is so common that there are in fact many people in the indexes who are matches on name alone. A simple technique to deal with this is the *extract*. In making an extract it is necessary to be accurate in recording what has been found. The idea is to write down every event or person that could be correct and successively to narrow down the possibilities to a handful of possible candidates. In the case of the GRO death indexes, the only clues we have to the correct death certificates are Name, Registration District and Age at Death. However, since we didn't know where Edward might have died, the only points we actually had were age at death and name.

The intention is to end up with a list where close matches can be examined against each other, as in the following chart. Because you start with the most complete list you can possibly make using this source, you know you can trust it and can now begin an elimination process. All obviously wrong ones can be quickly eliminated: first the children, then all the men who are more than five years too young or too old. This leaves a list of possible candidates that can be further winnowed on age and location.

An extract of Edward Price deaths for March 1914 to June 1915 from the General Register Office indexes found online at FreeBMD (www.freebmd.org.uk)

	Age	**District**	**Vol**	**Page**
March quarter 1914				
Price Edward	62	Chester	8a	543
Price Edward	88	Clun	6a	806
Price Edward	81	Droitwich	6c	267
Price Edward J	62	Bridgend	11a	1139
Price Edward R	0	Merthyr T.	11a	977
September quarter 1914				
Price Edward	0	Bethnal G.	1c	217
Price Edward	76	Birkenhead	8a 5	45
Price Edward	5	Prescot	8b	951
Price Edward A	67	Bromley	2a	537
Price Edward J	34	Kings N.	6d	17
Price Edward M	63	Marylebone	1a	95
December quarter 1914				
Price Edward	62	Kings N.	6d	6
Price Edward	43	Croydon	2a	394
Price Edward	89	Wolverh'ton	6b	681
March quarter 1915				
Price Edward	0	Llanelly	11a	1632
Price Edward	72	Bury	8c	713
June quarter 1915				
Price Edward	86	Ecclesall B.	9c	589
Price Edward	68	Ruthin	11a	578
Price Edward	1	Mansfield	7b	89
Price Edward	70	Edmonton	3a	729
Price Edward	2	Greenwich	1d	1121
Price Edward	1	Bedwellty	11a	143
Price Edward	55	Bedwellty	11a	190
Price Edward	48	Holywell	11b	289

By continuously extracting for up to 100 years after birth, the researcher will satisfy the 'width and length' part of our effective searching criteria.

Another technique that works well with deaths, but also any two lists of people that have elements in common, is to use one source to *discount* another source. We could have taken all those Edward Price deaths and matched them against probate information from the National Probate Calendar, because slightly more information is given in the calendar than in the death indexes from the General Register Office. For any Edward Price death that could be matched against a probate calendar entry, where the calendar entry could definitely show that this was the wrong Edward Price, it would then be discounted. In the Edward Price case it would not have worked as a technique, because the information Sarah had was so limited, but it does work when you know the names of other family members or spouses who would be expected to be named as executors or administrators of an estate, since the probate calendars shows this information.

Another technique used by all competent researchers for narrowing down a big list of possible candidates within an online index is *name and date combining*. This means using a combination of two or more names and/or dates to arrive at a narrowed-down list of candidates. It is particularly effective in census searches. For example, there may be many hundreds of girls called Alice in Stepney on the 1851 census, but when you progressively narrow down the search to any girl called Alice who was born in either 1849, 1850 or 1851 with parents William and Mary Ann, the choice narrows dramatically. Then you begin to realize just what a great tool name combinations can be, either in conjunction with age information and sometimes without. There are only forty occurrences of the above combination across the whole of England and Wales in 1851. Try it for yourself using a census search for your own first name, in combination with just one of your parents' names or both parents' names.

The story of Henrietta Hobbs and Frederick Hertzell

The next example shows how the *combining of a number of different sources* helped to get to the bottom of a mystery about names.

My client had come to me because she could not find her great-grandmother's birth in London around 1859 – not a very uncommon problem to encounter. There are a number of reasons why people cannot be found in the GRO birth indexes at that date and a big city is an easy place to avoid the census enumerator as well. This search, however, illustrates the use of source combination and whole-family reconstruction to get at a surprising truth. The name being searched for was Henrietta Hobbs. Although her father's name and occupation were known, nothing else was known about Henrietta's past.

The only documentary evidence for Henrietta's age was her marriage certificate and the 1901 census where she was found with her husband. She simply could not be found anywhere else. There is not a great deal of choice in the GRO indexes for girls with that name, and even fewer candidates appear when using online census indexes.

Gradually, by using a combination of age and place and variations on a first name, an unmarried Henrietta was found living with her brother and sister-in-law and another brother in 1881. She had been mis-indexed as Henritta. This was the first breakthrough. Using the information from the 1881 census, the marriage of this brother and his wife was found, first in the GRO indexes and then in the original parish register. The father's name and occupation on the brother's marriage entry matched that on Henrietta's own marriage certificate and was unusual enough to confirm that Henrietta had been correctly identified on the 1881 census and that she was with two brothers, William and Arthur. The discovery of the marriage of the second brother, Arthur, helped as well. At this stage the search process needed to look at Henrietta's siblings for both confirmation and clues.

So, from a mystery person who had no known brothers and sisters, whose birth could not be found and where the main evidence was only one marriage certificate, a family picture was emerging. This technique is the start of a process known as whole family reconstitution, where all members of a family are followed through. This enables a large amount of evidence to be gathered.

On 2 November 1878, William Frederick Hobbs, Clerk, and Susan Rainbow married at the parish church of Hackney. The marriage entry clearly shows the father of William as William Frederick

Hobbs, Dock Sampler. The witnesses are members of the Rainbow family.[10]

On 17 January 1885, Arthur Hobbs and Mary Ann Lay married at St Barnabas, Homerton; Arthur is shown as being 24, a Silk Salesman, and his father is William Frederick Hobbs, Dock Sampler (deceased).

One of the witnesses is William Fd Hobbs (his brother).[11]

These two men were surely brothers to Henrietta, as all three of them have fathers who match the name and occupation exactly, and this is the piece of evidence that allows the research in the census to be more certain.

The 1881 census showed William Frederick Hobbs and his wife Susan (Susannah), together with brother Arthur and sister Henrietta, (indexed as Henretta) all living together at 64 London Road, Clapton.[12] The house was shared with another family. The fact that a young married man would be providing houseroom to an unmarried brother and sister is a clue that possibly something had happened to the parents. Normally, of course, one would expect unmarried women at this date to live with their parents, or to be living somewhere else as servants. When I returned to the search, I bore this hypothesis in mind and did not necessarily expect to find Henrietta's parents together or still alive.

An extensive search within the census returns for a William Frederick Hobbs, a Dock Sampler, failed to find him. However, the 1871 census did have a family that fitted very well with what was now known about Henrietta, William Frederick and Arthur.

This showed at 11 John Street, Homerton: Mary Ann Hobbs, widow aged 43, with unmarried children, Alice Mary, aged 20, Eleanor, aged 18, William Fred, aged 16, Henrietta (here Henritta), aged 11, and Arthur, aged 9.[13]

I had so far failed to find any of the Hobbs family on the 1861

---

10 London Metropolitan Archives, Saint John at Hackney, Hackney, Register of marriages, P79/JN1, Item 086. Online at Ancestry.co.uk
11 London Metropolitan Archives, Saint Barnabas, Homerton, Register of marriages, P79/BAN1, Item 014. Online at Ancestry.co.uk
12 RG 11/304/71 p.38.
13 RG 10/326/86 p.24.

census, using any of the information that I now had, but I needed to do this to complete the final missing link to connect these children with a father, William.

Evidence from the census for Henrietta's birth date and place was therefore this:

1911 – Aged 51 born Mile End
1901 – Aged 41 born Stepney
1891 – Aged 31 born Bow
1881 – Aged 21 born Mile End
1871 – Aged 11 born Mile End

This is remarkably consistent and gave Henrietta a birth year of either 1859 or 1860. Because of this consistency of age and place, I trusted the information. The census was taken at the end of March or start of April each year, so her birth date was slightly more likely to be 1859. Her birth should have been registered in the district of Mile End Old Town, although Poplar and Stepney were also possibilities.

A search of the GRO indexes at freebmd.org.uk gave no Henrietta Hobbs in Mile End, Poplar or Stepney and none of her brothers and sisters either. A country-wide search for Henrietta Hobbs in the same indexes for the period 1858–61 inclusive resulted in only four entries:

Henrietta Jane Hobbs, March quarter 1858, Newington, 1d 240
Henrietta Hobbs, September quarter 1858, Shoreditch, 1c 183
Henrietta Hobbs, March quarter 1860, Bideford, 5b 137
Henrietta Eliza Hobbs, September quarter 1860, Shoreditch, 1c

If her brothers and sisters could have been identified in the GRO indexes in Shoreditch, then the story would have turned out differently. If the Shoreditch registration was correct, then she would be the only one in the family to have her birth registered, as there is no William Frederick Hobbs in the period 1853–6 anywhere in the country, or Arthur Hobbs or Alice Mary Hobbs. Therefore it struck me that it was unlikely this was her.

We now come back to the problem of what had happened to William Frederick Hobbs, Dock Sampler. There was no man with this name in the death indexes or in the census. It seemed most likely at this point that he was registered as just plain William Hobbs.

One other bit of family information was useful, which I have not yet mentioned. Henrietta and her husband had emigrated to Australia, but she had remained a staunch church-goer in the Anglican tradition. It thus seemed very odd that someone who was known to have been strongly Church of England would not have been baptized during her time in London. I found a Henrietta Hobbs baptism in the indexes now maintained by Ancestry.co.uk for 1871 at St Barnabas, Homerton. Knowing that St Barnabas was a church that had featured in two marriages in the family, I decided to take a further look, even though Henrietta would have been aged 11 or 12 at the time.

This was a breakthrough for several reasons, but mainly because it changed my thinking about the family. Four of the Hobbs children had all been baptized together on 6 February 1871. Their births are also noted beside the baptism date:

Alice Mary Ann (born 20 September 1850)
Eleanor (born 27 January 1853)
Henrietta (born 3 June 1859)
Arthur (born 20 January 1861)

The parents were shown as Frederick and Mary Ann Hobbs, of 11 John Street; father's occupation was 'Sampler'.[14]

The matching of four of the children's names, the address at John Street, which appeared before, and the father's occupation were now all very good evidence that this was the same family. You will remember that 11 John Street was where Mary Ann and the children were living at the time of the 1871 census.

So why were the children being baptized so late in life? I will come on to that.

---

14 London Metropolitan Archives, Saint Barnabas, Homerton, Register of baptisms, P79/BAN1, Item 003. Online at Ancestry.co.uk

A further extensive search of the 1861 and 1851 census indexes ensued. Armed now with more precise knowledge about the family, including birth dates and the fact that William Frederick senior appears to have been known only as Frederick, I eventually found a family on the 1861 census that matched in every respect except one, the surname. At first, I wondered whether the census enumerator had made a mistake with the surname, but it later transpired not:

7 Clayton Cottages, Stepney

Frederick Hirtzels, aged 42, Pensioner E I Company, born
    Middlesex, Stepney [E I is East India]
Mary Ann, wife, aged 33, Laundress, born Whitechapel
Alice, daughter age 11, born Stepney
Elinor, daughter age 9, born Stepney
Henrietta, daughter age 6, born Stepney
Arthur, son age 6 months, born Stepney[15]

You may feel that this is just a coincidence with regard to the children's names and ages, but in fact it would be very rare indeed to have two families with parents' names and children's names matching so completely, together with ages. And, knowing that Hertzell (and its variant spellings) is a German name and that people of German origins had a tough time in London at certain times, I considered it most likely that the surname had been changed from Hertzell to Hobbs to anglicize it, or in some way to alter their identification. This was my theory and I now needed to prove it with more documentary evidence.

I searched for Frederick Hertzell in the indexes of the Families in British India Society and found what I believed to be an entry for him. He had fought in the Indian Mutiny and been injured, and this is why he is shown as a pensioner of the East India Company in the census.

The entry on an Indian Mutiny medal roll reads:

---

15 RG 9/295/148 p.26.

Frederick Hertzell, private in the 2nd Bengal European Fusiliers, severe wound to left elbow Delhi 9 July 1857, invalided to Europe.[16]

I then found them on the 1851 census, this time indexed as Herlgeer:

15 John Street, Mile End Old Town

Frederick Hertzell, 33, Sampler, West India Docks, born
    Stepney
Mary Ann, wife 24, born Whitechapel
Alice, daughter 6 months, born Stepney[17]

The 2nd Bengal European Fusiliers was a regiment raised by the East India Company in 1854, and after the 1857 Mutiny, when the East India Company ceded authority over India to the British government, that regiment became the 104th Foot. Obviously, Frederick joined up after 1854 and left in 1857 when he was injured.

I was still very troubled as to the exact date Frederick died, why his son William Frederick had not been baptized as Hobbs and other factors, but I was able to quickly find all the children's births registered under the name Hertzell, not Hobbs, in the General Register Office indexes. I sent off for Henrietta's birth certificate and waited for it to arrive. I simply could not find a marriage between a Frederick Hertzell and anybody called Mary Ann. If Frederick had been at the baptism of his children, then he must have died in a very short time period between 6 February 1871 and the date of the census that was taken on 2 April 1871. I even decided to look at everybody called Frederick who had died in the March quarter in that district. Nothing was found.

As I was doing some very intensive searches among all the indexes held at Ancestry.co.uk for anybody with the name Frederick Hertzell and other names that sound similar, I came across two entries for someone of that name in the Criminal Register indexes

---

16 The Indian Mutiny Medal Roll (British Forces) transcribed by Kevin Asplin, IOR Reference 355.134.
17 HO 107/1553/841 p.20.

in The National Archives series HO 26 and HO 27. This led me to investigate these further. Here was a man with the same name convicted of unlawful wounding in 1865–6. Had a criminal conviction led Mary Ann to change the name of the children to Hobbs? This suddenly seemed a distinct possibility. She would have been aware the census was fast approaching; Alice was 21 and perhaps needed to get married, giving proof of her name; the shame of the conviction – all these things would have preyed on a mother's mind. There was no necessity for both parents to be present at a baptism; indeed, the vicar may have known of the circumstances and been sympathetic. In addition, under the law at the time, the baptism record was taken as being proof of your true name.

I decided that Frederick had not died by the time of the 1871 census, but was in fact in prison, so I made another search on the 1871 census for him, this time using the surname Hertzell. I found him in Dartmoor Prison.

This then led me to look for a newspaper report of the case and, with good luck due to the rare name, I immediately found it reported in *The Times* on 11 March 1865. It made sad but interesting reading, not least because it confirms that all the children were in fact illegitimate. Whether Henrietta ever knew the whole story behind this is hard to tell. It seemed that Mary Ann Hobbs was never Mrs Hertzell, which explains why I could not find a marriage, and why the vicar would have been quite happy to baptize the children into what was actually their true name anyway – Hobbs. This is assuming he knew the whole sorry story, which he may not have done.

The case of Henrietta shows how effective combining different sources can be and how necessary it is to look at more than one person in order to build a better picture and to gather extra information on all the known family members.

Sometimes the known facts about a family, combined with other people's muddled research, and disinformation spread on the internet, makes proper analysis of a problem the main factor in success, before any searching is done. I know of some very good examples from American families who were trying to connect up their immigrating ancestor with the correct family back in England.

Unfortunately, where many people have combined to work on researching one family and where some of those researchers have not been careful about documenting sources and have copied dubious information, the resulting mess can take quite a bit of untangling. In such cases it is absolutely vital that work proceeds only from the known facts, and these often have to be teased out not only from examination of original records, but also scrutiny of the work of past genealogists. This comes under the criterion of establishing the nature of the problem, and we look at this more closely in the chapter on planning.

Finally, I come to some basic techniques for getting over *known gaps* in the records. Some of these gaps can be very frustrating. I have already mentioned the loss of almost all the probate records pre-1858 for the counties of Devon and Somerset as a result of the bombing during the Second World War. In these cases the researcher has to become very proficient in using what records are left behind. For example, are there any surrogates made before the records were lost? In the cases of the Devon probate, indexes were compiled before the loss. If the will can no longer be found, finding an entry in the index would at least give a clue as to date of death and administration of the estate.

Whole-family reconstruction might mean that a way backwards can be found using a known sibling to your ancestor. First, try not to be discouraged or to believe that the task is hopeless. Persistence is going to be your key. Next, recognize that your search may not be easy. You are going to need good planning and to keep accurate records of what you have looked at, when you looked at it, what it told you, and what it did not tell you. Make sure that you consider the whole family and keep proper documentation on them. Always make sure that you contact others who are researching the same family. Other descendants may have extra clues.

Finally, try to focus on one question at a time, and concentrate on solving that question before moving on. Of course, you pick up lots of peripheral bits of information that need to be documented and that may or may not be relevant to your immediate quest. Very little information is ever wasted, so it makes sense to collect as much as you can.

Special techniques for search tools

The effective researcher needs to have a good understanding of how internet search tools work. Some of this is common sense, yet is often overlooked. Very few people take the time to read the instructions about the search engines on any website, but not doing so can waste your time. It is very important to read the instructions, and work out how the search tool returns results. It is vitally important to remember that all an online search can do is return a record that matches what you have entered. They do not find ancestors as such. Search engines are also very bad at second-guessing you. If you input PRIVE instead of PRICE, they will not usually point it out. 'Garbage In Garbage Out' is an old computer saying which is still true. Although any data website – Ancestry.co.uk, findmypast, Family Search, FreeBMD, and so on – will have their own peculiarities in search, there are still generalizations that can be made about searching effectively on all of them.

Search engines are designed to be very simple to use; you input a name, a date, a place, then press a button and, hey presto, up pops a result. A common failing of all user interfaces, or the carefully designed little boxes that you enter information into before searching, is that they do not signpost to you exactly how they work because it would be too complicated to explain in simple easy stages. It would destroy the easy-to-use friendly little search box if you had to go through screens of reading before you got to it. The user friendliness therefore overlies the complexity of their behind-the-scenes functions. Some will happily give you the option for searching using different name variants or with varying degrees of certainty allocated to the terms you search for. Ancestry.co.uk would be an example of this where you can choose whether to search on the exact term or whether to let the search engine come back with a huge number of 'fuzzy' matches, ranked according to its own definition of relevance. This, of course, may not be your own definition of relevance.

Many people abandon a search because they are too eager to move on when they get no result, instead of trying to work out why the result was negative. If this happens to you, you need to spend some time not only finding out how the search tool works, but also on better defining your search. Think about whether you are searching on exact name, what the date range is, whether you use just the surname, or whether you have to use both surname and first name. It is usually helpful and instructive to start with a wider search – for example, any instance of *this* surname within *these* dates – and see what happens, rather than to start out with inputting everything you know about a person. If I do not quickly find what I am looking for, I do a series of searches using just surname and date, or first name and place and then various combinations, and I often find it useful to get an idea of how common a name is in a particular place and time. This helps me to work out whether there could be multiple candidates. One good way to problem-solve finding a family with a very common name when you don't have a lot of detail is to search for the child with the most unusual name or the most unusual place of birth. Thus, in a search for John and Elizabeth Smith in London in the census, I would look for their child, Janet, born in Bethnal Green, or their child, John, born in Basildon.

Some search tools tell you what system they use for phonetic matching. Ancestry.co.uk uses both a mathematical system called Soundex and another phonetic system. Soundex and other systems are used for finding names in databases that are equivalent. For example, Smith and Smyth are equivalent names. This equivalence can be particularly important to spot those occasions when a transcription error would prevent you finding a record. The various census indexes that exist are particularly prone to transcription error.

Soundex is a piece of software that was originally developed back in 1935 for use with the 1880 US Census for the then new Social Security system. So, the first thing to be aware of is that it was never created with the genealogy researcher in mind. It has been supplemented with various other systems, but not one of them is anywhere near perfect. These systems turn letters into numbers so that a computer can spot matches of equivalent names. The Soundex system takes the vowels out of a name and substitutes numbers for consonants. For all Soundex and other phonetic searches, there is a high risk that information in the database is not found. BEACHCROFT is the name I most commonly search for, and I need also to find all these simple variants: BEECHCROFT, BEECHCRAFT, BEACHCRAFT, BECHCROFT, etc. The variations of this name normally occur in the use of the vowels, which makes Soundex an ideal system to bring back matches.

However, there is nothing as yet that is sophisticated enough to spot all true variants of a surname, and if you have a surname beginning with a vowel they cannot cope at all. In a search on the census for a family with the surname EDEN, Soundex would not find the transcription that has them as EDEW. This particular mis-transcription happened to my Edens, and they can only be found using name combining on the 1871 census. Therefore, although phonetic systems can help the genealogist with some matches or transcription errors, they do not take away the need to try a number of different strategies in order to try to get over their own constraints.

Another common failing among users when faced with a long list of results is impatience in not clicking through to the second, third or fourth page of results. An effective researcher would always either seek to refine the search to produce fewer results, and/or wade through all the results. On many occasions I have found that the record I am searching for was not on the first page of results.

If you truly cannot find someone, ascertain whether the data set exists elsewhere. For example, the England and Wales census now appears in a number of different websites and all of them have different transcriptions. So, make sure you search all of them.

Be prepared to experiment and take a note of how the search engine works. Does it bring up surname matches first, then place matches, or does it return results matched on surname, before matching on age? Does it return a ranked set of results according to the most matching across all criteria? Each one displays results in a different manner. You need to get used to them all. This actually requires a period of study to understand how website searches return results.

Always vary the amount of information you give the search engine to play with. In many cases, less information will find you the right result. You may need to refine a large number of results in stages. Any search engine that allows search by first name only is a great tool. Sometimes you have to abandon the surname altogether and search using only a combination of first name(s), ages and place. This is surprisingly easy at the parish level and is even effective in London registration districts if there is the facility to combine two first names from the same household: husband and wife, or mother and child, for example.

Dealing with negative results

Very early on in your researches you will find that you come across negative results. Many people cannot accept that a negative result can be just as useful as a positive one. It may not be the result you are hoping for, but *it is still a result*. The way negative results are handled is usually a distinguishing feature between the professional researcher and the amateur. While you might not be happy to have continual negative results, they are telling you something. There was a very wise gentleman I used to chat to at the Family Records Centre in London who told me that genealogists should learn to trust their results, and this simple statement I believe to be remarkably profound. If you have searched thoroughly, methodically, using all known name variants and across all possible time spans and you still do not find them, then the likelihood is that they are not there to be found, *because they are elsewhere*. Thus if a death search in England and Wales has proved negative across the widest possible range of dates, then there is a high probability the person died outside of England and Wales – perhaps Ireland or Scotland, or even further afield. If we consider British records of the nineteenth and twentieth centuries, it might be true that a record is missing, or your ancestor is not recorded for some reason in one or maybe two types of records, but it is unlikely that there are no records at all for him or her, and certainly within British records of the nineteenth and twentieth century it would be extremely unlikely that a whole British-born family would not appear somewhere. And do remember to swap to searching Ireland and Scotland if you get persistently negative results for a whole family. As we saw in the story of Henrietta Hobbs, part of the effectiveness of the search was that despite all the known problems of census indexing, when I combined the negative results in the census with the negative results I had had in the GRO indexes, it told me something. It told me that something unusual was going on and that I would have to question some of the basic 'facts' about the family, including possibly their surname.

Finally, it is very important when you have a negative result that you record where you searched and the dates. This not only prevents you from going over the same ground again, but a good list of properly recorded searches will help in the planning and problem-solving process, and we look at this in more detail in Chapter 7.

In conclusion, this chapter has set out to discuss what could reasonably be called effective searching. Although my examples here are from the English census and civil registration office records, the techniques are universal and can be applied across a wide range of records, whether British or not. My belief is that a large part of effective searching is actually to do with the ability to conquer those inner voices that tell you to stop now because you need a cup of tea; to switch to another search halfway through because you are not finding something; not to worry about writing it down because you are only doing a quick search – and any other of those little lazy things that prevent systematic, methodical and recorded searches. The question of trust in results and in the research process is so fundamental to good genealogy that we will come back to it again later on.

3

The Records Framework

Understanding the creation and keeping of records – what might be called the records framework – really helps you understand why some aspects of genealogy research are very challenging. When you have a good working knowledge of the records framework, whenever or wherever you are working, you should find many benefits, at least one of which is that you don't keep looking for records that do not exist. Unfortunately, the subject can be a little dry and is often skipped over; yet paying attention should greatly help your understanding of where to look, which is the subject discussed in the next chapter. I have tried to assume very little knowledge on the reader's part. This chapter therefore gives a basic overview of the various local administrations in England and Wales which have created records of use to the genealogist. It also examines what is meant by primary and secondary sources and evidence. All countries where you are likely to be researching have some kind of record-making and record-keeping framework and there are universal themes in all archive-keeping systems. You should be able to take most of the ideas here and apply them to other countries, even though my remarks are mainly confined to England and Wales.

Genealogists are used to searching for and using documents that have already gone through that slightly mysterious process that turns them into archives, but in order to have a full grasp of what is available and where it is held, you need to understand something about how records are actually created and by whom, as well as where they end up and how they are duplicated and disseminated. Almost all government records, both local and national, are created, stored and kept because of some law, somewhere. You must not expect everything to have survived; if it had, we would simply be awash with documents. Most records that were ever made have actually been destroyed, but then again most records are actually of little historical or genealogical value. Part of the job of the archivist is to determine what should be kept and what can safely be thrown out. This winnowing-out process is known as appraisal.

What is a record and is it different from a document? Yes, there *are* differences. Records may be made up of many documents (for example, we would talk about the records of the Royal Navy), and confusingly one document could also contain many records. An employment register maintained by a company could be one phys-ical book, yet contain the records of many employees. Normally a document will be a physical item: a sheet of parchment, a book, a letter, and a record will be the information contained on or within the document, and records in plural might be the sum of all the information in a whole series, or even a whole archive, of documents.

Records carry both evidence and information. This information was originally useful for the organization creating and holding the record, and it provides evidence of the organization's activities. Records are created by organizations either because of some busi-ness process, or because of a legal necessity. They are then held by the creating organizations – for example, church, school or govern-ment department – and referred to while they have a use to the organization because of the evidence and information they carry. Thus the records of a long-running legal proceeding will be kept by the courts, by the lawyers and in the form of copy letters by the parties on either side for as long as the case is running, and then for many years afterwards as evidence of the decisions and judgments made. At the end of this cycle of creation and use, they may go through a formal process of being reviewed for their worth as archives. This currently happens to all government records, or they may get destroyed (this happens to many business records), or they may get stuffed into a cupboard for years, until they are finally rescued by someone and donated to an archive.

However they come down to us to use as evidence in information gathering for genealogical purposes, it is useful to see them in two ways: as individual documents, but also as whole groups of records, created for a purpose, maintained for a purpose, but now very often being used for a completely different purpose than their original creators were thinking of. Archivists call these groups of records classes or series. It is a truism, but the creator of the record did not have the genealogist in mind when he or she caused the record to come into being. When older records were first described and catalogued at the Public Record Office in the nineteenth century, the archivists and keepers did not consider the family historian either; they felt their natural ally was the historian and it was the constitutional and political historians who then ruled the roost. The lives of ordinary people were not really thought to be of much interest. Partly for this reason, archives' catalogues still tend to reflect the interests of historians over genealogists in their catalogue descriptions.

It is particularly important to combine a basic knowledge of national history with some understanding of the record-keeping administrations. For example, some simple facts about France would help the researcher understand where to look for what he or she needs. The French Revolution not only swept away the old regime, but also caused a total reorganization of local administration in 1789, with 100 new departments of France, each with its own archives. To further complicate the picture, town halls also might hold records and Paris is divided up into its own districts, which again hold records. Vital records of birth, marriage and burial from 1790 are thus held very locally with no national indexes. To contrast this with England, we are blessed not only with a huge quantity of records, but a stable and expanding administrative system which has only seen one major internal upheaval: the Civil War period, 1638–60. Added to this, our records suffered relatively minor losses during the Second World War, although of course it is very annoying if your searches are personally frustrated because of bombing.

The growth in English records from the sixteenth century onwards is evidence of the growing powers of the state, population expansion and an increasing feeling that the written word was somehow more binding than oral testimony. There was an information explosion in the early modern period which continues today. After the Reformation, documentation was no longer simply the preserve of the Church. The civil parish had to find people who could read and write, and secular organizations such as firms and businesses needed to create records. At the same time, it became obvious that one copy was not enough; copies of documents needed to be made so that different authorities could hold and examine them. All of this led to more copies, as well as more originals and more 'authenticated copies' being produced. For example, copies of terriers (a type of landholding summary) would be held in the parish and also were lodged with the archdeacon. Bishops' Transcripts are another important example of contemporary copies, which meant that parish register entries were copied for the bishop to hold. All records therefore carry with them a hinterland of administrative history and use, which it is very helpful to understand.

The geography of administrative systems

As I have previously stated, records are created under jurisdictions. Broadly, records may be divided into national and local, and because of the record-making and record-keeping propensities of the Church and other religious organizations, they can also be divided into secular and non-secular. For example, a tax applied by the government to all men on a national basis would be a national record. A census would be the same. These records are also mainly held at a national level – for example, in The National Archives. On the other hand, parish records of baptism are created locally by each parish church and, for England and Wales, are now held mainly at the county, or local level, by the respective County Record Office.

In England, we have had a complex system of local administration, some of which is very ancient. The counties, upon which so much depends in genealogical research, were set up before 1066 with a few exceptions. The hundreds, an old system no longer used, may not neatly lie within county boundaries and appeared in the ninth century. The manorial system and its records are believed to have started soon after 1066. The Church, to make matters even more confusing, has always had a separate system of administration and districts. These often follow even more ancient geographic areas than the counties. If you have ever wondered why diocesan boundaries seem to have no relationship to any other 'modern' territorial areas, this is because they have origins that go back to at least the later seventh century and may represent the boundaries of pre-Christian kingdoms.[18]

These ancient administrations and record-keeping systems have not stood still, but have been tinkered with over the centuries. While it is not necessary for the ordinary genealogist to be an expert in the administrative history of the county or the manor, it is useful to have a passing acquaintance with some facts. There are two main reasons for this. The records created from each administration may not be held in the same place, so you need to know not only who created the records, but where they are now held. Second, where boundaries have changed over time, you can find yourself dividing your research efforts between two quite separate parishes or counties, manors or dioceses. If you are not aware of boundary changes, then you may end up missing vital information.

Problems of boundary and jurisdiction change are universal. In Great Britain, being an island nation, at least we know that our outer boundaries have not changed. In contrast, if you have ancestors who lived in Eastern Europe there may be several different countries and different administrative systems that you need to get to know. Many other places have similarly complicated histories of invasion and re-invasion that complicate the record-keeping history. If your searches take you into any British Commonwealth country, then you will find some records created as part of the British Empire that are held in London and not in the country itself.

Here, then, are some points to be aware of for administrative areas in *England and Wales*, and if you have ancestors elsewhere

---

18 Francis Pryor, *Britain in the Middle Ages, An Archaeological History* (Harper Perennial, 2007), p.113.

you need to discover the equivalents for the country in whose records you are researching.

The county

You will find frequent references to the county of your ancestors. For example, in the records of Chancery almost all the pleadings start with describing the plaintiff as Joseph Bloggs of x, in the county of y. Many finding aids are organized by county, so we search by county; parishes fit by and large (not always) into the counties. In fact, it is hard to imagine doing any genealogy without the county structure. Throughout England and Wales, the location of every town and village can be described in relation to the county it is in – or at least that used to be the case. Modern administrative and boundary changes have brought confusion. The two main changes to be aware of occurred in 1888 and 1965 for London, and 1974 for elsewhere. There has been some consensus among gene-alogists that the historic county boundaries should *always be used*, and you can find some really excellent tables and background information on the Genuki website (www.genuki.org.uk).

Should you be unlucky enough to have ancestors who lived on a changing border or in a detached part of a county, surrounded by another county, as happened in Wiltshire, you will definitely need to know about the exact location of county boundaries because this will affect where the records are held and where you go physically to research. In all cases, you will need to know where the place was in the past, as well as where it is now. A good gazetteer and maps published before 1974, and the local government changes of that year, will be instrumental in helping you. Occasionally you will need to check with a gazetteer published prior to any other nine-teenth-century changes, such as the Samuel Lewis *Topographical Dictionary of England* (1831 and 1833 editions) and the *Topographical Dictionary of Wales* (1833).[19] Lewis is available on

19 Samuel Lewis, *A Topographical Dictionary of England* (London, 1831, 4 volumes) and *A Topographical Dictionary of Wales* (London, 1833, 2 volumes).

Ancestry.co.uk and also free at Google Books. Here, for example, is the entry for East Ham which is now very much a part of London, but back in 1831 was not:

HAM (EAST), a parish in the hundred of BECONTREE, county of ESSEX, 6 miles (E) from London, containing 1424 inhabitants. The living is a vicarage, in the archdeaconry of Essex, and diocese of London, rated in the king's books at £14. 3. 9., and in the patronage of the Bishop of London. The church, dedicated to St. Mary Magdalene, is partly of Norman architecture. There is a place of worship for Wesleyan Methodists. The river Thames bounds the parish on the south-east, and Bow creek separates the counties of Essex and Middlesex on the west. An almshouse for three poor men was erected and endowed with £40 per annum, by Giles Breme, in 1621; besides which considerable benefactions have been made, for various charitable purposes, by the Latimer family and others. There is an old brick tower, fifty feet high, in the garden of Greenstead house, said to have been built by Henry VIII., for Anna Boleyn. Dr. Stukeley, the celebrated antiquary, who died in 1765, is buried in the churchyard.

Unlike the parish, no single administrative function has defined the county; instead, they have just been taken for granted as territorial areas. But you will find that Acts of Parliament, which have created records useful to genealogists, take the county as the basis of organization. An example of this would be the records of the militia which are organized by county, and more anciently the jurisdiction of the sheriff is by county; the quarter sessions were also organized by county, unlike the assize which consisted of a circuit of counties.

The parish

The parish is the smallest administrative unit, with the exception of the township created where parishes were very large, often in upland areas like the Pennines. Most parishes were in existence by the year 1200 and some are considerably older. Parishes vary greatly in shape and size depending on soil, topography and the population when they were formed. When you know the parish your ancestor came from, half the battle is won as regards finding out about records that might name him or her. There is a difference between the civil parish and the ecclesiastical parish and you may need to be aware of that. Because of the influence of the Church until relatively modern times, the main records we use, the parish registers of baptism, marriage and burial, and other parish chest material were (and still are) part of the records of the Church of England. It was only after the Second World War that individual churches started to deposit their parish records with the local County Record Office. A small number of older parish records are still held by the incumbent, and of course the current registers are still with them. Parish register research in the past always had to be done by visiting the relevant church and paying a small fee to look at the originals. To add further confusion, there are other parochial places, such as chapelries and townships, which may also have created records. In each case, it may be necessary to understand the exact administrative history of an area.

Two invaluable reference works are *Phillimore's Atlas and Index of Parish Registers*[20] and the website known as 'HistPop', or Online Historical Population Reports to give it the full title, which hosts the 1801 Abstracts of Parish Registers at www.histpop.org; from this report you can get detailed information about the parish registers from anywhere in England and Wales, organized by county and then by hundred. For detailed understanding of the churches and chapels and their surviving registers in any one county, the National Index of Parish Registers, edited by Cliff Webb and published by the Society of Genealogists, is also a vital reference tool. Volumes have been published that cover most, although not all, of England and Wales. Many of these volumes have useful introductions that give advice about other relevant sources. Although the need to know some of this information appears to have been dissipated by

---

20 Cecil R. Humphery-Smith (ed.), *The Phillimore Atlas and Index of Parish Registers* (Phillimore & Co, Institute of Heraldic and Genealogical Studies, 3rd edn, 2003).

much more parish register material being available online, it is still vital to know about gaps, surrogates, and who holds what. If you do not know about gaps in indexes and online offerings, then your search has not been complete.

Town and borough

From early Medieval times, certain towns had a special status and a sharp distinction developed between the rights of these towns and the rights of people living outside the towns, and also the records created. In essence, they acted in a variety of franchises, exempt from normal jurisdiction and not running parallel to the development of the countryside. Their main aim was to try to exclude themselves from inspection by the Crown. A borough is a community that enjoys privileges under the grant of a Royal Charter and this enabled institutions and customs that were different from rural communities. By the thirteenth century, they were beginning to become self-governing and to appoint mayors, aldermen, bailiffs and coroners drawn from the property owners and merchants of the town. The brunt of local administration was done, unpaid, by local men. Inhabitants of towns were also allowed to own their own land and tenements, which is not true of land held under the manorial system in rural areas. They also had the right to hold fairs and markets. Borough records can contain deeds to land, quarter session court records, and lots of records about regulation of commercial activity.

You will need to consult reference works such as the Victoria County History and gazetteers to find out if a town where your ancestors lived was an ancient borough.

The manor

The manorial system divided the country (although not all of it) into territorial units, each one of which was presided over by a lord of the manor, usually with his own farmed lands in the manor, known as his demesne. Unfortunately, for researchers the picture is very complex indeed, because the records were essentially private and individual manors vary widely in size. There is also the question of whether the records have survived and whether they have been deposited with a public archive. Some of them are still in private hands.

Originally, manorial land was part of the feudal system whereby land was held and farmed in exchange for service to the lord. By the end of the fourteenth century, this system had largely been replaced by tenancy in exchange for money as rent, although there were regional variations. Land was thereafter held by the local people under a tenancy system known as 'copyhold', which meant that the freehold belonged to the lord of the manor and transfers of copyhold land could only be made with the lord's permission. This system of permission-seeking created a rich array of records that are extremely useful to genealogists. Manors often cross other geographical boundaries, such as parishes, and did not have to be contiguous, so that parts of one manor may be geographically separated by another manor. The simplest way to find the manor your ancestors lived in is to use the volumes in the Victoria County History series, many of which are now available online at British History Online (www.british-history.ac.uk). You can also try the Manorial Documents Register maintained by The National Archives, not all of which is online. What is *not* online was in the form of a card index system which has subsequently been microfilmed and needs to be searched manually. If your ancestors lived in the English countryside it is very important to know not only the manor they lived in, but also the manorial customs for that place because those customs can affect the way property was divided up at death. Manorial records (although in Latin before 1733) are very important for tracing people through their land-holdings and are a prime source for any rural family, particularly in earlier periods.

In the example of East Ham earlier, the Victoria County History of Essex[21] tells us that the history of the manors of East and West Ham are interwoven and describes the areas that fall to each part. It also tells us that East Ham had the manorial custom of partible inheritance, with choice for the younger child, similar to the

---

21 W.R. Powell (ed.), 'East Ham: Manors and estates', A History of the County of Essex: Volume 6, British History Online, www.british-history. ac.uk/report.aspx?compid=42741&strquery=east ham

'gavelkind' system of Kent. (The gavelkind system meant that sons inherited an estate in equal shares, and if there were no sons, then daughters in equal shares. This is completely different from the more common system in England of eldest son automatically inheriting everything, known as primogeniture.) This would be important to know if you were expecting the eldest son to automatically inherit land in East Ham.

The system of copyhold land was not finally brought to an end until 1926 under the 1922 Law of Property Act.

The registration districts and Poor Law Unions

Before July 1837, there was no national system of recording births, marriages and deaths, except for the parish register system operated throughout England and Wales by the Church of England since 1538. There were thus no national indexes, but there was an increasing desire by the state to count and create statistics on its population, and in particular an interest in whether or not the population was increasing.

Also of concern to the authorities was the state of the marriage law, which during the eighteenth century had become more and more unsatisfactory. There were growing numbers of dissenters (non-conformists, or people worshipping outside the established Church). Registers were kept by the Jews and the Quakers and some other churches, but they were outside the system. Other religious communities were not keeping records at all. It was not until the parliamentary and constitutional reforms of 1832, and then reform of the Poor Law system in 1834, that finally something was done about civil registration.

Two Acts were passed in 1836:

- The Marriage Act – amended existing legislation and dealt mainly with marriage procedures; it also set up the procedure for marriage in a registry office. It was also known as the 'Dissenters Marriage Bill'.
- An Act for registering Births Marriages and Deaths in England (Wales was not mentioned, but has always been included by

implication) – to provide 'the means for a complete Register of the Births Deaths and Marriages of His Majesty's Subjects in England' and it repealed previous legislation regulating parish and other registers.

The new system began operating in the summer of 1837 – the first published civil registration indexes are those for September quarter 1837 – that is, all births, marriages and deaths in July, August and September. The provisions of the new Registration Act included the following:

- Superintendent registrars' districts would be formed, based on the Poor Law Unions.
- Each district would be subdivided into registrars' districts.

Each sub-district had its own registrar appointed by the Poor Law guardians and the superintendent registrars. But it is only the superintendent's districts that are indexed by the General Register Office. The system seems simple enough, but when searching for common surnames among unfamiliar place names you need to be certain which districts are going to be relevant to your search. For some districts that seem to be the same as towns, a large rural hinterland will also be part of that district.

The Poor Law Unions were groups of parishes that paid no heed to historic county boundaries. Therefore, places on the borders of counties may be found in the unions of neighbouring counties. For example, the parish of Holwell in Bedfordshire is actually in Hitchin Poor Law Union in Hertfordshire, and therefore any birth, marriage or death in the indexes in Holwell will be found in the district of Hitchin. It is vital that you take these boundary anomalies into account when searching in the indexes.

A very useful book is *Poor Law Union Records: 4. Gazetteer of England and Wales*[22] by Jeremy Gibson and Frederic A. Youngs Jr,

---

22 Jeremy Gibson and Frederic A. Youngs Jr., *Poor Law Union records 4: Gazetteer of England and Wales* (Federation of Family History Societies, 1993).

which is the fourth volume in a series describing poor law records and a gazeteer of the places within each Union. Maps can also be purchased from the Institute of Heraldic and Genealogical Studies, showing the districts at three different times.

The Poor Law Union areas were not only used for the basis of the registration districts, but also for the census districts from 1841 onwards.

The Church of England, ecclesiastical jurisdictions

The Church played a very important part in the lives of our ancestors and the records it created and kept are best understood according to church hierarchy. Prior to 1858, church courts dealt with probate, matters relating to marriage: marriage licences and allegations, as well as moral conduct crimes (adultery, heresy, prostitution, drunkenness, and so on).

At the top level administratively are the two provinces of Canterbury and York, both with archbishops. That of Canterbury also had a jurisdiction that covered all of England and Wales. Each province is broken down into dioceses. The diocese of Canterbury was created in AD 597, but the Welsh ones of Bangor, St Asaph, St David's and Llandaff were created even earlier. There are currently forty-three in England (forty-four including the diocese in Europe). The diocese is an ecclesiastical administration under the jurisdiction of a bishop. Diocesan record offices are often amalgamated with a County Record Office, but for the purposes of finding records, genealogists will definitely need to know which diocese their ancestors lived in, and be aware that diocesan boundaries have changed over time. Welsh diocesan records are kept at the National Library of Wales. The church court associated with a whole diocese was the consistory court.

The archdeaconry is the smallest unit of church court administration, and again the records are usually to be found in the relevant County Record Office. A group of parishes formed a deanery and several deaneries were grouped to form an archdeaconry.

Bringing jurisdictions together

The most important recent innovation that will help you find and locate the diocese as well as other jurisdictions is the English Jurisdiction 1851 maps function on the Family Search website (http://maps.familysearch.org/). Using this will enable you to find the following information:

- The ecclesiastical status of the parish or place, whether that is Ancient Parish, Ecclesiastical Parish, Chapelry, or Extra Parochial (outside the parish).
- The names of other places within a parish: hamlets, villages, wards, divisions, and so on.
- When and from what other place it was created.
- The mother church, if a chapelry.
- The year that parish registers and Bishops' Transcripts began.
- Other notes concerning records and where to search.

This is a pretty impressive effort, which is a great help when faced with finding records and understanding boundaries. After you have searched for a place, you can use the Jurisdictions tab to find out the names of the jurisdictions that relate to that place. Included jurisdictions are: Parish, County, Civil Registration District, Probate Court, Diocese, Rural Deanery, Poor Law Union, Hundred and Province. By clicking on a hyperlinked jurisdiction name, you can see a highlighted view of the boundaries of that particular jurisdiction.

Other administrative systems

Apart from the geographical divisions discussed above, the other main record-creating body of interest to genealogists is national government. For England and Wales, the records of central government are held at The National Archives. The records are held within a hierarchy that reflects the government bodies or departments that created the records. Generally, the records created by central government relate to the process of governing the whole country and it is here, for example, that you will find the records of the Home Office and the Colonial Office and other government departments. We look at this in greater detail in the next chapter, as well as finding records from non-governmental organizations.

Primary and secondary evidence

You may remember that I said that records carry *evidence*. This is an important point to grasp. Evidence may also come from other things, perhaps books or even artefacts. For example, an engraving on a ring or a pistol might be a source of evidence. A source is simply where you get your information from; there are two types of sources identified by historians: primary and secondary.

For the historian, a primary source is a record or artefact created at the time of the event. An original birth certificate is primary, so is a letter, so is a contemporary index. Secondary sources for historians are works published by other historians, containing interpretation of the primary sources. You will sometimes see a list of primary and secondary sources at the back of a book, and the primary sources will include manuscripts and records from archives, and the secondary sources will include published works. For example, *London Life in the 18th Century* by M. Dorothy George is a secondary source, and the original militia attestation papers in series WO 96 at The National Archives are a primary source. Historians generally have it easy compared to genealogists. For the purposes of evidence-gathering when building connections between people, genealogists categorize and treat their sources a little differently from the way primary sources are used by historians, because the historian's definition of primary and secondary does not always work for genealogy very well. For example, the family tree drawn up by my father, and found by me in his papers, is technically a primary source as evidence of what my father thought was his pedigree at that time. However, to me as the genealogist it might be worthless as good evidence as to the real family tree. So, yes, it is a primary source in the sense used by historians, but only one that has to be checked against other even more primary sources, such as the documents that were used to draw it up. The census is another example of a problematical source, for a similar reason: its tendency to be inaccurate. It is a primary source for much statistical information about the population at the time of the census and much other unwitting testimony as well. However, the way the census was compiled means that information once collected from households was subsequently written out again into books, adding in a layer of possible mistakes. And that means that the information about your family on the census might not be correct in all its details. So primary sources and their evidence do not necessarily mean correct information that proves a genealogical link – although it is primary evidence for what someone thought and wrote at the time. Of course, people not only get things wrong, they may also lie.

It is not the publishing of a source that turns it from a primary source into a secondary source (many published editions of records would still be considered primary). It is the interpretation of that source that becomes secondary; therefore my father's hand-drawn tree is a secondary source as far as genealogists are concerned because it is only his interpretation of the evidence he has collected from primary sources. It is better to think of all published trees, whether in a book or on the web or on bits of paper, as secondary sources, and only the original documents as primary sources. Understanding these subtle distinctions is all part of understanding and being able to judge how reliable your sources are, a subject I will come back to later on.

In addition to this, genealogists often have to use sources that are derived from other sources. Indexes, transcriptions and computer databases would fall into this category of derivative sources. The creation of these types of record follow after (often long after) the original creation of the primary source. These derivative sources can be high in information, but score less well on the strength of the evidence they bring us because they do not come direct from the original document, but instead have been compiled or gone through a secondary stage which has rendered them prone to error, and therefore made them suspect. This is why you will hear the mantra of getting as close as possible to the original source in order to verify your evidence.

This chapter has introduced some important facts and concepts underlying much genealogy research. The following chapter expands on this by looking more intently at archives and how to find records.

4

Find What You Need

This chapter is about learning to think like an historical researcher so as to locate with confidence the records you require to take your journey further. You will need to be aware of geography – that is, the place where your ancestors were located, and where any records relating to that place are now to be found. You need to bear in mind the jurisdictions and administrations discussed in the previous chapter. You must also get used to using a whole variety of media and resources: books printed on paper; electronic books; original documents; images of original documents; old-fashioned paper catalogues; online catalogues; and all manner of internet resources, including search engines like Google.

As far as your own research goes, there are five things to keep in mind:

1 The sort of records that have genealogical value.
2 The information they contain.
3 The periods of time they cover.
4 Whether they are likely to have survived.
5 Where you can find them and in what format, whether that be online or offline.

And there are three main places where we can search both for records of our ancestors and the background information that we need about those records:

- Archives; both in person and online.
- Libraries; both in person and online.

- Other online sources, of which there are many.

It sounds hard, and it is true that knowing exactly what *could* be available as well as what is *not* available is something that takes quite a bit of effort and experience. Nevertheless, there is plenty of help available in published guides and on the internet, and the trick is to get your mind thinking along the right lines. The most basic of the questions you need to start with will be 'Which ancestor am I tracing? What clues do I already have as to his or her geographical location and the time span in which I need to search? Do those clues lead me to believe that I can narrow down a search to just a single parish, town or county?' Geographical knowledge is absolutely vital because the more narrowly you can define the search, then the more narrowly you need to look for records and information.

Having answered the questions about who you are searching for and where, only then can you turn your questions to 'What records are there likely to be?' and 'Where are the originals held?' Next you will have to ask, 'Are there duplicates of those records [known as surrogates]? Where are they available? Are they online?' These questions are relevant across all types of research and across different countries as well. Obviously, an ability to use the advanced features of a search engine is also very useful.

You may also find it helpful to break down questions about records into consideration of *why* your ancestors would have been recorded. We all know about baptism, marriage and burial, but you might like to think also of the following ways in which people might have got themselves into official records: for example, occupation and tax, or crimes and court cases, which of course contain not just information about criminals but also about witnesses, victims and lists of juries. Who needs to create records about people in the first place? The simple answer is normally the government, both local and national, the law or legal system, and often the Church. Other bodies that create and record information on people could be the press, the armed forces and other employers.

Very rarely are we blessed with an exact address, and usually we know only that our family came from a particular area, which might be a county, town, village or parish. If we are unlucky, it could just be a country. You will need to find out what records

77

survive and where they are held for the geographic area that your ancestors lived in. Therefore, the question of how you find what you need must be jointly answered first by *geography* and *event*. Where is this ancestor located, what event in my ancestor's life am I looking for? The date of the event will obviously be an integral part. You need a good combination of these two factors for success.

If your geographic knowledge stops at only a country, then your search will probably have to start with seeking out any nationwide indexes that exist, and of course you will need to be precise about a date and name. This should be done in conjunction with some background reading into the main records used for genealogy research in that country. A census with a national surname index would be an example of an obvious place to start. The ability to find out about records worldwide and, increasingly, to search them, comes to us thanks to the internet. We no longer need to rely on hard-to-find paper catalogues. The success of a search when you only know the country will depend on how common the name is and the period that you are researching. In general, the further back you go, the more difficult it is likely to be.

In all cases, you should be armed with a good genealogy text-book that concentrates on record sources for the country or administrative region you are interested in, such as Mark Herber's *Ancestral Trails*,[23] or, for England and Wales, Amanda Bevan's *Tracing Your Ancestors in The National Archives*. There are many excellent country-wide guides for all English-speaking countries that will introduce you to records and sources for that particular country. There are also basic guides to research in Europe and other countries available. Specialist bookshops, often linked to genealogy sites, can help. Much of this can be found online with simple inter-net searches using your favourite search engine. A basic knowledge of the legal system of the country in which you are searching is also important. Be prepared to spend some time on this background research – it may not all fall into your lap right away.

Just as important as knowing where the original document has

---

23 Mark D. Herber, *Ancestral Trails* (Sutton Publishing & Society of Genealogists, 2nd rev. edn 2004).

ended up and where you can view it is the knowledge of what records or research are already in print. Genealogists hear 'check the original source' time and time again, but we must not be slaves to the original document. To be frank, we would not need to be so very concerned about our sources if all those who have inexpertly indexed something, or inaccurately jumped to the wrong conclusions, had done a better job in the first place. But when you have a reliable printed source, then it may do just as well as the original document. For example, many of the original English seventeenth-century hearth tax returns are now being published as part of a scholarly project organized by the University of Roehampton. There is no longer any real need for the average genealogist to go and check the original hearth tax returns for the counties that have been covered. If you neglect published material because you think it untrustworthy, you are leaving out a whole host of potentially useful clues, as well as background material to help put your family into their historical context. However, you do need to keep all your critical faculties about you if you use *only* printed or transcribed sources to build a family tree, because you might be adding errors into your connections.

Be prepared to use archives, libraries, the internet and any number of different research guides. But first, and most importantly, you need to make more than a passing acquaintance with the types of record sources genealogists use. Here is a list of the most commonly used sources for England and Wales. In fact, there is an astonishing variety of records that contain information about people. Those listed below are in no particular order:

Civil registration: birth, marriage and death, also divorce.
Parish registers: baptism, marriage and burial, and Bishops' Transcripts.
Marriage allegations and bonds.
Probate: wills, administrations, inventories, bonds and Acts.
Personal memorabilia: letters, diaries.
Census returns.
Memorial inscriptions.
Poor Law records.

Trade directories.
Land registrations, property records, insurance records.
Manorial records.
Newspapers.
Local and national elections: voter records.
Apprenticeships, trades, professions.
Schools and universities.
Taxation: local and national.
Criminal courts.
Equity courts.
Ecclesiastical courts.
Ships' passenger lists, naturalization records, other immigration records.
Army, Royal Navy, RAF, Royal Marines.
Merchant shipping.

Each of these can be subdivided into many different kinds of records. Many other countries have similar kinds of records, although few in quite such abundance as we are blessed with in England and Wales (and Scotland as well). However, most countries have carried out historical censuses of their population, kept records of births, marriages and deaths, and have national archives that collect records of central government. The main differences between Great Britain and other countries will be in record survival, record starting dates, and the administrative arrangement. For example, in Canada civil registration is organized by province; in the USA it is by state, and there are no national indexes. In the UK it is by country group: England and Wales, Scotland, Ireland.

Many families cross country boundaries and this is no longer such a problem to the genealogist. Using a combination of internet research, and one or two people based locally who are prepared to look up records that are not found online, you can cover a huge amount of ground. For example, below are the records used to discover the ancestry of one particular family, which covered England, the USA, Latvia and Lithuania. Some of this was done using original records; some using digital images of originals; some using indexes and transcripts.

England Census, 1841–1911.

USA Census, 1880–1930.

Civil Registration in England, 1841–2007.

Civil Registration in Maryland, USA, 1878–1950.

Memorial Inscriptions from cemeteries in Maryland.

Newspapers from the UK and the USA.

Civil Registration in New York, USA.

Parish registers for a number of Devon, Buckinghamshire and London parishes.

Records of the Goldsmith's company, London.

UK naturalization records.

Russian Empire Census of 1897.

Ships' passenger lists, UK and USA.

Family stories, letters and photographs.

Other people's research (much discredited by our findings).

Probate records from England.

Church records in Germany.

Tax and local records from Lithuania.

Finding and using all of these sources was the result of application of knowledge, good indexing and a methodical, step-by-step approach.

So, in summary, the first answer to a question like 'How do I find what I need?' is figuratively to get yourself up out of your chair and down to the library or on to the internet in a quest to read about the records that will have been created for the geographic area in which your ancestor lived. Be prepared to do some background reading about sources for that country or area. Use online web portals and search engines to make speculative searches. This can be very complicated because laws, administrative systems and geographic boundaries change over time. The more narrowly you can focus on a specific time period and define the geographic area, the more success you will have, although it may still result in a negative search. To help you start out, what follows is a short introduction to archives and how they are kept and described, and also what you might expect to find in libraries and by using the internet.

The archive-keeping system

An archive is a collection of records created by an organization, usually with the original hierarchy of the creating body preserved for its historical evidence and importance. Not all records can become archives because they are too ephemeral, are not considered to be of enough historical importance, or simply for pragmatic reasons such as they may contain duplicate information and are too voluminous to be stored. And of course many records do not survive. All national systems of archive-keeping are based upon the very real need to assess records before they are deemed worthy of permanent preservation. Collections of letters and miscellaneous records held by libraries and other bodies may not strictly fit the definition of 'archives', but these distinctions are only of importance to archivists and librarians and need not bother you.

A basic knowledge of archive descriptions and archive-keeping systems is, however, very helpful.

Archive catalogues are not organized like library catalogues, but try to reflect the hierarchy of the original record-keeping systems. You will also see reference to visiting 'an archive' when in fact what you will be visiting is a 'repository' or a record office. Again, you need not be too bothered about this distinction.

Archives and repositories do the following:

- Hold the historic records of an organization or organizations (like schools, guilds, businesses and churches).
- Ensure the long-term preservation of the records.
- List and describe the records, usually in a catalogue.
- Provide access to the records for the general public (with some privately held exceptions).

In England and Wales, there are four separate types of archive.

The first has a national remit and includes The National Archives (TNA), the national libraries such as the British Library Manuscripts Collection, and the National Library of Wales, the Courts of Law, and some special national archives such as the Parliamentary Archives (previously the House of Lords Record Office).

The second type is made up of the local authority record offices, run by all the counties (except Avon) and unitary authorities and boroughs, and these are generally known as the County Record Offices. London also has borough archives. The defining characteristic of these archives is that they acquire archives from a particular geographic area, but from all types of institutions and individuals.

The third type is publicly funded specialist repositories; university libraries and archives fall into this category. They may have a very specialized remit. For example, King's College London archives houses the Liddle Hart Military Archive. Museum archives also come into this category.

These first three types are all publicly funded.

Finally, the fourth type is privately held and funded archives. This includes privately held family papers, business archives still held by the business, and other specialist collections. Just to confuse matters, some of these may have a national collection policy; trades union archives would be an example of this. Records that are of use to genealogists will be found in all four types of archives, although the heaviest use is made of the big national collections and the local authority record offices.

Using the internet to find what you need

As mentioned earlier, there has been an explosion of information relating to genealogy arriving on the internet. Those of you who are not using the internet to find what you need are missing out, and are no longer mainstream genealogists. At first, genealogy records on the internet were easy to disregard or to dismiss as likely to be inaccurate, and there was still a general mistrust of any information found online. This is no longer the case. Using the internet to locate information about the records themselves, information about who holds the records, and even digital images of the exact records and documents you need, is now an everyday and normal part of genealogy. There are now whole books on internet genealogy. There is not room here to go into too much detail about using search engines or the differences between using a search engine and starting with a gateway site. If you find yourself confused by these terms and feel unsure of yourself in the online world of genealogy, then two books I particularly recommend are Peter Christian, *The Genealogist's Internet*,[24] and Stuart Raymond, *Netting Your Ancestors*.[25]

Leaving aside what is available on the data websites such as Ancestry.co.uk, which is a huge topic in itself, I am going to concentrate my advice in this section on locating original records held by archives, with online searches. In other words, you search online for a description of the record series and work out where it is held, although you might physically have to make a visit to actually search within the records. Fortunately, finding out what records exist, and where they are kept, is now relatively easy thanks to two initiatives that can be searched online: the National Register of Archives (NRA), and the catalogue of catalogues – Access 2 Archives, known as A2A. Both of these databases can be found at The National Archives website. A third site, ARCHON, also hosted by The National Archives, lists contact details (www.national-archives.gov.uk/archon/) for record repositories in the whole of the UK and also for institutions elsewhere in the world that have substantial collections of manuscripts noted under the indexes to the National Register of Archives.

The National Register of Archives (NRA)

The website www.nationalarchives.gov.uk/nra/default.asp is the quick guide to what is mainly held within the third and fourth types of archive and some of the second type. It contains unpublished lists of records that would be impossible to find unless reported and held on the National Register. The NRA index can be searched by the following categories: corporate name – records relating to businesses and organizations; personal name – records relating to individuals; family name – records relating to particular families and estates; and

---

24 Peter Christian, *The Genealogist's Internet* (5th edn, The National Archives, 2012) with online updates at www.spub.co.uk/tgi4.
25 Stuart A. Raymond, *Netting Your Ancestors* (The Family History Partnership, 2007).

place names in the UK and overseas. It is often worth checking the NRA when you need to do speculative searches for material relating to a particular place. There is also a national register for Scotland, held by The National Archives of Scotland. It is not useful for individuals unless they are well known. However, the Scottish Archives Network (www.scan.org.uk/) is similar to A2A and provides a way to search across fifty-two Scottish archives, as does Archives Wales (www.archiveswales.org.uk/).

Access 2 Archives (A2A)

For most searches relating to English genealogy, however, it is A2A (www.nationalarchives.gov.uk/a2a/) that has become *completely indispensable*. A2A is particularly valuable for research across boundaries as you can search for names and other terms across geographic regions. For example, a search for the Hertfordshire parish of 'Datchworth' will bring up not only material held at Hertfordshire Archives and Local Studies (previously Hertfordshire Record Office) but also material relating to Datchworth held in other county archives. This would have been very difficult to discover otherwise. However, I would still recommend a search of *both* A2A and the NRA as a belt and braces approach. One of the drawbacks of research in the county record offices before online catalogues were available was that there was very little material relating to neighbouring counties available at each record office. Thus, if you had ancestors on a wandering boundary or who migrated to a nearby county, it was difficult and time-consuming to find things. Now you can more easily work out what is held where.

Private archives

For the genealogist, any records held in private archives will be the most problematic. In some cases, like the few London Livery Companies that have not deposited their records with the Guildhall Library, a part-time archivist may be prepared to do some free research for you. Some business archives have the facility to have researchers visit and use their records, but others will only allow access to a few selected academic researchers. In all cases, a very polite enquiry with exact details of what you are looking for will be required.

Some privately held items may possibly have been sold and now be housed in libraries and museums abroad, notably in the USA. For example, the Huntingdon Library in California holds a large number of UK documents, but again these are listed in the NRA along with a number of other overseas repositories.

To find lots of extra information about county resources, as well as using A2A, the web portal Genuki should be used to search for any indexes and to give you an overview of what might be online. Finally, don't forget also to use a search engine like Google. I often find myself starting with a general online search for a specific set of records, even if I could also check the NRA. This can produce some very useful results very quickly.

Visiting and contacting archives

Not all the information you need is going to come from online indexes and searches, although they can point you in the right direction. Sooner or later your research is going to take you physically to an archive because what you want is not available any other way.

The British genealogist is usually going to need to come into contact with the County Record Office for the county where their ancestors lived, and very often the primary reason for a first visit will be to check findings from the IGI, or other indexes in the original parish registers, or to look at other parish registers that are not yet indexed.

Visiting a County Record Office for the first time can seem intimidating, but it needn't be if you go prepared. That means reading its website, checking on opening times, booking a seat in advance if you need to, bringing the right identification, and so on. In the reading rooms you will not be allowed to use pens, so make sure you have a pencil (this is to protect the documents). There will be a list of other rules: no mobile phones, no eating and drinking, cameras may not be allowed.

But the number one rule is that you must go with some purpose in mind and knowing what records you would like to see. Mostly, people start with parish records. The records are not displayed on the shelves, like a library, so there is no browsing the actual records, although there will normally be a range of printed material for you to look through – such as card catalogues – and looking at these can be very productive.

Every time a TV programme shows a history or genealogy presenter in an archive store room with rows of boxes, there is a sigh of dismay from the archives profession, because the general public are not able to browse the shelves like this. Those scenes are always staged especially for the TV and the actual records are under lock and key for their own protection.

These are some of the terms you might come across in an archive:

- List – In the context of an archive a list is the most basic descriptive tool; it is just a list of records – for example, file titles and dates. It is not the same as a catalogue.
- Calendar – A calendar seeks to describe the records better than a list, by itemizing names, places, and perhaps giving a summary of contents. The calendars of state papers are a good example of where the calendar gives a very good idea of the exact content of these letters and papers, so that the researcher has a precise idea what it is going to tell them *before* they look at the original.
- Finding aid – This is an overarching term used by archivists that covers catalogues, guides, calendars and lists.
- Research guide – Heavily used by TNA, the research guides seek to guide the researcher through the records, subject by subject, using background information and extra description about records to help pinpoint what you need to see.
- Catalogue – In archives these are not arranged like library catalogues, but as a series of descriptions of, first, organizations, then classes of records, according to function, then individual records.

A large amount of contact from the general public with an archive now comes via email. The ease of this has undoubtedly led to a huge number of enquiries that previously they would never have had to deal with – mainly from people doing family history. So you need to be aware that if you do send an enquiry like this, your email is just one among many received by the archive that day, all of which have to be answered.

You need to have a specific question. Examples of good questions to ask are:

- 'Do you have the records of xxxx parish in your collections?'
- 'Are there any indexes to the Poor Law records?'

An example of a bad question is, 'I am researching my great-grandfather who I think was in your county in 1850 – can you send me his documents?'

Archivists are busy people and under-funded as well, so they appreciate a precise question about the records they hold rather than how to do research. They cannot tell you how to do your research; it is up to you to find that out.

You will get the best service if you do the following:

- Keep your question short and to the point.
- Do not go into lengthy detail about your family history (they are not interested!).
- Ask questions about the records they hold, not about your family.
- Give precise places and dates.
- Have already explored and made yourself familiar with their online catalogue (if they have one).
- Have found the reference for the documents you want to ask about.
- Don't assume you know more than they do, even if you do.
- Say thank you.

Do not expect:

- The archive to do your family history for you, although some of them do have a research service that you can use to pay for

their staff to do research; many of them keep lists of independent researchers who will also work for a fee.
- An immediate response.
- Everything to be free – archives are always short of money
and they need to recoup some of their costs.

The National Archives (TNA)

TNA deserves a special mention in any book about genealogical
method, simply because of its size. You probably know that it is
not really the place to start your family history, although that is less
true nowadays than it used to be, since it has developed so much
information that seems aimed at the beginner.

TNA is the home of the records of central government of the UK
that have been selected as worthy of preservation. It also holds the
records of the law courts of England. Previously called the Public
Record Office (PRO for short), TNA is housed at Ruskin Avenue in
Kew, Surrey, on the outskirts of London. Material that is specific to
Scotland is housed in Edinburgh in its own separate National
Archives, now called the National Records of Scotland (NRS).

The vast majority of us now visit TNA website (www.national-
archives.gov.uk) more than we would ever have physically visited
the building. If you live a long way from TNA, there is no longer
any need to feel at a great disadvantage. The website is rapidly
building into one of the best internet resources for family historians, military historians, academic historians and archivists. This is
a deliberate policy on behalf of TNA to make their records more
accessible to greater numbers of people. However, the website is
huge and takes some getting used to.

The catalogue is at the heart of all TNA activities. To the unini-
tiated, it may seem ridiculously complicated and designed to stop
you finding out what you want. However, this is really not the
case. It seeks to describe and make accessible, by listing in a hierarchical order, all the records in the archive (held on 167
kilometres of shelving) within 10 million descriptions of varying
quality and detail. Notice that I say records, not documents. This is

an important distinction. It would be impossible to describe all the separate documents held by TNA. However, the task of cataloguing is made possible because individual documents fall into categories or types, called series or classes, and the series are arranged according to the department that created or had custody of the records and the activities that they were originally created to record.

This means that to fully understand the records you need some understanding of how the various government departments that created the records worked and were organized, and what kind of information is likely to have been retained, etc.

Within those 10 million descriptions there is a very wide variety of information. The more important the government department thought a record series was, the more detailed the description, sometimes down to the document level. But for many a record series there is little or no guide as to what exactly it contains.

Therefore, like other archive catalogues, TNA catalogue is not a searchable index of documents, but a searchable index of record descriptions, arranged in hierarchical stages. The catalogue reference, which you need to order an original document, or for remotely ordering a copy to be sent to you, as well as for recording what you have looked at, consists of a number of elements:

- The department code (always 1–4 letters) – ADM (for Admiralty) WO (War Office) or HO (Home Office) or FO (Foreign Office), etc.
- The series description (always a number, 1 through to four figures) – e.g. WO 364 or WO 10.
- The piece or item number – e.g. WO 364/1100.

There are national and international standards for cataloguing records in archival systems, so it is worth paying a bit of attention to the way they are organized because it is knowledge that can easily be translated to many other institutions that hold archives. There is normally some sort of description of the creating organization. In the case of TNA this equates to the government departments, but it could be a school, or a business, or any other organization. At the next level down there is a description of the type or series of records within that organization and there will be a handful, or perhaps hundreds of series depending on the size of the organization, and then at the next level down is a description of the individual items. It is all these descriptions that go to make up the entries in the catalogue and what you mainly will be searching. You can visualize it like this:

Metropolitan Police (description only)
Service Registers (description only)
Register 1 (a document you can search)
Register 2 (ditto)
Pension Registers (description only)
Register 1 (a document you can search)
etc., etc.

Why you need to know about these hierarchies of arrangement makes more sense after you have been faced with a brief entry in an online catalogue that leaves you with lots of questions. For example, you can now search TNA catalogue for individual names of criminals who appear in the records of the Central Criminal Court. You might, for example, be searching in a random fashion for the surname Greenaway and come across an entry online that gives you this information:

CRIM 1/1/7 – Defendant Henry Greenaway, February 1840

Knowing what the reference codes means gives you the extra information that CRIM = Central Criminal Court, CRIM 1 = Depositions from that court, and Henry Greenaway's record is the seventh piece in the depositions. Working from this piece of information, the enquiring genealogist could then ask what other records of this court might be relevant to find out more about Henry. Checking within the descriptions will show whether these also have been name indexed, or whether they need further investigation. If they are not indexed and also need further investigation, then there is nothing for it but a visit to the archive.

My family is not indexed! What do I do?

In general, when you are searching the higher-level catalogues such as NRA, you are not likely to find your own family listed in the index. This is because, like most catalogues, it only indexes specific terms, places, names of organizations and so on from the description. It does not act as an index to the records themselves. You therefore must not abandon the search and conclude that the records hold nothing of interest to you.

However, you may find that some members of your family do appear in indexes in several other places where the indexing has been done at a deeper level in the records. Places to search would be within A2A, and on TNA catalogue. Some County Record Offices also have good online catalogues or sets of online records within which you will find people. This seeming inconsistency between what you are likely to find on online archives' lists and catalogues can be very confusing, until you understand some of the distinctions between them.

It might be helpful to think of it like zooming in on a map from a great height. The first level would be the general map of the whole country; you can see the outline, the major towns and some of the major features. The map gives you an overview and would be like a general description of the records and where they are held. At the next level within the catalogue you get a list of what might be held in individual boxes, or the titles of individual files. This would be like zooming down to an A–Z of a particular town. The final level (which will depend on how detailed the indexing and description of the records is) would be so detailed that you could see the individual houses and fields and all the names and numbers associated with them. It is at this final level that most genealogists want to work, yet the majority of records are not yet described at this very detailed level; using my map analogy, the zoom function simply does not work down here. This level of detail would mean that each record, document or page has been looked at and indexed for all names, dates and places. When you do find a good index to a particular set of records, where every document or page has been included and all names on every page included and you still don't find the people you are looking for, then you can start to have confidence that they are not there to be found.

It is important to remember that the work of cataloguing and indexing records is very skilled and labour intensive and it is also completely inconsistent between archives, particularly between different County Record Offices. Thus some records have been indexed, others have not. Only experience is going to help you make sense of it all.

Using libraries

We are all familiar with libraries. In the past the answer to the question about where to start your family history was usually by visiting your local library to see what reference books they had in their genealogy section. This is still good advice and not to be disregarded, even though so much is now online. The useful thing about a library is that you can search and browse for books using subject categories. Although your local library will not (normally) contain records, they will be able to order books from other libraries for you and you may find that they have on their shelves some of the older reference works which are still indispensable to genealogists, as well as the latest 'how to' books. Some libraries also act as repositories for local history collections, and in these cases you can see original records from the local area. In addition, there are many printed indexes and printed publications from local record societies that are extremely valuable to the researcher. I find that a large academic library with a good history and reference section is still invaluable. There is something about working with books that cannot be had from searching the internet.

Detailed and advanced background reading, by which I mean of historians in peer-reviewed journals, will often open up totally new sources. Paying close attention to other people's footnotes and sources has proved really successful for me in the past. However, it does require access to an academic or big reference library or to the online academic journals known as JSTOR. You can also search for

and find out-of-copyright books on Google Books and at www.
archive.org, and academic articles on Google Scholar.

Two specialist genealogy libraries deserve particular mention.
The Society of Genealogists has a very large collection of resources
and books all held together in one place in central London, and
their library catalogue can be searched easily online at www.sog.
org.uk. Because the Society is run by genealogists for genealogists,
the library has a very big collection of parish register material as
well as deposited family papers and books relevant to genealogy.
The Family History Library in Salt Lake City is run by the Church
of Jesus Christ of Latter-day Saints. Their catalogue is available
online; they have microfilmed much rare material, not just parish
registers, and all of it can be called up into your local family
history centre. British researchers tend to forget, or don't register
in the first place, the usefulness of the network of local family
history centres which are all over the world. Being able to call in
microfilm of parish registers from far distant places means that
you don't always have to travel to visit the original documents. See
below for more about this service.

The finding and using of surrogates

Ideally, you would have already become familiar with the archive-
keeping system in the region in which you are interested before
finding and using duplicates or substitutes of those records. Archivists call these surrogates. However, due to the amount of records
now making their way online, in practice this is very unlikely. You
will almost certainly have been happily using surrogates, printed
sources and online databases without any thought or care for any
of the preceding information. If you have never come across any
problems in tracing your family tree, you may feel that ignorance is
bliss and is certainly less hard work! My guess is, however, that you
are reading this book in order to expand your knowledge and help
you pass some research blockages.

So, what are surrogates and why do we need to know about
them? A surrogate is a faithful duplicate of a document, either on

microfilm or microfiche, or increasingly a digitized image. The original could be a bound register book which is now stored in an archive. But that register book has been photographed in its entirety or in part, and transferred to microfilm. That microfilm in turn could have been duplicated and now exist in libraries and other places around the world. Many parish registers and other records have been copied like this by the Church of Jesus Christ of Latter-day Saints. They have the biggest collection of surrogates in the world. They also have local centres in almost every country and city from which you can order up these duplicate or surrogate records. The benefit to the archive is that by providing a surrogate, the original gets to be preserved away from hundreds of hands that will cause it damage. The benefit to genealogists is that they can access records in locations near to where they live, for which in the past they would have to have travelled to the archive. For more on the holdings of the Church of Jesus Christ of Latter-day Saints, go to www.familysearch.org/Eng/Library/FHLC/frameset_fhlc.asp.

Another way of providing surrogates is by digitizing records and providing access online. Any website that allows you to view the original image from the record is providing a surrogate. Normally, this is done by permission and with the help of the archive that holds the original. Examples of this include the original English and Welsh census images 1841–1911, created by the Home Office in the first instance and then by the Registrar General. They are now in TNA, and have been made available to the public in two stages: first by microfilm and subsequently online at Ancestry.co.uk and findmypast, as well as other genealogy websites.

Don't confuse surrogates with either transcriptions or indexes. A surrogate can be used instead of the original, with some caveats because pages can always be missed out by mistake during filming. Most genealogists understand that errors and omissions creep into transcriptions and indexes and therefore these sources need to be checked with the original record. But if you check with a complete surrogate, then you will have checked the original. You don't need to worry that, having found all your ancestors on the census, you then need to visit the original enumerators' books.

Where you do need to be careful is in situations where the

surrogate only *partly* covers the original record or, more often, contains some volumes from an original series of records, but not all of them. In this case, you will only have done a part search and may need to see the original in order to complete the search. There are many examples of this, particularly with what is available online, but also in the holdings of the Church of Jesus Christ of Latter-day Saints. In each and every case, you must ask yourself, 'Who holds the original? What information can I find out about the original record? Does that compare with the surrogate? Can I be confident that they are the same?' If you are really pernickety and not confident about the surrogacy process, you may find yourself checking page numbers to make sure that all of them do occur in the surrogate and that pages have not been left out of the filming or scanning process. Unfortunately, examples of this type of gap do occur as well.

Indexes and transcriptions provided by the Family History Societies

Family History Societies, of which there are over 160 in Britain as I write, have been at the forefront of indexing and transcribing records relating to their area of interest. You may need to join the relevant county or borough society to take advantage of their knowledge and indexes. Many of them have also produced indexes on CD-ROM which you can purchase. A full list of all the societies can be found at the website of the Federation of Family History Societies (www.ffhs.org.uk/). A large proportion of societies are making some of their indexes available on findmypast as part of the subscription and pay per view packages on that website. The Society of Genealogists also has a large number of indexes and transcriptions, particularly of parish register material, and you can check its holdings in the catalogue on its website (www.sog.org.uk). Be very aware that these indexes may not be complete. It is extremely important that you find out exactly what parishes and time spans are covered.

Family History Societies are also likely to have special indexes that you may not be able to access in any other way – for example, particular marriage indexes or indexes to some of the more obscure records. The Federation of Family History Societies also plays a role in indexing, by publishing the National Burial Index, and you can find out more about that by visiting its website.

The finding and using of transcriptions and indexes online

There are many places to begin an online search for these types of records. You can just start with a search engine; you can look through the lists of records held by the major data websites, such as Ancestry.com; or you can use a genealogy portal such as Genuki (www.genuki.org.uk). I have previously mentioned Genuki only in passing, but it is a very important resource, particularly in the context of helping you find online resources. It is a volunteer project to provide genealogy information relating to all of Britain and Ireland, divided by country and county, and then by type of resource. The information on each county differs because different groups of volunteers work within each county section adding links and information. Some counties have really excellent links to many sources – Kent is one. Others are more sparse. Another place to start a search, particularly for records outside of the UK, is the excellent Cyndis List (www.cyndislist.com). This huge genealogy portal contains links to websites and resources from around the world and is often the place I start to find out about records from different countries.

Visiting several subscription sites and using more than one search engine and genealogy portal will help you to find out what is available. This is not something that can always be accomplished with one search term; get into the habit of using several keywords and in a different order – for example, use 'Kent parish registers online' as well as 'online parish registers Kent'; and try the phrase 'civil registration' as well as 'vital records'.

Examples

Let's work through some examples of combining geography and event to find what you need, whether that is original, index or surrogate. This example uses detailed local information and reference works.

Here is a simple checklist, with some sample answers for a baptism search in the county of Durham, to help you visualize what I have been trying to describe:

What am I looking for?	Birth information
Where?	Darlington, Durham
When?	1800–1801
What records will I need?	Baptism registers
Which church?	St Cuthbert, Darlington
Is there more than one church in this place at this date?	No, but there are also records of a Quaker Meeting and also Catholic records
Who holds the originals?	Durham Record Office, Durham
What copies exist elsewhere?	Society of Genealogists holds a transcript of the registers 1798–1812 on microfiche; Latter-day Saints Family History Library catalogue has copies and Bishops' Transcripts for the same period (FHL BRITISH Film 1514686)
Are they indexed by anyone online?	Not available on the IGI, but part is available on FamilySearch.org.

Taking this information, I can now plan my research either by making a visit to Durham Record Office or by visiting the Society of Genealogists in London, or by doing a part search online and then reserving the rest for a physical visit, or by going to the local Church of Jesus Christ of Latter-day Saints family history centre and calling up the relevant film.

Finding Harriet

I have long been perplexed by my 3 x great-grandmother, Harriet Beresford. Harriet was born about 1820 and died in 1876 of pneumonia. She married a well-to-do solicitor on 13 October 1840, and on her marriage certificate her father's name is given as Benjamin Beresford (deceased). She and her husband lived a comfortable middle-class life in the centre of the London legal world. On one census return, her husband had put that she was born in Judd Street, Holborn. It is not often that one finds such a specific place of birth as the actual street given on the census returns, so you might imagine that it would be relatively easy to follow the clue up and find Harriet's baptism. Not so far. From some family notes in my possession, made by an unknown person, comes the suggestion that Harriet may in fact have been born in Ireland, or at least be of Irish descent.

My first task was to work out what was needed and where to find it. The aim was to confirm Harriet's birth (the event); and if not her actual date of birth, then her baptism and thereby the names of her parents. I knew the location was Judd Street, Holborn. There were then two questions to ask: 'What parish is Judd Street in?' and 'Do I need the original parish register, or are there any indexes available that might include the parish?'

First, did Judd Street still exist? A quick look in the modern London A–Z showed me that it did. It runs south of the Euston Road, parallel with the Gray's Inn Road, a stone's throw from what is now the British Library. I could see from the A–Z that there are four local churches marked. Using both my *London Parish Map*[26] and the *A–Z of Victorian London*[27] together, I discovered that Judd Street is in the parish of St Pancras. Therefore, I needed to start the

---

26 *London Parish Map: A Map of the Ecclesiastical Divisions within the County of London*, 1903 (London Topographical Society, pub. no. 155, 1999).
27 *A–Z of Victorian London* (London Topographical Society, pub. no. 136, 1987).

search in the baptism records of St Pancras in the period around 1820.

The next question must be, 'Where are the originals?' Another two indispensable reference books were brought into play: *The Phillimore Atlas and Index of Parish Registers* and the *National Index of Parish Registers: Volume 9, London and Middlesex*.

From these reference sources I found out the following: St Pancras baptism records from 1660 to 1936 are held at the London Metropolitan Archives. Bishops' Transcripts of these baptisms between 1813 and 1880 are also held there. However, baptisms also appear on the International Genealogical Index (the IGI). There are also a number of independent and non-conformist chapels in the parish, some of them with records starting earlier than 1820.

But, hang on I said to myself, I have already checked the IGI for Harriet's baptism and could not find it. Where does that leave this search? I needed to work out exactly what the IGI covers in respect of the St Pancras records. Luckily, there is one website that helps, commonly known as 'Hugh Wallis' (http://freepages.genealogy. rootsweb.ancestry.com/~hughwallis/).

This allows you to find exactly which parishes in any county are covered by the IGI and also to spot any gaps within the parishes, of which there are many. Using this tool, I saw that St Pancras baptisms for 1813–24 are indeed covered by the IGI, and moreover that the independent chapels in the area are also covered by the IGI where the records exist. Therefore, at the time I did this, I decided to trust this information and turn my attention to another way of finding out about Harriet's birth. Perhaps she was born in Judd Street, but her parents moved away before she could be baptized? Perhaps she was not baptized at all, or perhaps she had a private baptism? If there was indeed an Irish connection, perhaps she had been baptized in Ireland? I could equally, of course, decide not to trust the IGI and actually attempt a physical check in the original baptism register held at the London Metropolitan Archives. This would not necessarily mean a physical visit since many of these London parish register records are now available online, although they were not when I first started this search.

My next step at this stage was to see if I could find out whether there were any more people with the surname 'Beresford' on the census in 1851 who had been born in Holborn. They could possibly be siblings or other relatives of Harriet. This search was inconclusive.

I looked again at Harriet's marriage certificate. This was at St Mary Lambeth. What was a Holborn girl doing getting married in this quite different parish? For those of you who do not know London, you will have to take my word for it that residents from north of the River Thames do not normally get married south of the river in Lambeth. Perhaps, I thought to myself, the church was fashionable in the early Victorian period for some reason, or perhaps she was living in the parish by then.

Could there be a Beresford family in St Mary Lambeth on the 1841 census? This would be only six months after Harriet got married. If you are asking yourself why I had not simply done a census search for Benjamin Beresford across all of London, indeed over the whole country, the answer is that of course Harriet's marriage certificate specifically told me he was already deceased by 1840. Other efforts to find him in any index had also failed. However, further searches of the 1841 census, concentrating this time on St Mary Lambeth, also drew a blank (at least for the time being).

At this point, I had put the search to one side until I could concentrate on a personal visit to the London Metropolitan Archives. However, subsequently, many of the parish registers of London were recently made available and partly indexed at Ancestry. co.uk. These could be a very useful short cut, saving me hours of research. I decided to look specifically at *any* Beresford events, baptisms, marriages or burials, at St Mary Lambeth. This quickly led to my first real clue, the marriage of a Caroline Beresford, also in 1840, daughter of a Benjamin Beresford (deceased) Gent. She looked to be a probable sister to Harriet. Using Caroline's married name, I then located her on the 1851 census to discover that she had been born in Shoreditch. Here was another geographic clue. Assuming that Caroline and Harriet were indeed sisters, could I find Caroline's baptism and thereby get to more information about Harriet in that way?

Shoreditch is a large area and might be used in the sense of Shoreditch the parish, or the general district. Caroline was born in about 1814 or 1815, so the next task was to work out the parish. St Leonard's Shoreditch is the main church and the records of St Leonard's are not indexed by the IGI. Once again, the originals are held at the London Metropolitan Archive. If you wish to make a search at the archives, in order to find your film you need to know that the modern-day borough is Hackney. This highlights a point about many archive collections. As they are usually classified according to the organization depositing the records, you often need to know the modern name or modern geographical place of that organization.

Checking on Ancestry.co.uk showed that the images (although not an index) from the baptism register for 1814 and 1815 are available there as well. I searched each page of the baptism registers for both years, hoping to find Caroline. Unfortunately, a baptism for Caroline did not turn up in either of these two years.

Analysing what I had discovered, I now appear to have two sisters, about six years apart in age, both married within six months at St Mary Lambeth, after their father has died and both born in nearby districts of London, neither of whose baptisms I can find, although I have looked in the right places. If I cannot find any baptisms, then perhaps the search should turn to a burial date and location for Benjamin. Did he die in London? Questions that I could ask concerning Benjamin's death would not only concern the actual burial, but also probate records including death duty. How would I now find what I needed? Probate records prior to 1858 were held by the Church, so I would need to look in several church courts for the right area of London and Surrey, for Lambeth at this date was in Surrey, not London.

Although the geography of the Beresford search includes the very vague (possibly Ireland), it also includes the very precise: Judd Street. Other records that could help might be the rate books for St Pancras to look at the people who lived or owned houses in Judd Street and also in St Leonard's Shoreditch, which would be a much longer search without a known street and no indexes; and although these may not tell me anything very specific, they might confirm the movements of the Beresford family. We will come back to the search for the Beresfords later on in Chapter 6.

Meanwhile, a summary of what I have done to find what I need is this:

- Used modern maps and contemporary maps to understand the geography.
- Used relevant genealogy reference works.
- Checked where the original records of baptism are now held and searched in some of them.
- Checked what parts of the original records are available online and searched within them.
- Checked where any indexes and surrogates are.
- Searched online for burials.

I could also have found out what the Society of Genealogists has in their library for St Mary Lambeth and St Leonard's Shoreditch. What I have not done at this point is expand the search much in terms of date ranges examined.

In conclusion, remember that people are not normally recorded by an official source unless there is some reason for it, and if they are not found on a census or in records of births, marriages and burials, the search might not be feasible. For example, I was recently asked by a potential client to try to find out where her foreign-born grandfather, a chauffeur, had lived and worked while in London in the period 1902–6. Unfortunately, it was an impossible quest. The only official 'index' that would give an address would be the census, which didn't occur in those years. As a foreigner he would not have voted, so would not be on any electoral roll, and even if the employment records of any of the private companies he worked for should have survived and be accessible, which is very unlikely, trying to track down which one would be completely impractical. In other words, the geography was too vague and there was no event that might be recorded officially for this search to have any success.

There is no simple one place to go, or even search online, that will provide you with everything you need. Try not to let yourself be beguiled by quick and easy information on a website, as it usually hides a much more complex record-creating and record-keeping system than it describes. The archive-keeping process is complex and easily misunderstood. Finding resources for genealogy is a process that will combine libraries, reference books and maps, surrogates online and on microfilm, original records and visits to archives with online search tools, websites and catalogues of many different types.

5

Has It Been Done Before?

This chapter is about the wonderful community of genealogy; what other researchers' work might exist that would be relevant to you, how you can search for it, and under what circumstances it can be trusted.

My own research interest was sparked by a long pedigree roll in a tin, and for a short time I visited various relations with the aim of coming away with more branches to my tree, preferably also in nicely presented pedigree rolls. I did get handed some useful and interesting information, varying in quality, but the initial thrill soon palled. I wanted to be able to discover things for myself and not have it all handed to me on a roll. From talking to other genealogists I know that many of us feel the same; we do not particularly want to add a hundred new names from someone else's research because that steals from us the thrill of the chase. To have discovered a new ancestor all on your own is a peculiar kind of pleasure. Just plugging into someone else's work is boring by comparison. Nevertheless, when you are stuck and need help, then finding others to share the burden, or who may have extra family knowledge, can be thrilling. There is a whole community of fellow genealogists out there – some of them related to you and working on your family. Some will be willing to help you; others will be secretive and want to work in isolation. Some will have websites or seemingly authoritative publications; others perhaps will have direct memories of people you need to know about. And, as we shall see, it is quite probable that at least some of your family has already been written about and actually published, either in book form, or via a family tree available on the internet.

During recent years the explosion of interest in family tree research has been fed by the social networking sites that have become common currency on the internet. More and more people are using evidence they have found in other people's trees to build their own trees. It was ever thus; it has just become so much easier and quicker. What is new is that more and more people are co-operating and building trees online. Most of us used to do our family history research on our own in a fairly isolated way, but there is also now a vast genealogy community 'out there' ready and willing to help you with answers to questions, and even help with actual research. This community ranges from magazines, and their own online forums, to various well-established discussion groups on Rootsweb, to Facebook groups, to members of the various Family History Societies, the Society of Genealogists and many other history societies and specific surname interest groups worldwide.

People have been writing out genealogies and drawing up pedigrees for a very long time. Some cultures have an oral history of genealogies; Celtic cultures had bardic genealogists; there are genealogies in the Bible; and there are genealogies carved in stone. The need to know who our father's father was and have a personal link with the past seems to be a basic human desire. Today, exciting advances with DNA testing mean that more and more we are discovering those very deep ancestral links, together with information about human migrations across the world, and there is a sharper awareness than ever before of our close cousin-ship to each other. Using the internet, people can now find records about both their ancestors and their living cousins and then link up with those distant cousins to trace their shared ancestry. While it can be certain that Y-DNA tests will not give you anything other than the truth, there are pitfalls with taking other people's research work at face value. But in one way nothing has changed; it has simply become vastly more complex with so many more people working away at their ancestry, and there remain very good reasons why you might need to find out whether anybody else has done work on your ancestors. And there are very many reasons why, having found someone else's work, you need to be able to subject it to a proper scientific appraisal, because just as long as there have been pedigrees, so there have been mistakes or uncritical connections drawn up.

Some efforts are also being made to link (using documentary sources) all living individuals together. This supreme effort arises from the Church of Jesus Christ of Latter-day Saints' ambitions, driven by religious beliefs, and is mirrored by sites such as Ancestry. com with their World Tree projects (Ancestry.com was originally set up and run by members of the Church of Jesus Christ of Latter-day Saints). This type of ambition might have seemed laughable only a few years ago, but technological advances and the power of thousands of people working together make this now a much more real prospect, at least in those countries that are rich in record sources.

Thus there are several intertwined issues. How do you find out if someone else has previously worked on a branch of your family? How do you trust their work? How do you find others researching, or with knowledge of, the same family, and how do you work together once you have found each other?

What work has already been done?

The quick answer to this question is 'a huge amount', and the work starts earlier than you might think. In the fifteenth century, a growing interest in pedigrees in Britain was mirrored by the growth in the heralds' concern for genealogy; perhaps particularly this was linked with a growth in the economy and a rising class of people who wished to have the right to bear arms. Although the heralds were previously interested in coats of arms because the right to a coat of arms depended on lineage, it was obvious that they would get involved more generally in proof of pedigree. But there was then no such thing as critical history writing and the pedigrees that the heralds produced (still useful to us today) are full of errors and pitfalls for the unwary. The heralds were not above making up a lineage if the money was right, but this does not mean that all their work should be discredited. The work of the heralds is most commonly consulted today by means of the printed volumes of

Heralds' Visitations. These give family trees for the upper-class families in most counties from the sixteenth and seventeenth centuries. The heralds' work continues today at the Royal College of Arms.

There was also a growing interest in antiquities and genealogy for its own sake, not just for legal or heraldic purposes. During the sixteenth century in the reign of Queen Elizabeth I, it became fashionable to be interested in genealogy and heraldry; this fashion was driven by a new gentry class who wished to take their place among the social elite. However, you must not be altogether surprised if many of these newly drawn-up pedigrees do not stand up to proper scrutiny.

The genealogist Dugdale (1605–86), working in the seventeenth century, showed an understanding of bringing evidence together in a proper fashion to draw reasonable conclusions and it was Dugdale who introduced the system of giving a reference note for every statement made. Dugdale's *Baronage* was a work about extinct families and he was therefore under no pressure to gild any lily in discussing their origins.[28] The same could not be said of other writers, and the English had to wait until the nineteenth century for a proper 'scientific' attitude to genealogy, first introduced by the works of J. Horace Round (1854–1928), who made his name as a critic of the made-up pedigree, and G. E. Cockayne (1825–1911), who produced the seminal work *The Complete Peerage*.[29]

Interest in genealogy remained strong in the seventeenth and eighteenth centuries and a number of part works were produced, most of them still on library shelves today, such as Burke's *Peerage*, and *Landed Gentry* among others, produced in successive editions and with a seeming authority.[30] Unlike Dugdale, they were based on

---

28 Sir William Dugdale, *The Baronage of England* (1675) (reprinted 1977).

29 George. E. Cockayne, *The Complete Peerage of England, Scotland, Ireland, Great Britain, and the United Kingdom Extant, Extinct, or Dormant* (1st edn, 8 volumes, 1887–1898; 2nd edn revised by the Hon. Vicary Gibbs et al., 1910–1959 and continuing).

30 Founded in 1826 by Irish genealogist John Burke, and continued by his son, Bernard Burke, *A General and Heraldic Dictionary of the Peerage and Baronetage of the British Empire* (Vol. II, 5th ed. London: Colburn and Bentley, 1832). Revised editions were frequently published by H. Colburn and R. Bentley between 1832 and 1917, and continue to this day under different ownership.

extant families, and because of no wish by the editor to offend the families they described, they are more than a little prone to error – and even downright falsification. Some of these fantasies have been incorporated in other works that are still being published today. It was Burke's *Peerage* that was attacked by J. Horace Round in a number of polemical works, and early editions of Burke's should be used with extreme caution. However, Collins's *Peerage*, and Sir Egerton Brydges's 1812 edition in particular,[31] can still be useful to the serious genealogist, if used with common sense and as a starting point, rather than taken uncritically. Also very useful are the county antiquarians and genealogists who published with increasing frequency during the eighteenth and nineteenth centuries. Where these show their sources, they can be used as a terrific guide to the gentry families of that county. An example of these would be George Ormerod (1785–1873), who wrote *The History of the County Palatine and City of Chester*,[32] a work that combines topographical and manorial history with the family history of notable Cheshire families, and was based on original documents held at Chester Castle, among other things. George Ormerod was a founder member of the Historical Society of Lancashire and Cheshire. If you are interested in finding out more about who to trust among the past works of English genealogists, then the works of Sir Anthony Wagner should be sought out.

For most of the well connected, there is little point in re-doing work into lineages that have already been extensively worked on and revised by good genealogists. If you can get an ancestral line back to a well-known gentry family, the nobility or a monarch, there is probably – unless you are particularly dedicated or determined to root out new sources – little left to do as far as actual pedigree research on that line is concerned. The lineages of the kings and queens of England and Scotland have been very extensively researched, as have those from Europe, so it would be ludicrous to repeat any work that has already taken place. Historical research

---

31 Sir Egerton Brydges, *Collins's Peerage of England*, 9 Volumes (London, 1812).
32 George Ormerod, *The History of the County Palatine and City of Chester* (London, 1819).

into the life and times of your ancestors would in this scenario be a different matter, and of course it is the getting and proving of your line back to that 'gateway' ancestor that is usually where the work needs to be done.

Any genealogist who has been working among the families of the better connected and written about soon comes to an understanding of how interconnected they all are. This interconnection is not unique to the royal families of Europe, or the county gentry families of England, but must in fact occur in the pedigree of everybody living. Simple mathematics will tell you that, with such a great increase in population in Europe since the ravages of the Black Death in the 1340s and 1350s, we cannot help but all be descended from a relatively small pool of people. Advances in knowledge about DNA and ancestry now also point to a pivotal moment for the whole human race: about 170,000 years ago when it is believed only 10,000 modern humans had been left alive. [33] This is what is known as a near-extinction moment. As for Europe, it is also now known that 80 per cent of modern European lines are derived from ancestors who were already in Europe before the last Ice Age 10,000 years ago.[34] No doubt further advances in DNA analysis into our deep ancestry will shed more light on the interconnected web of ancestors from whom we all descend.

It is not an original idea in genealogy circles that all Europeans are likely to have at least one line of descent from the Emperor Charlemagne (747/8–814). J. Horace Round was fond of asserting that he could trace back any Englishman of any social class to Edward III, which is surely an exaggeration given the lack of probate and parish register information that would be likely to get in the way, but no doubt you get the picture he was painting with this assertion. An American genealogist attempted to do that with the monumental work called *The Plantagenet Roll of the Blood Royal*,[35] which focuses on American lines of descent from Edward

---

33 Stephen Oppenheimer, *Out of Eden, the Peopling of the World* (London, Constable and Robinson, rev edn 2004) p.16.
34 Ibid, p.250.
35 The Marquis of Ruvigny and Raineval, Melville Henry Massue, *The Plantagenet Roll of the Blood Royal Being A Complete Table of All the*

III. Recently, mathematicians have modelled how far back we would have to go to find a common ancestor for everyone in Europe and it turns out that this is only back to AD 300. It is more than tempting to see us all as one big family, and a little further explanation sheds light on these huge and perhaps surprising revelations.

One of the most fascinating aspects of genealogy is that of 'pedigree collapse'. This is caused by cousins intermarrying, either wittingly or unwittingly, and thus one ancestral line collapses or disappears because cousins share an ancestor. In communities where much intermarriage among third and fourth cousins has occurred, descendants will have many less ancestors than in communities where people have freely moved around and chosen partners who are much more distantly related. For example, work on Prince Charles's ancestry shows that his pedigree has suffered a 37 per cent collapse. In the whole of human history we cannot help but have far fewer ancestors than the binary doubling up of ancestors for each generation would suggest, simply because when taking this doubling up (2, 4, 8, 16, 28, 56, etc.) back every twenty-five years to represent a generation, by the time you get back to AD 800, there would be more people in your tree than had ever been alive at something like 263 trillion.[36] Therefore we have all got distant and not so distant cousin marriages in our trees. In some societies where it is socially acceptable to marry close relations (for example, in Japan or some of the Indian castes) the amount of pedigree collapse will be very high. In any small isolated communities with between 300 and 500 people, after six or so generations there are *only* third cousins or closer to marry. One of my own dearest wishes is to find a connection between my family and my husband's family to prove to him that we are (in fact, must be) distantly related. We often see press stories about politicians or other famous people having surprising ancestors or links to others – for example, it was widely reported in 1994 that successive Prime Ministers Margaret Thatcher

---

Descendents Now Living of Edward III, King of England (London, England: T.C. & E. C. Jack, 1905–1911).

36 The work of genealogist Robert C. Gunderson as quoted by Shoumatoff, Alex, *The Mountain of Names: A History of the Human Family* (New York: Simon & Schuster, 1985), pp. 231ff.

and John Major had a common ancestor in one Samuel Crust of Boston in Lincolnshire and were in fact fifth cousins. This type of story is always reported as being very surprising, a fantastic coincidence, yet it is probably just symptomatic of all English people's very deep ties with one another. I am fully convinced that with more and more of us doing genealogy and with the discoveries in DNA evidence that are also happening, the wonderful web of interconnectedness that encircles us all is going to become more and more apparent.

Published works showing pedigrees of many families grouped together, such as the Heralds' Visitations, the county antiquities and pedigree works, and works concerned with the peerage and baronage, are just one example of material that could be of use to you – although they come with caveats and need to be supplemented with background reading about how they were compiled. There is also now a very large amount of deposited working papers from amateur genealogists. The Society of Genealogists has a very big collection, having always encouraged the deposit for safe keeping of work done by its members. The Society's Document Collection is therefore a miscellaneous collection of manuscript research notes on around 14,000 families, arranged by surname; this can be searched for (at no charge) on the Society's website. They vary enormously. Some are very extensive, with pedigrees, documents and extracts from sources. Others are much more sketchy. The gems of the collection can be amazingly useful. For example, work deposited on the Scattergood family in the Society's library includes all the birth, marriage and death certificates purchased for the nineteenth century. It is therefore always worth checking the Society's surname collections as it could potentially save you a lot of money and time.

The question of how to find the disparate genealogies and family accounts among the hundreds of possible local and county histories, biographical studies, national and local journals and transactions of archaeological and record societies has been variously solved in the past by the publication of bibliographies, or lists of printed material. The most important of these are now looking very dated (although of course are still useful).

For England:

G. W. Marshall, *The Genealogist's Guide* (1903).

J. B. Whitmore, *A Genealogical Guide* (1953).

G. B. Barrow, *The Genealogist's Guide* (1977).

T. R. Thomson, *A Catalogue of British Family Histories* (1980).

C. R. Humphrey-Smith, *Armigerous Ancestors, Heralds' Visitations: A catalogue and index of genealogical resources in the Visitations of the Heralds and related documents* (1997).

For Scotland and Ireland:

M. Stuart, *Scottish Family History* (1930).

J. P. S. Ferguson, *Scottish Family Histories Held in Scottish Libraries* (1986).

B. de Breffny, *Bibliography of Irish Family History* (1974).

E. MacLysaght, *Bibliography of Irish Family History* (1980).

Finding individually printed family histories, which were usually produced in small print runs and privately published, can be very difficult. The library of the Society of Genealogists is a good place to start, as well as the catalogue of the Church of Jesus Christ of Latter-day Saints Family History Library in Salt Lake City. Google Books and other internet library sources can also be worth trying. You should also try the British Library Catalogue and the US Library of Congress. Secondhand bookshops are always worth visiting (although you would be very lucky to pick up something of direct relevance to your own family history) and their online counterparts at Abe Books and Amazon as well.

County Record Offices may also have deposited papers and pedigrees and these will normally be catalogued under the name of the depositor. Naturally, these should be used with a great deal of care, particularly when they represent the work of people who were putting together lines from parish registers in just one county and without the benefit of being able to check against another source. I had a really excellent example of this in a long-standing case to reconstruct a family in eighteenth- and seventeenth-century Essex.

The client's work had been based on a deposited set of papers at Essex Record Office, which included a family tree drawn by hand and for which the work had been done only from parish registers, long before much of the indexing work such as the IGI, which we now take for granted, had come about. The research was not helped by being on a common surname. Suffice to say, the tree that had been faithfully copied by the client and then published by him, both privately and in extracts in family history magazines, was riddled with errors – with children assigned to the wrong families and unproven lines written as fact. For a very long time the tree cast its shadow over the research as I struggled to sort out the real relationships and explain to my client why and how I thought the tree was wrong. So much time was spent on it that it would have been much cheaper and easier never to have seen it in the first place and to have started from scratch.

The Americans have always been a step ahead of the British when it comes to amateur publishing and depositing genealogy work in libraries and repositories. For example, deposited work in the library of the Daughters of the American Revolution constitutes a core of their collections, where they have thousands of family histories and a file collection running to an estimated 300,000 folders. These files are a mixture of documentation submitted with applications to membership, subsequent donations by members, and items donated by the public. Among the type of records included are Bible records, family studies, and research notes covering the eighteenth, nineteenth and twentieth centuries.

There are also some very useful American journals and magazines. The PERiodical Source Index (known as PERSI) is to be particularly recommended as an index to American work. PERSI is the largest and most comprehensive subject index to genealogical and historical periodical articles, written in English and French, in the world. It has been created by the foundation and department staff of the Genealogy Center of the library in Fort Wayne, Indiana, and is widely recognized as being a vital source for genealogical researchers, covering works from the eighteenth century up to the present, and containing more than 1.8 million index entries from almost 10,000 titles. British people should not be sniffy about consulting it, since many of us share the same roots, although it might be slightly galling to discover that Chuck Norris from Texas has already done much of the Norris family history for you. Naturally, as with any other work done by someone unknown, you must be prepared to check it out against original sources and not assume that because something has found its way into print, this means it is the gospel truth or the last word on the subject.

Another potentially extremely useful source is the work done by members of the Guild of One-Name Studies. As their work involves collecting instances of *all* the occurrences of a particular surname, then their members may well have information that would help you. You can easily find out if a surname is registered with the Guild and being actively researched by checking with their website at www.one-name.org. Most of the surnames being studied are the more unusual ones, although there are some much more common names being studied – such as Gray and Gallagher. If you do find that your surname is among those being studied, then get in contact with the Guild member running the study as they are bound by the rules of the Guild to help members of the public with enquiries. You have nothing to lose and may find some extremely useful work has already been done. It is also well worth joining the Guild even if you do not intend to register a surname study because of the depth of knowledge that Guild members have. They are a very dedicated bunch of people and run an active email list and publish an excellent magazine, *The Journal of One-Name Studies*, which has much to interest the ordinary genealogist as well as people who want to find out more about particular surnames.

There are now thousands of Y-DNA projects set up across the globe, with the aim of proving ancestry. The biggest provider of family history DNA testing or 'genetic genealogy' is Family Tree DNA (www.familytreedna.com/projects.aspx), and there are now also thousands of surname projects registered there.

In summary, the various types of previous research you will come across include:

- Pedigree rolls drawn up by the College of Arms or professional genealogists, often printed and made available in the older publications, or from private work and passed down the generations in a family.

- Hand-drawn trees and notes passed down by amateurs and collected by many genealogy libraries, particularly in the USA and at the Society of Genealogists in London.
- Printed family histories in libraries, both physical and online, usually the work of one dedicated amateur.
- Burke's *Peerage* and many other reference works that concentrate on the upper strata of society.
- Genealogy journals, the best of which are in the USA, but also the *Journal of One-Name Studies* and PERSI.
- Family trees online at Ancestry.co.uk and on many other genealogy websites.
- Hundreds if not thousands of individually hosted websites.
- Parish register reconstructions online such as those hosted by Sussex Weald.
- Websites and surname profiles linked to the Guild of One-Name Studies; Y-DNA projects.
- Notes, family Bibles and other trees drawn up by your own relatives.

Pitfalls with other people's research

Unfortunately, it is very rare to come across any previously done amateur genealogy research which contains absolutely no errors. There are some exceptions of course, but mainly you will still need to check at least some of the research. There are some very obvious pointers that show the work needs to be thoroughly checked and could, in fact, be a complete fiction. Some of the obvious ones that I have seen are:

- No dates given at all.
- Some dates given, but normally only the year.
- No sources shown (where has the information come from?).
- Birth and baptism dates muddled up.
- Death and burial dates muddled up.

- Missing generations.
- Children's dates that cannot possibly belong with parents' dates; for example, children born when the mother was too old or too young.
- Firm connections made without proper evidence.
- Over-reliance on just one source (normally the IGI, or the census).

The top three are, of course, genealogical 'no-no's'. Any tree with missing dates or no sources is immediately suspect. Some would say they should be thrown out, but of course they still provide clues and can represent the truth. As a researcher, I would far prefer a tree with no dates but the right children assigned to the right parents, than a tree with lots of dates but no source information and erroneous connections.

Other problems with someone else's research might not be obvious and therefore much more difficult to deal with, unless each fact is rigorously checked. An example of this would be where an otherwise good and trusted genealogist has simply made a mistake, or there has been a printing error in a book. Even famous genealogists sometimes get things wrong. On the other hand, it has not been unknown for unscrupulous professional genealogists to produce what look like perfectly referenced and researched trees, but which actually are works of fiction.

Don't believe that things in print must be right. Pressure to publish quickly or cheaply means that mistakes creep in and facts are not always checked. Historians also make mistakes, particularly, in my experience, in their citations and document references. It certainly would not be true to say that printed work is more trustworthy than work found on websites; either could be excellent or worthless. One essential skill of the genealogist is learning how to weigh up other people's work whatever medium you find it in. The disentanglement of errors that have been perpetuated in print and made their way on to the internet, and then referred to by others, has been a notable feature of the American genealogist's life for some time. Unfortunately, the tendency for people to copy trees from websites into their own records means that it is becoming common everywhere.

Probably the most difficult previous research to be critical of (at least until it trips you up) are the family trees, notes on family history and family Bible information that has been passed down to you from the previous generation. Time and again I have heard people say '... but my aunt can't possibly have got it wrong'. Oh yes she can! Even baptism and burial information from family Bibles, or indeed papers of any kind, needs to be checked, since the dates might have been added many years after the event.

If I were pushed to try to give a general rating on reliability for the list of sources above, it would be almost impossible to generalize, except to say that in the main the family tree information supplied by the general public on websites like Ancestry.co.uk tends to be the least reliable unless it has impeccable source notes, and that the websites and profiles linked to the Guild of One-Name Studies would be more reliable, again with a caveat about sources being shown.

Finding lost cousins

In the past, the genealogist who wanted to contact others researching the same family would have limited places in which to advertise; a popular place would be the small ads in the genealogy magazines. That has changed completely and many people now register their research and surname interests online in the hope that other researchers will contact them. There has been a huge growth in recent years in using social media sites to do research and contact others at the same time, and many of the familiar data websites, such as Ancestry.co.uk, also offer a place to advertise your family trees and invite connections with others. More and more people use blogs or websites to talk about their ancestry and provide details of their family trees. Indeed, some very large and complex family reconstructions and tree building have now appeared online, hosted by individuals who wish to share their passion for genealogy.

Probably the number one reason for finding others researching the same family has to be that you hope they have more information about your ancestors than you do. In fact, this often turns out to be the case. Even if they know nothing very precise about the ancestors you seek, just filling in your knowledge of the wider family can have great benefits. You can also make effective research friendships. In one example I know about, a distant cousin who made contact after finding her surname on someone else's website was able to provide a photo of an unknown ancestor that had pivotal information written on the reverse of the photo. Putting together the two stories from families that had become separated in the nineteenth century was enormously helpful in finding out more about the family. I have come across many examples like this. Just having someone else with whom to share the triumphs and the frustrations of research, albeit that they are on the other side of the world, can also be wonderful.

The Church of Jesus Christ of Latter-day Saints was one of the first organizations to deliberately provide a means of linking people with others working on the same families. Their Pedigree Resource File and Ancestral File, both of which can be searched online, contain information submitted by individuals on a very large number of trees, mainly from the USA. These submissions are not checked or edited and can, and do, contain misleading or erroneous information, sometimes with very basic mistakes.

On the other hand, people working on surname research, like the Guild of One-Name Studies (www.one-name.org), usually make a great effort to get people with the same surname to contact them, and some Guild members co-ordinate surname projects that see a number of researchers all working on the same surname, reconstructing family trees to discover links, and eventually to understand the history of the surname, where it came from, and information about the first people to have the surname. The emphasis in the Guild is on serious documented genealogical research.

Genes Reunited (www.genesreunited.co.uk) is one of the larger social network sites for family historians, and combines this with some databases and search tools. The idea here is to link up family members. However, the emphasis is not on proper documented research but on social connections, so extra care has to be taken when taking any of the trees on Genes Reunited at face value. The fact that you have to make your tree available for everybody to see is one of the off-putting factors behind Genes Reunited, as also with similar websites. This means that your information is not really secure. When you share your information using a third party website, you need to check the terms and conditions carefully as the information uploaded on to a third party website might be deemed to belong to the third party. This has put off many people from uploading information.

A need for more personal security in sharing details of families with strangers online was behind the founding of the website Lost Cousins (www.lostcousins.co.uk), which provides a novel and useful way of connecting with people who are almost certainly related to you. This is done by automatic matching of entries on the census, using data you and your 'lost cousins' have entered. This method provides a high degree of certainty that you will in fact be 'lost cousins', plus security that nobody else can see your tree or details of your family. You are then free to share details of your trees with each other privately by email or other methods.

One of the most off-putting parts of sharing research and working with other people has to be the small minority who ask for information and then take other people's hard work, which could be the results of years of research, and publish it online as though it were their own research. For this reason, many of us have been put off making our genealogy research available online. As most family tree software programs have the facility to have the information within them converted into a standard format known as a Gedcom, it is possible to quickly and easily share all your information with someone else by sending them a Gedcom file which they can just import into their own software. There is then no barrier to them sending the same information elsewhere or publishing it. There is no doubt that you have to build up a certain amount of trust before you share information with a stranger and this is even more important if your files contain details about living people, such as birth and marriage dates, and other bits of data that can positively identify these people and so leave them open to others perpetuating fraud. If you do share information with others, it is a good idea to hide birth and marriage dates for those who are still living.

Hobby genealogists do not have to register with the Information

Commissioner under the Data Protection Act in the UK, and in fact are not bound by the law. However, information about living people needs to be treated with care. Even information about the dead can come as a shock to relatives if they are unaware of the truth of paternity events. If you uncover secrets from the past, they can have the very real potential to affect people's lives, and so the utmost caution should be used when corresponding with strangers who are distantly related.

6

Analysing and Working
with Documents

Having understood the background to the creation of the
records we need to use, and found the actual documents
necessary to progress our research, we can now turn in
eager anticipation to reading and understanding the information
and evidence they present us with. The genealogist worth his or her
salt knows how to strip all the relevant information from any document or record, and that process is often more rigorous than those
employed by many professional historians using other types of historical material because genealogists really have to make the sources
work for them. Sometimes all we have are just one or two documents providing evidence for the whole of a person's life. Correctly
analysing and interpreting individual documents is therefore of vital
importance when there is so little to draw from in the first place.

The process of analysis starts with a detailed knowledge of the
record, who created it and when, what it was used for; and also the
history of record-making and record-keeping. It is followed by a
close examination of all the evidence: what the document says;
what it might have been expected to say; perhaps what it omits to
say. The process is much more than just harvesting names and dates
from the document, although of course that process of correctly
gleaning names, dates and places is important as well.

No document, whether parish register, census page, hearth tax
return or soldiers' attestation papers, present the researcher with
'the truth'. There is always the possibility that a lie was told, a truth
was withheld, a mistake made, a word misheard, a clerk was lazy,

or something was not copied correctly. We can never be totally sure, even on an official document such as a birth certificate, that all the facts presented to us as evidence on the document are correct. The only thing that a document can tell us is that it is someone's version of the truth at that point in time. The whole process of genealogical analysis becomes an investigation into the creation of the document, the use of the document originally and secondarily and, by extension when talking about whole record series, the storage and other record-keeping aspects of the document. A deep knowledge of the records themselves needs to go hand in hand with careful scrutiny of the evidence presented.

Document analysis is the breaking down of all the written evidence – and other evidence such as what the document is made from, whether it has seals and signatures – into its component parts in order to come to conclusions. In some disciplines, analysis is an end in itself; in genealogy it is a means to an end. We need the process of critical analysis for the simple reason that it produces new facts and allows us to weigh up the evidence correctly. Document analysis is also known as diplomatics, a branch of the historical sciences, and is used by archivists and record-keepers to work out whether a document is authentic or faked and the quality of evidence it gives. Genealogists need to take the diplomatic process even further, and ask extra questions.

Questions surrounding authentication or validity of a document or record include:

- Is it signed? A signature, or autograph cross, would sometimes be enough to make the document valid.
- Is it sealed? A seal was the primary way of authenticating a document from the Medieval period in England until the seventeenth century, and they continue right up to the present day for some documents.
- Is it witnessed? Witnesses are extremely important for both verbal and written agreements; an un-witnessed will is not valid.
- How has it been copied and do both parties have a legal copy? For example, in the past, two copies of an agreement would

be made and a wavy line cut between the two. Both parties would take away their half as proof of the agreement between them. This is known as a chirograph or indenture.

The actual meaning of the document or record is obviously very important; by this I mean not only what was written, but what contemporaries would have understood by it. This, of course, might differ from what you understand by it, or how it appears on the surface. There are some wonderful pitfalls the researcher can fall into when working with conveyancing documents before 1841. As the result of trying to get around feudal laws (whereby only the Crown could hold freehold land, which was then granted to tenants, and enrolment fees were charged), what are known as fictitious actions were drawn up. A fictitious action is a legal action that sounds as though it took place, but in fact it did not. Examples include the Common Recovery and the Final Concord or Fine. You may also come across the conveyance of property by Lease and Release, the purpose of which was to subvert the enrolment process and to sell freehold privately. A Lease would be drawn up for one year in return for a nominal payment; the Release, which would actually contain the conveyance, would be dated the next day. The real payment would be made together with the Release. Thus the Lease and Release together constituted the sale of the property, although on the surface they look as though they are a rather mystifying lease for a year. If the two documents become separated, then the only way to tell that this was actually a conveyance of freehold property, and not simply a leasehold agreement, is by the very specific wording – which should contain the words 'bargained and sold'. The cleverness of this is that by only concerning themselves with interests and rights, no mention of freehold was made and therefore there was no necessity to have it enrolled and made public with extra fees.

The common form of wording on any document can also be important, either as a pitfall since you don't understand its significance because this is the first such document you have seen, or because it does not match the common form you are expecting and you want to know why. The common form is that wording which, on a modern form, would be printed out, and you would just fill in the blank spaces with your details. For example, the common form for the start of the plaintiff's suit in Chancery in the mid-seventeenth century starts like this:

> Humbly complaining showeth unto your honour your orator [name of plaintiff] of [parish] in the county of [county] [followed by occupation of plaintiff].

Dating

Dating is an essential part of document analysis and it is absolutely vital to genealogists to make sure their notes record the correct dates taken from documents. Dates on documents can include the date of creation of the document or record, the date of witnessing the document, and dates added later by clerks and record-keepers, such as can occur in legal cases, or on document wrappers. Make sure you note down any dates with particular care.

I mentioned in Chapter 1 that problems can occur if you do not understand the move from one dating system to another in 1752, but in using documents from earlier than this it is even more complicated, as dates were often referred to only as regnal years, or saints' days, or exchequer years, and legal documents were created and held in the four main legal 'terms' of the year. These were the four periods of the years when it was allowable or feasible for lawyers to come to town to transact legal business: Michaelmas, Hilary, Easter and Trinity. There was an exceedingly complicated way of working out how long these terms ran, and naturally it varied over time. You can read more about it in C. R. Cheney (ed.), *Handbook of Dates for Students of English History* (CUP, 1995). These legal terms were abolished in 1873. You will also frequently come across reference to the English quarter days; Lady Day, the feast of the Annunciation on 25 March, Midsummer Day or Nativity of St John the Baptist on 24 June, Michaelmas on 29 September, and Christmas Day on 25 December. In Scotland different quarter days were used, being Candlemas 2 February,

Whit-Sunday fixed at 15 May, Lammas on 1 August, and Martinmas on 11 November.

What basic facts do we therefore need to establish about any document?

- Who wrote it and on whose authority?
- Does it conform to the regulations of the administration whence it has come?
- What does it say?
- How is it written?
- Who is involved in the issue of the document? Is it a draft (no witnesses, no seal, with obvious crossings out); is it a fair copy?
- Why was it drawn up?
- Is it believable?
- Where and when was it made and issued?
- Where is the document now?
- What importance is the document to the beneficiary?
- What advantage is it to the creator?
- Who are they informing?
- Who is the document most important to?
- What piece of legislation has brought the document about?

Let's now turn to some actual documents, to see how much evidence can be squeezed out of them for genealogical purposes. My first example is a short will which, on the surface, appears to tell us not very much until it is both dissected and put into historical context. It is the will of Thomas Hoare held by the Buckinghamshire Record Office in Aylesbury and given here in a true transcription, keeping original spelling and line breaks:

the xxxi th of January 1626

In the name of god Amen I Thomas Hoare
of Aylesbeary in the county of bucks cordwayner
beinge sicke of body but of perficke rememboran[ce]
thankes be to god for it I do ordaine this may last
will and testament in mannoure and foarme

following first I give and bequeath my
soule into the handes of almighty god my
Saviour and redeemer by whose mearitor I hope
to be saved and my bodye to the grounde from
whence it came to be buried in the churchyarde
of Aylesbeary at the discreation of my
executrix

Imprimis I give and bequeathe to my daughter
Agnes Orton xiid to be payde her within
one month after my desease
It[e]m I give to my daughter Auradrye xiid to be
payde to her when she doth demande it after
My desease and also to her daughter xiid

It[e]m I give and bequeathe all the rest of my
goodes and chattels landes and tenements
unbequeathed unto my wife whome I doo
ordeigne to be full executrix of this my
last will and teastament

and I doo ordeeine to be overseerers of this my last
will my trusty & wellbeloved friends John
Forriste and Jones Orton & I give to either
Of them for theire paynes vi d a peace
Sealed and de[c]lymend in the presence of John Forrist
Chistopher Arden Jonas Orton

The will was proved in the peculiar of Aylesbury,
Buckinghamshire, on 5 April, 1627 by Elizabeth Hoare,
widow and executrix[37]

This is a very short but typical will of a seventeenth-century small tradesman. It is correctly witnessed, contains a signature or mark of the testator, names an executor and carries a date. These elements make it a valid will. It comes from the holdings of the correct church

---

37 Centre for Buckinghamshire Studies – Ref: D/A/WF/26/229.

court, and is held together with many other wills from the same court. It is a court copy and not the original will. We can be sure of authenticity and validity although, as it is not the original, we cannot be sure that it is a completely accurate copy. We trust that it is because the clerk who copied it would presumably not have held his job long if he made many mistakes.

The fact that it was proved in the Peculiar Court of Aylesbury is evidence that Thomas Hoare held property only within the bounds of the jurisdiction of that court – that is, only in Aylesbury itself. Therefore, at the time of death, we would not expect him to have lived and worked anywhere other than Aylesbury.

Date of Will – The date of the will is 31 January 1626/7 [1627 in New Style dating].

Implied Date of Death – The date of proving the will is 5 April 1627, therefore Thomas probably died sometime in February or March 1626/7. He says he is 'sicke of body' and it was common practice for a will to be drawn up quickly if an illness was likely to prove terminal. The executor(s) would have had to appear at the peculiar court with the will, after the death. By law this had to be within four months of the death, although the actual process of probate being granted could take longer.

Place – His last place of residence is Aylesbury, Buckingham-shire.

Place of burial – The church at Aylesbury (the burial register could be checked to find a precise date).

Occupation – His occupation is cordwayner, which was a shoemaker (after a type of leather which comes from Cordoba in Spain[38]).

Widow – The grant of probate tells us that her name is Elizabeth and she is sole executrix.

---

38 *Oxford English Dictionary* (1956 edn).

Children – He names only two, his daughters Agnes Orton and Audry (no surname given).

Children's families – Agnes is married to a man named Orton; Audry has a daughter, but surprisingly no married name is given to her. Had Thomas forgotten it? Did he know it? Her bequest is unusual because Thomas says 'payde to her when she doth demande it' instead of the more usual paid to her within one month or six months after 'my decease'. This might imply that Audrey is far from home, not living in Aylesbury.

Age of Thomas – Our only clue is that he is a grandfather. We can only be sure that Thomas is probably above the age of 40, and more likely to be 50 or even 60.

Overseers – The appointment of overseers was normally for the purpose of making sure the executor(s) did their job properly. In this case it may have been the selection of good friends who Thomas could be sure would provide assistance to his wife if she needed it. As the actual administration of the bequests could only have been a small job if we take the will at face value, the appointment of overseers might imply that Thomas's affairs were slightly more complicated than the will seems to disclose, or appointing overseers might simply have been the custom among the folk of Aylesbury at this time. Further investigation into the practice of other testators in Aylesbury would be helpful here.

Probate Court – We know from the grant that this was proved in the Peculiar Court of the Prebend of Aylesbury. Peculiars were places outside the normal jurisdiction of the archdeacon and would grant probate only within their boundaries, in this case the town of Aylesbury. (Some further research found that the Prebend of Aylesbury at the time this will was proved was one John Hackett, BD, Rector also of St Andrew, Holborn.)

Format of Will – The common language of wills is used, and it is probably safe to assume that Thomas was neither an ardent Puritan, nor had Catholic sympathies. Wills at this date were often written out by clerks using a common language at the sick bed.

What can the timing of this probate process, when fitted into any larger historical context, tell us? At the time this will was written, the Puritan movement was making attacks on the church courts. (During the Civil War, which broke out in the 1640s, the church courts were temporarily suspended.) However, the church courts were only responsible for overseeing the deceased's personal possessions. These consisted of moveable goods, credits and leasehold property, not freehold or copyhold property, which was termed real estate. Inheritance of any copyhold property would come under the jurisdiction of the relevant manorial court and issues surrounding freehold property would be determined by local customs and common law. However, by the time of Thomas Hoare's will, the use of the words 'last will and testament' was evidence that in practice the church court was overseeing the wishes of the testator in disposing of all property, although they still did not get involved in disputes about real estate.

Thomas does not mention any property by name. We might conclude from the bequests in this will – that is, money given to two daughters and a granddaughter and everything else to his wife – that Thomas did not have any sons. This may not be a correct assumption.

Most administrators or overseers were widows or next of kin; sometimes creditors might be involved, or reputable neighbours. It seems likely therefore that John Forest and Christopher Arden are either neighbours or have some kind of kinship to Thomas or to his wife; Jonas Orton is probably, although not definitely, the husband of Agnes Orton, who is named in the will as Thomas's daughter.

Of the people mentioned in the will, we can be certain of the following only: Thomas Hoare had two daughters, Agnes and Audrey, and Audrey had a daughter. Thomas does not name his wife, yet the probate grant names her as Elizabeth.

What can we imply from the bequests? Thomas gives no money to the poor and leaves only bequests totalling 3 shillings. I think it is fair to assume that Thomas did not have much money to dispose of. However, the appointment of overseers for such small sums might suggest some complications behind the scenes.

What other records could we choose to check in order to place the evidence from this will into a wider context? First, we could check the actual wording of the grant of probate, the Act Books, and other records of this Peculiar Court. An inventory may also have survived. Second, we would check records of Chancery to make sure there was no dispute over this will; third, we would look at the parish registers for Aylesbury to confirm further details about this family. The wills of the three overseers and of Thomas's widow, Elizabeth, should also be looked for. Manorial records for Aylesbury and any other town records could be checked as these might enable Thomas's house or shop to be located; and a check on any other copyhold property should also be done.

What this will *does not tell us*, yet is also known from other sources about this family, shows how precarious it can be to make assumptions from single documents.

Elizabeth is Thomas's second wife. His first wife was Julyan Tripplett and they married at Aylesbury on 12 February 1592. Agnes and Audry are the children of Thomas and Julyan and therefore not daughters of Elizabeth. Thomas had four other children who are not mentioned in his will, two of them being boys. They may not all have survived into adulthood. Agnes Hore (or Hoare) married Jonas Orton on 15 January 1617/8 at Aylesbury. Audry married Thomas Harris, and at the time of this will was living in Virginia in one of the very early American settlements there. This is why her father doesn't expect any money to be got to her quickly after his death. The fact that Elizabeth was his second wife makes the appointment of overseers, one of whom is his son-in-law, more sensible. Perhaps Thomas could not totally trust his wife to pay out the bequests to children who were not her own, even though he leaves the residue of his estate to her. If his sons were still alive at the time of making the will, and if Thomas did have properties, 'all the rest of my goodes landes and tenements', then by virtue of this will one might believe that he had disinherited them and his other daughters. However, it is also very likely that money or property had already been given to his other children.

I hope this has shown how much information can be taken from a very ordinary and short will, and how putting it into the historical context and also into the wider family context can alter how you interpret and view the evidence.

My second example is from another will, sixty years later and in Wiltshire:

In the name of God amen I Sarah / Bayly of Warminster in this County Wilts Widdow: being not in / Good health or Body: But of sound and perfect mind and memory / Praised be therefore given to Almighty God doe make and ordaine this my / p[re]sent Last will and Testam[en]t: in manner and forme following (this is to say) / first and principly I commend my Soule into the hands of God Almighty: / hopeing through the merritts death and passion of my saviour Jesus Christ / to have full and free pardon and forgiveness of all my sins & to inhereitte: / Etermal life: and my body I commit to the earth: to be decently buryed / At the discression of my Executor hee after named: And as touching the / Disposition of all such Temporall Estate; As it hath pleased Allmighty / God to bestow upon me I give and dispose thereof as followeth /

Imp[rimis] I will that my debts and Funerall Charges shall be paid and discharged / ff: I give unto my Grandchild Sarah Naish my white whitle and a / paire of sheets: ff I give unto my grand child Thomas Naish the / sum[m]e of Ten pounds to be well and truly paid him: By my Executor / when he shall come or attaine to the age of Twenty one years.ff I / give unto my Grandchild John Naish the sum[m]e of Twenty pounds / to be well and truly paid him: By my Executor when he shall come / or arrive unto the age of Twenty one years; ff I give unto my / grand child Mary Naish the sum[m]e of Twenty pounds; All of / Lawfull moneys of England to be payd by my Executor as aforesaid / And all the rest and residue of my personall Estate goods & Chattells / Whatsoever I doe give and bequeath unto my dear and loving / Sone Thomas Naish whome I make and ordaine my full and / Sole Executor of this my last will and testament. And I doe / Hereby revoke disanull and make voyd all other or all former wills / And Testaments heretofore made by me made In witness whereof I / the said Sarah Bayly to this my last will and Testament have / here unto sett my hand and seale containing haulfe a sheete of / paper this twenty fourth day of January: Anno dom[inus] 1687:

Signed Sealed and Published   Sarah Bayly [her marke]
In the Presents of

John Adlam
Elizabeth Hibberd [her marke]
William Hibberd [his marke]

[This is the original copy with original signatures.]

Proved at Salisbury 5[?]th May 1691

[Note on reverse:]

An inventory of ye Goodes of Sarah Bayly late deseassed
Impr[imus] her Wering Aparell Apraised At £3-0-0
Ff: one bed and beding belonging to [word crossed out]
& one tester bedstead appraised at £5-0-0
In Money & Bondes £70-0-0[39]

This will is perhaps a little more interesting in its tone. It is also an original will showing the original signatures and marks on it. The language here:

> *hopeing through the merritts death and passion of my saviour Jesus Christ / to have full and free pardon and forgiveness of all my sins & to inhereitte: / Etermal life:*

displays some more directly Protestant elements than does Thomas Hoare's will sixty years earlier. The other immediate thing to note is that although Sarah is a widow she is not a poor one, as the

---

39 Wiltshire and Swindon History Centre, Archdeaconry of Salisbury, P2/B/1133.

short inventory of her possessions includes £70 in both money and bonds. These bonds may have been documents drawn up to show that she or her late husband had lent money to someone else. It was common practice in a time before a modern banking and credit system for neighbours to lend each other money, and when this was done a bond would be drawn up. These were essentially private documents, but they provide much material for disputes in Chancery at this date. The will also paints us a picture of Sarah and brings her vividly into the mind's eye wearing her white 'whitle', which was a woollen blanket worn by Westcountry women, sitting up in her tester (four poster) bed. This was a time when a pair of sheets was an expensive luxury and would be something to pass on in a will.

We learn from this document that Sarah made the will on 24 January 1687, which in new style dates would be 24 January 1688: although as it was not proved until May 1691, we can assume that she probably died in the first half of 1691. She mentions her son Thomas Naish, and we can therefore infer that her marriage to Bayly is at least a second marriage for her. Her grandchildren, Sarah, Thomas John and Mary, may be recorded in order of their ages, but they were all under the age of 21 on 24 January 1688. We can tell from the inventory of her goods that Sarah's possessions were her bedding, her clothes and her money. It might well be that she is living in the house of her son Thomas Naish in Warminster. It was common practice during the sixteenth and seventeenth centuries for the widow of a man to be left the bed and bedding from a household and we might also infer that, as a grandmother of four, Sarah is at least 50, possibly quite a bit older, and this would give us a clue as to the range of years for her birth. We also know that Sarah's husband is already dead by January 1688, and that gives us a clue as to when to start the search for his burial or probate documents. What this will does not tell us is the first name of that husband, the names of any of her other children or grandchildren, or any other family names. In fact, it might mislead us if Sarah had had more than two marriages. If the marriage to Bayly was her third marriage, then simply looking for the marriage of a Sarah Naish or Nash to a Bayly would not work. We would have to look at other sources, and in this instance it might prove better to start first with the baptisms and evidence for Thomas and his children.

The direct evidence from Sarah herself in this will is only the following:

Sarah's name at the time of making the will.

Her normal place of residence is Warminster in Wiltshire.

She is a widow.

The date of making the will.

The name of at least one of her sons.

The names of some or all of her grandchildren; those named were under 21 at the date of making the will.

Her personal possessions mentioned and the legacies she leaves.

She doesn't sign her name, but makes a mark.

The indirect or inferred evidence is the following:

The children are listed in order of their ages.

That Sarah was previously a Naish, but has subsequently married a Bayly.

Sarah has been involved in lending money.

Sarah is living in the house of her son Thomas whom she names as executor.

Her named grandchildren are also in Warminster at the date of making the will.

Sarah died in Warminster and is buried in Warminster.

The social status of Sarah as implied by her money, her bonds and four poster bed is of the middling type: tradesmen, shop-keepers, farmers and yeomen.

We can definitely use the pieces of direct evidence to make further searches, while keeping the inferred or indirect evidence up our metaphorical sleeves in order to test them out as hypotheses as we gather further evidence.

We next look at getting the maximum evidence from the census, using an example from 1851. There is a great deal of information on the process by which each census was taken, and as one of the more commonly used records for genealogy there is no excuse for not finding out about it. In the week before census night, the enumerator left schedules with all the households in his particular area. Everyone in the household on that night was to be included. On the Monday after the night of the census, the enumerator returned to collect the schedules. If they had not been filled in, then he (and it was always a 'he' in 1851) had to ask questions of the householder (or whoever was in at the time) so that he himself filled in the schedules. Those schedules were then copied into a book, several of which were bound into folders and given to the registrar. After checking, they made their way to the census office to be checked again.

Below is a transcription of a very unusual household from the 1851 census of Midhurst in Sussex; the full reference is The National Archives: PRO: HO 107/1654/104 pages 4–5.

The place is enumerated as North Street, parish of Midhurst, Sussex. The 1851 census was taken on the night of 30 March 1851.[40] The person filling in the household schedule is William Bayly, Perpetual Curate of Midhurst, also Headmaster of Midhurst Grammar School. We therefore might expect William to display some accuracy in the recording of the household. The 1851 census was the first census where the relationship between the people in the household and the head of the household was asked for, and also the place of birth information included both county and parish. A final column asked whether the person was deaf or dumb, although in my example here nobody was, so I have left it out of what is otherwise an exact transcription, with my own comments in square brackets.

---

40 You can find dates and other useful information for the census 1841–91 in Susan Lumas, *Making Use of the Census* (PRO Publications, 3rd edn 1997).

Name	Relation to Head	Condition	Sex	Age	Rank Profession or Occupation	Where Born
William G BAYLY	Head	Mar	M	51	Perpetual Curate Of Midhurst, LLD	Herts [looks like actual birth place Hants]
M BAYLY	Wife	Mar	F	43		Marlow Buckinghamshire
L BAYLY	Daughter		F	14	Scholar At Home	Midhurst Sussex
H BAYLY	Ditto		F	13	Scholar At Home	Midhurst Sussex
W BAYLY	Son		M	12	Scholar At Home	Midhurst Sussex
M BAYLY	Daughter		F	11	Scholar At Home	Midhurst Sussex
L BAYLY	Ditto		F	7	Scholar At Home	Cheltenham
A BAYLY	Son		M	6	Scholar At Home	Cheltenham
F BAYLY	Ditto		M	9	Scholar At Home	Cumberland
C BAYLY	Daughter		F	5	Scholar At Home	Cheltenham
An Infant	Ditto		F	2 W		Midhurst Sussex
H BIGMOUTH	Visitor	Mar	F	41	Lawyers Wife	Marlow Buckinghamshire
E DUVINS	Governess	U	F	26	Teacher Of Language	France
H PHILLIPS	Governess	U	F	25	Teacher Of Music	London
P DANIELS	Nurse	Widow	F	68	Nurse	Maidstone Kent
M PITHER	Wet Nurse	Mar	F	21	Servant	Hampshire
M HALL	Servant	Unmarried	F	26	House Servant	Cumberland
S TIGGORE	Servant	Unmarried	F	24	House Servant	Bognor Sussex
E BURT	Servant	Unmarried	F	21	House Servant	Fernhurst Sussex

S BLUNDON	Servant	Unmarried	F	19	House Servant	Heyshott
M SEATON	Niece	Unmarried	F	9		Southampton
W HULTON	Ward		M	6	Scholar At Home	India
G RAINE	Teacher	Widower	M	28	Teacher Of Language	Moscow
J TURNER	Pupil		M	17		Bepton Sussex
C SPEEDY	Pupil		M	14		India
J SENES	Pupil		M	14		Easebourne Sussex
H HULTON	Pupil		M	13		India
E LEECH	Pupil		M	15		London
W LEECH	Pupil		M	9		Hertfordshire
A WILKINSON	Pupil		M	11		Petersfield Hampshire
J COOK	Pupil		M	13		Petersfield Hampshire
C YALDING	Pupil		M	12		India
R YALDING	Pupil		M	10		India
W HUTTON	Pupil		M	9		India

There is potentially an enormous amount of information that can be taken away from this household return, even though the head of household looks as though he has been rather lax in filling in the schedule correctly. He omits his own parish of birth and then is inconsistent with other places of birth. The impression I get after studying the return is that William has done this in rather a hurry and, given the sheer number of people he has to account for, I suppose who can blame him for not filling it all in fully.

It seems obvious that William G. Bayly is running a small school at his house, as well as acting as Perpetual Curate of Midhurst. The total number of actual male pupils is eleven, ranging in age from 9 to 17. Also in the household, aside from William's own children, numbering nine in total – one an unnamed infant only 2 weeks old – are two other children: W. Hulton, who is described as 'Ward', and M. Seaton, who is described as 'Niece'. The rest of the household consists of two female governesses and a male teacher, plus four live-in servants and two nurses for the little children. All William's children are being educated at home (no small expense). Finally in the household is H. Bigmouth, described as a visitor and 'Lawyer's Wife'. I notice that she has the same birth place as Mrs Bayly and suspect that she is a relative, probably a sister, visiting in order to see the new baby, and perhaps also to generally make herself useful in running the house while the new mother rests. The work of running such a household must have invariably fallen heavily on William's wife. At first I thought William was having a cruel joke on his sister-in-law. Bigmouth is not a name that is recognized as a surname in any English civil registration index, yet I suspected that this person is Helen, younger sister to his wife. Full names are more usually given in the census, but William has just put initials. This of course makes it much more difficult to find most of the people in this household if you do not know the address and are relying on modern name indexes. After some reflection on the name, I followed the census forward and found in 1881, living with the widowed Maria Bayly, her sister Helen *Weymouth*. It then seemed a bit more likely that, in fact, this is an enumerator's mistake rather than a joke by William. However, it would not be possible to say either way without knowing exactly what William had written. If William's handwriting was bad, it would not be surprising to find other enumerator's mistakes in this entry.

Another fact that can be inferred from the census return would be the large amount of moving about that William and his family have done. Looking at the children's birth places, it is possible to track them in Midhurst in the period 1836 or 1837 to around about 1840, then a birth in Cumberland, followed by three births in Cheltenham, with the final child being born in Midhurst. While it was common for curates to move around the country, without other evidence to suggest that the family was actually living away from Midhurst, then it is possible that Mrs Bayly simply went to stay with relatives to have some of her children. Everybody's year of birth can of course also be inferred from the census.

Another piece of evidence from this census return is the

interesting international aspect to the house and school. One teacher is French; another has an English name yet was born in Moscow, and the majority of the boys come from families stationed in India with the East India Company (until 1857, India was ruled by the East India Company). This was a household that looked outwards to the wider world and embraced both foreign language and music teaching for its children.

We now examine a completely different sort of record and comment this time on the surrogate as held by Ancestry.co.uk and indexed by them as 'Slave Registers of Former British Colonial Dependencies'. The original records are held by The National Archives (TNA) in the record series T71. This database, filmed and indexed by Ancestry.co.uk, is a very good example of an incomplete filming and index of a surrogate. If you look at the source information on Ancestry.co.uk, you will discover a list of places and dates included, followed by a list of places and piece numbers not included, although you need to know where to look to find this information. You also need to be able to match this up to TNA catalogue in order to make complete sense of what has been filmed and what has not. In other words, what is available on Ancestry. co.uk is not the complete set of records as held by TNA, and it should be used with care. It is also an example of a record surrogate that is stripped of all the contextual information and help given by TNA into their holdings, and the understanding of how the registers were created and held. Therefore when looking at documents that are surrogates, or partial surrogates, another question to ask of the document would be, 'Does the provider of this record give the same, or information consistent with that given by the custodian of the record?'

The background to the creation of these registers is that in 1807 an Act was passed that prohibited the trading of slaves from the coast of Africa. It was not until 1834 that the holding of slaves was abolished. TNA research guidance on these records says this:

> There are some registers of slaves created to monitor slave holdings and the importation of slaves into British colonies

between 1814 and 1822, duplicates of which are in the series T71. The first registration for each colony is a complete list of all slaves. Subsequent returns usually only record increases or decreases to the slave populations such as births, deaths, bequests, purchases etc. Many of the returns record where the slave was born so it is possible to identify slaves born in another country and several returns indicate if a slave was exported or imported since the last return.

All of this information is vital to making sense of the registers and this is all before one actually examines any of them. To put these registers further into their record-keeping context, it is also useful to know that the records in the series T71, although first created in the colonies as proof that the 'negroes' they held were not recently traded and were held lawfully, ended up as duplicates within the Office of Registry of Colonial Slaves and Slave Compensation Commission because, under the terms of the Slave Registration Act (1819), a central registry of slaves in London was created, subject to the control of the Commissioners of the Treasury. Under this Act, no slaves could be bought, sold, inherited or moved between the islands unless they had first been entered into the appropriate island register. In 1821 the governors were instructed to send copies of the island slave registers and associated indexes to the London registry. Therefore the record-making and record-keeping history of these registers is complex and there are varying degrees of help, not all of it available with the surrogate images held by Ancestry.co.uk.

The entry I am discussing appears in the Registers for Antigua, indexed by Ancestry.co.uk as St George Parish, and the reference for the register at TNA is T71/245. In TNA catalogue the entry is simply Antigua, 1817–1818 and no mention is made of parishes.

The page has a number 1 in the top left-hand corner and is headed Original Return.

Name and description of Person making the Return etc	Slaves in Possession			
	Names	Sex	Colour	Reputed Age
Marie Antoinette Proprietor	Antoinette	Female	Black	Twenty Four
	Amelia	Do	Coloured	Eighteen
	Total Two			
	Marie x Antoinette her mark July 30th, 1817			

Antigua. I Marie Antoinette do Swear that the Return now by me delivered to be Registered contains to the best of my knowledge a true faithfull and accurate account and description of all the Slaves belonging to me and being within this Island And I do further Swear that no one of the said Slaves has been to my knowledge imported into this Island contrary to the existing Laws for abolishing the Slave Trade. So help me God, Marie Antoinette her mark

Sworn before me the 30th July 1817

Robt. French

The first thing I would point out is that the information that this is from St George's parish on Antigua comes from Ancestry.co.uk and is not included either in the information on the image of the page that holds this entry, nor from the catalogue of TNA. In other words, this information would need to be double checked with the original register. This page, number 1, holds two other returns, very similar to this one, which I have not reproduced here, but browsing other pages in this sequence and other entries shows that this is in fact a typical return, although it contains a few surprises. We tend to think of slave-owners as white male plantation owners, but this entry shows otherwise.

There is no evidence to suggest that the entry is anything other than exactly correct; it is sworn and witnessed and the date is consistent not only with other entries, but with what is known about the history of these registers. However, this is obviously a copy of an original. We can tell this only after browsing the other entries that follow. They are entered in alphabetical order all in the same hand, with no original signatures or marks. The book has therefore been made up after the event from another record. It is a copy and, if you had alighted simply on one entry following the index on Ancestry.co.uk, you might miss this bit of information. A variety of different dates is testament to the varying length of time it took to get all slave-owners sworn before the responsible officer; presumably they had to come into town to do this, and from a remote part of the island, this could take some time. What lists were used to check that everybody had made a return?

From the entry itself we learn that Marie Antoinette is a person of unknown status except that on 30 July 1817 she testified that she had two female slaves, Antoinette and Amelia, aged around 24 and 18. Marie cannot sign her name and has made a mark. The return has come from the Island of Antigua (parish of St George). This is what we can be certain about. What is unknown but might be inferred is that Marie is possibly a freed slave herself, although this is speculation, but her lack of proper surname might be a clue to that. With two young women to help her, she may be farming a small piece of land. As proprietor on her own, it is unlikely that she is living with a husband, although again we cannot be certain of that.

These four different examples have shown us that evidence from any document can be direct (that is, what it says), and also inferred (what we can draw from it, but it does not tell us directly). The inferred evidence may mean that we have to make assumptions. The document can be a contemporary copy; the Harris will is an example of this. Or it can be an original – like the Sarah Bayly will. It can be from a good-quality surrogate, such as the census returns, or it can be from a less complete surrogate like the slave registers. All of these types of document and their degree of primacy may affect the evidential value that we should place upon them. The genealogist needs to understand and work with all types of evidence, and in particular not let any assumptions from inferred evidence take over the research. On the other hand, it is quite OK to develop theories as long as you recognize that theories have to be tested.

Historical interpretation

I said in Chapter 1 that there are many misconceptions about customs and life in the past, and that the misinterpretation of records, and ignorance of the law as it was commonly applied, can lead one into difficulties. The past is neither exactly like today, but nor is it totally different either; basic human nature doesn't appear to change very much. People are still people with emotions, motives and ways of behaving. A familiarity with the different culture of society or communities in the past is not something that can be acquired overnight or by reading a genealogy textbook; it normally has to be earned through direct experience with the record sources over time. As with much else in genealogy, before coming to conclusions about the life and times of our ancestors it is necessary to put away all our preconceptions and assumptions and to approach the documents with a totally fresh eye. Do not allow your own self to come between you and the records. If you are someone for whom an inner monologue is all the time persuading you of new theories, you have to first of all learn to quieten down that voice and absorb what you are being shown.

Sometimes one has to stand back and consider a family within a wide historical context in order to try to make sense of their movements, their decisions and what happens to them. Sometimes the historical context will just be local – a crop failure here, a local tragedy there. Annoyingly, every family is different and it can be very hard to make sensible generalizations about all families in the past, and I know if I do so here, then plenty of people will point out my errors. Even so, a good knowledge of the customs and culture surrounding the people you are researching will help, particularly when you get stuck and wonder 'Why did they do that?' This is not necessarily the kind of history that you studied at school, which tended to concentrate upon kings and queens and other constitutional and political matters. The study of history divides into a number of sub-disciplines and those that may be of particular interest to genealogists are legal history, cultural or social history, economic history, demographic history, local history, urban history and rural history.

Background reading about past times (and particularly the local history of the area where your ancestors lived) is important, but so is finding out as much as you possibly can about each type of record. There are some books aimed squarely at the genealogy market that take a particular type of record and explain the history and background as well as how genealogists can use and interpret them. One recent example, among many, is *Census: The Expert Guide* by Peter Christian and David Annal.[41] However, the real need – now that so many people wish to move their research further back – is probably for greater explanation of the older, more difficult or obscure records. An extremely good way to understand and familiarize yourself with some of these is to read the publications of the county and local record societies.

The London Record Society, like many others, publishes a new volume every year, providing a scholarly introduction, and then good transcriptions of a set of records or a particular manuscript to a high standard, which allows you to read the original in a modern typeface. A good example is Volume 33 of the London Record Society, the subject of which is the Chelsea Poor Law Examinations 1733–66.[42] This is a collection of 469 interviews, known as 'examinations', with paupers and unmarried mothers in the parish of Chelsea over a thirty-three-year period. In his interesting introduction, the editor Tim Hitchcock explains the legal context, gives guidance on in-depth extra reading, and explains what happened in practice in Chelsea, rather than what the law *said* should happen. He points out that in Chelsea the interpretation of the law was subject to the character of the magistrates, the type of examination being transcribed, and even the experience of the clerk writing it all down. Contrary to what one might expect of magistrates at this date, who are often held to have been corrupt, he found no evidence of corruption while studying the records. Reading through the actual examinations shows how any number of misconceptions might need to be re-examined. You don't think people in the past

---

41 Peter Christian and Davd Annal, *Census: The Expert Guide* (The National Archives, 2008).
42 Tim Hitchcock and John Black (eds), *Chelsea Settlement and Bastardy Examinations, 1733–1766* (London Record Society, 1999).

moved around very much? Here are many who have come to Chelsea from all over the country, and with many other stopping-off points on the way. You don't believe people in the mid-eighteenth century lived to be very old? Here are people in their seventies, eighties, and even a man of 90. You don't think that respectable tradespeople might fall on hard times and have no one to support them? Here are many men in just that situation. You think that people always got married in the bride's parish of origin? Most of them here were married elsewhere. You think that marital break-down only happens in modern times? Here are plenty of stories to convince you otherwise.

What, however, do these documents tell us about each individual case aside from the genealogically necessary clues as to name, marital status, children, age and locations? They have to be handled with care because they don't actually give us very much insight into any human emotion or what people felt about their situation. They are formal documents drawn up for a purpose.

Bearing in mind that your family might be exceptions, I will try to cover a few general points that may help you make better sense of records and what they tell us about our ancestors:

- It is hard for us now living in a secular society to understand how people in the past were so much ruled over by the Church and religious belief systems. Strong beliefs had a big influence on day-to-day living. Persecution of those who did not conform could be harsh. However, this does not mean that everybody was a church-goer or non-conformist worshipper, particularly in the large towns where it was becoming more common by the mid-nineteenth century for children not to be baptized.

- We are so used to having to supply proof of our identity that we have forgotten what it could be like not to have to supply a birth certificate, passport or driving licence for the most trivial of things. The baptism certificate used to play the part of the birth certificate, but for the vast majority of people they would never need to show it or supply a copy to anyone, and thus society as a whole placed much less emphasis on docu-mentary evidence for jobs or before marriage, or even to travel abroad; even passports in order to leave Britain were not required until the First World War.

- Class structures tended to be more rigid in the past, with less likelihood of people marrying others from totally different classes. While no doubt there were cases of serving girls marrying the master, and hard-working young men of humble background who rose above their original place in society and were accepted there, it was not common. Nevertheless, there was a circulation over many generations from rich to poor and poor to rich. Many genealogists have pointed out the likelihood of the families of the younger sons of gentry gradually descending down the social scale until they end up with only a surname to show where they came from. The plot of *Tess of the d'Ubervilles* by Thomas Hardy includes just such a family.

- There was generally a far stronger feeling of 'shame' or 'scandal' in the families of those people who transgressed social rules, or where there was mental or physical disability, than there would be nowadays. However, this varies from century to century and probably from place to place as well.

- Women were by and large the property of their husbands and could quite literally be ruled over by them in many ways that we would consider astounding today. Until the Married Woman's Property Act of 1882, any property that a woman owned automatically legally belonged to her husband. The upper classes got round the restrictions of the law by using private marriage settlements and trusts for female heirs. This does not mean that women did not run businesses or have an economically active life as spinsters or widows, but it does explain why there are so few probate documents for married women.

- Early widowhood for both men and women was common, but so was relatively quick remarriage. Any man left with children to look after needed a woman to do that for him, and any woman without a wage earner in the household needed to find one. Many of these arrangements must have been pragmatic rather than romantic, and even first marriages were often ones of convenience or business rather than romance.

- Regions could have very different characteristics and customs, even though they were geographically close to one another. This bred a great deal of insularity and fearfulness of strangers. An 'alien' was someone from another county as well as someone from outside of England.
- Poverty might strike at any time, and certainly over a working man's life there were waves of poverty that came and went depending on whether he was fit enough to work, how many children needed support at any one time, or whether he had children of working age in the same household. This meant that a couple recently married might be in a more secure state than a couple with three children under the age of 6, then relative ease might be found again as the children grew up, until finally old age would once again mean poverty.
- Words have changed in meaning, sometimes greatly so over a period of a couple of hundred years. Dialects and even strong regional accents are now dying across the British Isles, but in documents you will come across dialect words and words that no longer mean the same to us as they did to our ancestors. You may need to look up dialect words or use a scholarly reference work, such as the full *Oxford English Dictionary*, to make sure you understand a meaning.
- Lawyers have their own peculiar way of expressing things, both now and in the past. Be aware that lawyers' language could be distorting how you interpret a document.

Finally, good analysis of documents can be carried out by anyone who can ask basic questions of documents and who can avoid putting their own preconceptions into the minds and lives of their ancestors. Really great analysis of documents, and the evidence they provide, only comes with plenty of practice, coupled with background reading about types of record source written by authors well practised in their use.

7

Planning and Problem-solving

So, you got stuck and you are now at your wits' end with a genealogy problem? First, you are not alone; we all get stuck at times with research. This chapter aims to show by a series of steps how problems can be overcome with both research planning and careful analysis of problems, but if you have come here first in search of inspiration, you should make sure you also read Chapter 2 on effective searching.

To help you work out what extra sources you might need to investigate, I have devised a handy list of sources and ideas in a series of questions, the answers to which will help you plan out exactly what you need to do. Making sure your research matches up to the standard of proof in genealogy (which we look at in the final chapter) also helps with all problem-solving. When you have got a problem or got stuck, you need to take care that you have done the following:

- A systematic and exhaustive search.
- Found reliable evidence and interpreted it correctly.
- Rebutted any contradictory evidence.
- Documented your facts.

If you have not done all of this, do not get discouraged. Now is the time to start putting it right. As well as helping you plan your research and solve your problems, this chapter also provides an introduction to proving relationships and documenting what you do, and all of these things taken together should help with even the most difficult problems.

First step – analysis

Your first step is analysis of the problem. This is simply breaking it down into its constituent parts, checking your facts, and sifting out what is conjecture and what is documented evidence. An important part of this analysis is writing out the problem. Very often the act of writing it out will mean that something is brought to mind that you had previously overlooked. And I don't mean think it through silently to yourself; I mean physically write it out as though you were explaining the problem to someone else. Try imagining that you are instructing someone to do some genealogy research for you. What would they need to know? What have you already done? Where did you do it? What sources of evidence do you have? Are your sources from original documents, from indexes; is it family hearsay? Do you have primary evidence or is it only secondary? How much weight can you put on your sources? Think of yourself like an investigator on a crime scene. If it helps to write out everything on a large sheet of paper, or a board, then do that.

There are several things that have to be part of this analysis. The first is a careful check of all the documents you have that provide evidence for this person's life. Here you may also need to bring to bear the document analysis skills discussed in the previous chapter.

In applying my own advice to the search for the Beresfords when I did this exercise for the purpose of this chapter, I quickly realized that I needed to double-check the 1861 census as I had not got a copy of it and no note that I had looked for it. The realization that there is another obvious source to check is very common, yet often people declare that they have searched everything. I also decided that I should give most weight to the evidence from the death certificate as to Harriet's birth being between July 1819 and July 1820, while keeping in mind the possibility that she was a little bit younger than this. Then I thought about the witnesses to both the marriages of Caroline and Harriet – could there be any clue there? I decided to document them as I had not previously done that.

It also occurred to me at this point to check what sort of street Paris Street was, by using the Charles Booth maps of poverty (available online at www.booth.lse.ac.uk), and I found Paris Street had been given the code purple for a mixed area. It struck me that possibly Harriet and her sister were living by themselves or with an elderly relative in modest rooms after the death of both parents. This theory would be supported by the fact that I had not previously found any Beresford entries in Lambeth on the 1851 census. Of course at this stage this is speculation, but speculation and building of theories helps set up ideas to test in the records. I am aware that I must not get wedded to these theories without further evidence. I must not let my enthusiasm run away with me. Therefore, even though I had previously written quite a lot about the research in Chapter 4, re-thinking it from the point of view of all the evidence gleaned from the original documents had subsequently clarified parts of the problem for me and given me new ideas to ponder.

One very helpful type of analysis is the creation of a timeline or chronology of information. This seeks to show in strict chronological order all the events over a number of years in a family's history. It helps clarify thinking, identify gaps, and raise questions that may resolve the problem. Below is what the Beresford information looks like in a timeline, with documented facts in bold.

Benjamin Beresford came from Ireland [source: family story]
about 1814 – Caroline B. Beresford born Shoreditch [source: 1851 census]

1819 or prior – Harriet Beresford birth [source: marriage certificate, 'full age' in October 1840]

Between 16 July 1819–16 July 1820 – birth of Harriet Beresford [source: death certificate, 16 July 1876 'age 56']

about 1820 – Harriet Beresford born 'Judd Street, Holborn' [source: 1871 census]

1819–1820 – Inferred fact – Benjamin Beresford and his wife alive and living in London

about 1823 – Harriet Beresford born 'Grays Inn, Holborn' [source: 1851 census]

1819–May 1840 – Death of Benjamin Beresford between these dates

31 May 1840 – Benjamin Beresford dead before this date [source: marriage certificate of daughter Caroline]

31 May 1840 – Marriage of Caroline Beresford of 'Paris Street' to George Frederick Nye [marriage register at St Mary's Lambeth, after banns] Witnesses with the surname Nye, difficult to read the handwriting and the first initial

13 October 1840 – Harriet residing in Paris Street, St Mary Lambeth [marriage certificate, after Licence]

13 October 1840 – Marriage of Harriet Beresford to Richard S Taylor 'both of full age' Benj. Beresford described as 'Gent' deceased [source: marriage certificate]

13 October 1840 – Witnesses to Harriet's marriage shown as J L Gawler [?] and John Seager

1851 Census – Harriett born 'Grays Inn' abt 1823

16 July 1876 – Death of Harriet Taylor 'age 56' at Field Court [source: death certificate]

[Paris Street and Little Paris Street described in the Charles Booth notebooks as mixed, some poor, 'ladies collecting rents', but this description is more than forty years later than the marriage certificate, so it is difficult to know how true it would have been for the earlier period.]

New ideas that occurred to me after writing this timeline were to investigate J.L. Gawler and John Seager, the witnesses to Harriet's marriage. Further, a source that had still not been looked at, because the research had mainly been online, was the parish rate books for either Judd Street, Holborn, or Paris Street, Lambeth.

Timelines can also be used together with information about the country as a whole, or the particular town or county where your ancestors were living. Events in your family seen against a back-drop of local events may throw a whole new light on a family and thereby some of the problems you may be having with them.

Second step – present the analysis in another visual way

Putting your facts in a diagrammatic way also helps thinking and can quickly highlight where there are gaps in your knowledge. In this case, I am using a drop-down chart to show the information I know about the Beresfords. Immediately I did this, I was reminded that there could well be one or two other children in between Caroline born in about 1814 and Harriet born in about 1819. The text-based chronology approach had not brought this home to me.

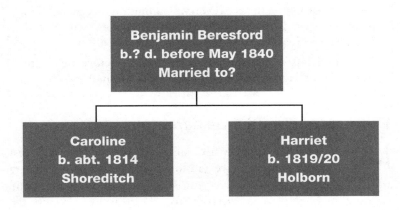

This prompted me to try yet another search on the London parish registers online with Ancestry.co.uk, this time asking the search engine to find burials of anybody with the surname Beresford between 1819 and 1840. My technique here was to see if I could pick up the burials of either Benjamin or any of his children. Systematically going through the results and checking the online images from the burial registers, I discovered the following. There was no Benjamin Beresford, but this entry was found:

Burials, St Mary, Paddington Green, 1835
'Catherine Ann Beresford of Paris Street, West Lambeth, March 7 [1835] age 20'.

No other evidence exists (so far) for Catherine Ann, yet the coincidence of her age (born about 1814/15), and the address being Paris Street, makes me wish to include her as another possible sister of Harriet. If this is so, then it gives a good starting point for a rate book search for Paris Street between 1834 and 1840. It also puts yet another parish into the list of possible places to search, so I add St Mary, Paddington Green, into my growing chronological list like this:

1819 – May 1840 – Death of Benjamin Beresford between these dates

1835 – 7 March – Burial of Catherine Ann Beresford of 'Paris Street, West Lambeth' at St Mary, Paddington Green, age 20, possible sister [source: St Mary, Paddington Green, Burial Register 1835, accessed online via Ancestry.co.uk]

31 May 1840 – Benjamin Beresford dead before this date [source: marriage certificate of daughter Caroline]

Third step – build a research plan

My research that started with a simple search for Harriet Beresford's birth is becoming ever more complex as new results are added and new ideas occur to me. It is time to make a proper plan. A formal research plan aims to bring together your known facts, the date ranges you need to seek, your aims, the resources you are going to use, and where those resources are held. It will build into a solid tool by becoming a research log as you progress since you can also utilize it to record your findings. You can use the research plan as well to make a systematic survey of all the surviving records that could be searched, and note any gaps that occur in the records.

The aims of the research are self-evident, yet necessary to state because it helps the focus of the research. My aim is to find more evidence for Harriet's birth and information about her parents. In fact, so stuck am I with the family that any new piece of evidence about any of them, including Caroline and her husband, and the new discovery of Catherine Ann, would be a good outcome. I therefore set out my aims and a short summary of my starting point or background:

Aim of the research: **To locate Harriet Beresford's birth records and more information about her family in order for positive identification to be made.**

Background to the research:

All that we know for certain at this point is that Harriet was most likely born about 1819 or 1820, probably in the district of Holborn, but by the time of her marriage she was living in Paris Street, Lambeth. Her father was dead by the time of her marriage in 1840 and there is no knowledge of her mother's name. She married an up-and-coming young solicitor and is likely to have come from a similar background to her husband's, although this is supposition on my part. Harriet lived all her married life in the legal quarter of London and died at the age of 56. She has not been found on either the 1861 census or the 1841 census. Allied to this is a family story about Ireland.

I make the research plan in the form of a table with headings. You could use a spreadsheet if you prefer.

Records to search	People to search for	Dates	Repository or website	Comments
Census – Middlesex or London	Harriet Taylor	1861, 1841	Try census searching on Ancestry.co.uk, Origins Network, findmypast, and www.freecen.org and any other relevant census indexes	Repeat searches in as many census databases as possible since they all have different indexing problems
Baptism records: Shoreditch, Holborn and possibly also St Mary, Paddington Green, and St Mary, Lambeth	Caroline B. Beresford

Harriet Beresford

Catherine Ann Beresford | 1810–1840

1815–1840

1810–1835 | London Metropolitan Archives holdings on Ancestry.co.uk | Discover whether there are any gaps in these registers, but also search across London |

Records to search	People to search for	Dates	Repository or website	Comments
Census, and parish registers of St Mary, Lambeth	J L Gawlor and John Seager	1840s		Investigate these witnesses
Rate books, St Mary, Lambeth	Beresford in Paris Street	1830–1840	London Metropolitan Archives – not online	

Fourth step – record new results, analyse and adjust the plan

Following my plan, I started to put it into action. By browsing the marriage registers for St Mary, Lambeth, I found that J.L. Gawlor and John Seager were witnesses to other marriages at the same church and therefore were probably churchwardens or people who were called upon to be marriage witnesses when family was not available. This gave me new information, but it did not help the search for Harriet.

I made another search of baptism records online as this was easy to do, and this time I looked for any baptisms for a Caroline Beresford within the London Metropolitan Archives holdings on Ancestry.co.uk. Once again, the search produced a result in St Mary, Lambeth, which caught my eye, where I could see a Harriet Beresford, daughter of a Caroline Beresford, in 1832. The dates were not what I was expecting, but perhaps my assumptions needed challenging. I investigated further by once again looking at the original images to verify the information from the index.

Here I found three 'adult' baptisms, all on 17 October 1832, at St Mary, Lambeth:

Caroline, adult daughter of Caroline Beresford of Paris Street
Catherine Anne, adult daughter of Caroline Beresford of Paris Street

Harriot, adult daughter of Caroline Beresford of Paris Street

This was the proverbial turn up of the books! Could this be the Harriet Beresford I sought? How could she be an adult in 1832? Was she much older than thought, or were all three of these girls teenagers and not, strictly speaking, adults in 1832? If this was not the family I was looking for, then could it be possible that there were two families with girls called Caroline and Harriet living in Paris Street about the same time? Why were these baptisms into the established Church necessary late on in life?

Suddenly the research had taken a new and unexpected twist.

As I think about what this knowledge tells me, the following questions occur:

a) I have now found three girls, but are there more children?
b) Why no baptism as babies? Could they be Catholics or non-conformist?
c) Did they need baptism certificates for some reason in 1832? Why baptize now?
d) What does the use of the term 'adult' mean in this context?
e) Are the girls living with relatives, or with their mother?
f) What sources have I still not searched?
g) What else can I do online? Should I revisit the census?

As the military saying goes, no plan survives contact with the enemy, so no genealogy research plan remains unaltered following new discoveries. Following adjustment, my plan now looked like this:

Records to search	People to search for	Dates	Repository or website	Comments
Census – Middlesex or London	Harriet Taylor	1861, 1841	Try census searching on Ancestry.co.uk, Origins Network, findmypast, and www.freecen.org and any other relevant census indexes you can find	Repeat searches in as many census databases as possible since they all have different indexing problems

Records to search	People to search for	Dates	Repository or website	Comments
Baptism records: Shoreditch, Holborn and possibly also St Mary, Paddington Green, churches	Caroline B. Beresford Harriet Beresford Catherine Ann Beresford	1810–1840 1815–1840 1810–1835	London Metropolitan Archives holdings on Ancestry.co.uk	Probable baptism found for all three of them as 'adults' in St Mary, Lambeth, 1832. Mother Caroline Beresford
Census for Paris Street, Lambeth	Caroline Beresford	1841, 1851	Do an exact address search for Caroline Beresford using findmypast census street indexes	DO THIS FIRST
Rate books	Caroline Beresford in Paris Street, Lambeth	1830–1840	London Metropolitan Archives	
Probate	Caroline Beresford, Benjamin Beresford	1820–1858	Probate records for Lambeth and Holborn	Make sure I know which court to search
Civil registration indexes – deaths	Caroline Beresford	1837–1851		Date searched will depend on whether I can find her on the census
Post Office and other Directories of London	Benjamin Beresford, Caroline Beresford	1820s–1840	London Metropolitan Archives, www.historicaldirectories.org and TNA	

Fifth step – look at old sources in the light of new discoveries and add new sources to the plan

At this point in the research, I felt reinvigorated. My confidence was growing that I was on the right trail and now I could see that it was worth reinvestigating the census, this time focusing just on the name Caroline Beresford, rather than Benjamin Beresford. Focusing on one person with a street address would enable me to be more inventive with spellings and variations on Beresford, which is a surname that can be spelled a number of different ways. And if I could find Caroline on a census, then I could also search for her death in the GRO indexes.

We will come back to this search later on. For now, though, we will look at adding new sources into your own plan using a record source checklist. I mentioned earlier how important it is to make a survey of all the existing record sources that could be relevant and to be aware of any gaps in the records. The checklist below will help you do this.

Record source checklist

As well as making a research plan, another very useful aid to solving problems is the use of a record source checklist. In fact, the two should go hand in hand, as a checklist can be combined into a research plan to produce a really comprehensive no-stone-unturned approach. I have devised a simple checklist for blocked research, using questions to prompt you to find out or write down the answer. It is not completely comprehensive, but should provide enough pointers to get even the most stuck search going again. Even if your research is not in England and Wales, you should be able to adapt this for any country in which you are researching. Use your answers to form the basis of your research plan. The source list encourages you to broaden your search, to expand away from well-known sources, and reminds you about sources that you should, or could, have checked when you have temporarily forgotten about them.

A: Dates

What is the earliest known date for this person?

What is the latest known date?

What are the dates for other family members?

Are there any conflicting dates – babies born before women were old enough to have children, or after the mother was too old?

B: Geography

Which parish and county are they in?

Which ecclesiastical jurisdiction is that?

Do you know the manor?

What is the registration district or Poor Law Union?

Have you got a map of the area and its surroundings? Is it contemporary or modern?

What were the main transport links at the time your ancestor was there? How can you find out?

Do you know which parishes adjoin? How many parishes are within a 15-mile radius?

Have the boundaries changed?

Does any part of the town or parish fall into another county or registration district?

What local newspaper served the area?

C: Census and Civil Registration

Have you found the family on each of the census returns 1841 –1911?

Have you purchased or found relevant birth, marriage and death certificates when searching in the period from 1837 up to date?

Have you looked at original documents, not just transcripts and indexes?

D: Parish records

Have you checked the parish and each adjoining parish for *all* vital events: baptism, marriage and burials for all family members?

What years did you search and do you need to expand your searches?

Have you looked at original documents or just indexes and transcripts?

What index coverage is offered by the IGI or other indexers, and have you identified any gaps?

Have you checked all of the following sources, well known and more obscure?

If you don't know what some of these sources are, then make it a priority to find out:

Baptisms and Bishops' Transcripts
Marriages, Banns Books and Bishops' Transcripts
Burials and Bishops' Transcripts
Churchwardens' accounts
Rate books
Settlement examinations
Militia lists
Glebe terriers
Other parish material

Could they have been non-conformist? Have you checked non-conformist records?

E: Ecclesiastical jurisdictions

Have you checked each jurisdiction level for the following, starting at the PCC and PCY level and working downwards?

Wills
Administrations
Other probate material such as Act Books
Estate duties
Church courts

F: Manorial and estate records

What manor do they live in?
Have you checked whether manorial rolls survive and where they are held?
Who was the major landowner at the time?
Are there surviving estate records which could have lists of tenants, or throw other light on rural life?

G: Legal jurisdictions

Have you checked ...

> Assize courts?
> Quarter sessions?
> Other local sessions?
> Chancery and other equity courts?

H: Contemporary printed sources

Have you checked which newspapers and trade or street directories cover the area?
Are there poll books?
Is there an antiquarian history of the county?

I: Migration

Do you understand the major transport routes into and out of the parish or town?
Is the parish open to incomers or closed?
Does the parish have large amounts of waste land for incomers to settle on to, or is it all parcelled up and held by one large landowner?
What might be the economic factors affecting migration into or away from these places?
What is the local history of the area?

J: National sources

Have you checked ...

All census returns, including whether census returns from 1801 to 1831 can help?
GRO indexes as well as local civil registration indexes?
Hearth tax?
Protestation oath rolls?
Other tax records?

K: Printed sources and other help

Who has published records or indexes for this county or parish?

Check the county record societies, British Record Society, List and Index Society and relevant Family History Society.

Are you quite sure that you have found all the printed material that relates to the parish, hundred or other area?

Do you understand the history of the area? Have you checked the Victoria County History? What gazetteers and other directories could help?

Have you looked at all the online material for your parish or county? Check that you have searched the following and followed up any links included:

www.genuki.org.uk – Genuki
. Online Parish Clerk – www.onlineparishclerks.org.uk/
www.britishislesgenweb.org/ – British Isles Genweb Project

L: Online catalogues

What results do you get from the following ...

Access 2 Archives?
The relevant County Record Office online catalogues?
The National Archives – catalogue and digitized documents?

Specific problems and possible solutions

It might be that you have analysed your problem, surveyed your sources, made a plan, undertaken extra research, and you are still stuck. In this section I look at some common genealogical situations and what you can do to resolve them. A very common problem is that the parish given in the census or other records for the place of birth is searched and the correct baptism is not only missing, but no evidence of the family name in the right period is found there either. In these scenarios it is important to remember that a stated place of birth does not mean that the birth actually occurred there, or if it did occur there that the child was baptized in that parish in the Church of England. The family may have moved into the parish shortly after the birth and the person simply grew up thinking they had been born there. The mother may have been away on a visit – perhaps with her own parents. Or, vice versa, the child was born in the parish, but was baptized elsewhere. The birth place might have been given as the nearest town, rather than the actual parish, which could lie just outside the town. Consideration should of course also be given to the fact that the child could have been illegitimate and therefore registered or baptized under a different surname. Or, as happened in the case of one of my ancestors who had several completely different places of birth on the census, she had been born in Devon (I can only assume while her mother was staying with relatives), but not baptized until several months later – and then not where her parents were actually living, but in the parish where her paternal grandparents lived. It took me some time to work out that tangle.

If you have no clue as to parents, let alone grandparents, then there are some techniques that might prove helpful. The main one is what is known as whole-family reconstitution and we met it briefly in the search for Henrietta Hobbs. This technique involves research into all and any part of the family: siblings, children, cousins, and so on. The aim is to reconstruct the wider family and to put the family into its historical context as much as can possibly be done. Follow the family in all possible census years and get certificates for each vital event during the period of civil registration; similarly for parish records in the years before 1837. Then add in other sources as relevant for the place and date. This means following everyone from birth through to burial. Aim to be really thorough. The Beresford search is a good example of how information gleaned from siblings can provide a breakthrough. If I had doggedly stuck to just a search for Harriet Beresford, and rejected other results, I would still be stuck. Researching the wider family will also prompt you to make sure you cover all possible years in all possible parish registers, or other records of vital events, and this will ensure that any burials of children are found. This may help in cases where there appear to be two potential candidates. If you want to try this approach, there is an excellent little book that describes the technique in great detail and deserves to be on every genealogist's bookshelf: Andrew Todd, *Nuts and Bolts: Family History Problem Solving through Family Reconstitution Techniques*.[43]

A related technique is to start a one-name study for a specific region. This means collecting everybody with the same surname in one place. Start with the parish or wherever it is thought that the person you seek came from. Make an extract or list of all people with the same surname, regardless of whether you can fit them into your family tree, from the parish registers and any material in the parish chest, such as Poor Law documents. Don't forget to include baptism, marriages and burials. Depending on the date ranges, branch out into other sources such as street directories, census, manorial documents, probate records, anything that covers the area at the same time. Gradually expand the search to include nearby parishes. Eventually you will build up a network of interrelated people that you can fit into trees, and hopefully connect up with your own family. I asked a group of people who had taken this technique as a starting point for a deeper investigation into their surname, and their family's heritage, whether collecting all the surnames in this manner had solved their original problem and the response was that about 20 per cent of them had indeed solved their

---

43 Andrew Todd, *Nuts and Bolts: Family History Problem Solving through Family Reconstitution Techniques* (Lancashire: Allen & Todd, 2nd edn 2000).

original problem. The system is not guaranteed, but it may be all you can do – and so is therefore worth trying. All of those people I asked had eventually turned their search into a worldwide one-name study registered with the Guild of One-Name Studies and had thus taken their genealogy to a new level. With an uncommon name, you might find yourself easily able to record all the instances of the surname in the GRO indexes, while with a common name you would need to start off only within the parish, or perhaps a group of parishes. You may even find yourself using more general surname-studies techniques to investigate origins – for example, there are surname distribution maps and tools that can help pinpoint localities for names. The Guild of One-Name Studies has much information on its website about how to go about a one-name study.

A refinement to the whole-family reconstruction plan is a whole-community reconstruction, also known as finding out about the neighbours. This is a useful technique prior to the nineteenth century when more people lived rural lives and were closely associated with the land. The aim is not to stick with one family name, but to reconstruct the whole community over a period in time, by using land and estate records and probate records. Where a family own or lease land, keep a list of the separate parcels of land to help track it, where it is, and who inherits. This is a very useful technique that can be used with both probate and manorial records. As you do this, you should make sure you read as much as possible about the local history and events within the community that may have affected your ancestors. As mentioned above, plotting local events in a timeline against events from your ancestors' own lives may also bring up some interesting correlations that could open up new avenues for you. Unfortunately, this technique is most difficult in big cities, which had large, impermanent and shifting populations.

Another common problem is identification in a situation where you have someone in one area who also appears in a different period of time in another quite separate area, and you wish to know whether they are one and the same person. The main technique is to research both ends of the story with the aim of finding evidence that either links them, or disproves the theory. If there are two men called Jack Jones in the census in 1851, you know they are separate people, but if you have Jack Jones in 1841 and Jack Jones in 1851 and the ages match up but the places don't, then make more searches until you have exhausted all possible sources. Try to kill one of the candidates off or eliminate him by finding him elsewhere. Things I like to do when faced with a problem like this is first to try to discover how many people there are born in the same place with the same name. That should show you how many potential candidates are involved. Then follow them all up to marriage and death. Then look at what you are left with after you have done that.

For each bit of evidence you have that has a problem, subject it to a test. Could the place be wrong? Could the name be wrong? Could the date be wrong? If the date is wrong, could the year be more than two years out? When weighing up the facts you have discovered, concentrate on those that need better evidence or verification, and then make them the heart of your research plan.

Some other suggestions

Keep a full list of the sources you have used and the dates searched, and review this regularly to see where you may have forgotten to search a source or a year. We look at documenting your sources in the next chapter.

Follow up *all* connections to the family that you find: any business associates and their roles; also godparents who may turn out to be related; and others mentioned in wills and as witnesses to documents.

If you have connections that are not certain, always look for evidence to disprove them.

Use long date ranges for searches.

Use the same source but indexed by different people; for example, don't just search the census on Ancestry.co.uk, but try findmypast and FreeCen as well as other data providers like Origins, or Family Relatives.

Expand the variations on the surname that you try and pay particular attention to whether the first letters in a surname could be mistaken for anything else; for example, Knight and Wright often look very similar in some types of handwriting.

Many British surnames belong to a particular district or region, and mapping the distribution of your name will help you to work out whether that applies to your own name(s). It can even point to a particular place of origin, which can help you to concentrate searches in one geographic area. There is specialized software to help you do this, like the Surname Atlas and Gen Map UK by Archer software (www.archersoftware.co.uk/) and you can also do it free online at the website http://gbnames.publicprofiler.org/.

If you have a subscription to Ancestry.com (not .co.uk), they also provide online maps personalized to the surname, based on the 1891 census of England and Wales.

Staying with names – this time, first names – it is possible that the naming patterns in a family give helpful identification clues. The Scottish have a tradition of naming patterns that help identify parents and grandparents like this:

- First-born son named after the paternal grandfather.
- Second son named after the maternal grandfather.
- Third son named after the father.
- First-born daughter named after the maternal grandmother.
- Second daughter named after the paternal grandmother.
- Third daughter named after the mother.

This can cause families to have two children with the same name if the grandparents had the same name. The process started again if the parent remarried, so it is common to find half-brothers or half-sisters with the same names. In fact, I have seen this in English families as well, with two sons having the same name but different mothers. Not all Scots families followed the exact pattern, but many that did continued it after leaving Scotland and it can be a good clue not only to their origins, but also the names of grandparents. Naming patterns are not used to the same extent by the English, but they do occur in some English families, although not normally in such a formalized way. In my own family, Samuel and Thomas occur over and over again. Helen and the related Eleanor are also common. Small clues like this can provide evidence that relationships exist between people, or that certain people need greater investigation.

If repeated use of uncommon names occurs in a family, this can lend weight to a family being ancestral, even though you cannot make a strong connection using documentary sources, although obviously that evidence on its own would be pretty weak. But take care to know what names are common or uncommon in the area, as it just might be that your region is full of people with the same 'unusual' name.

Occupations are very important as identification tools and often provide supporting evidence for other sources. Usefully, occupations often passed from father to son. Thus in a Welsh community with every other person called Williams, it is often possible to identify the Williams family you are after because they have a distinctive trade such as blacksmithing. Any tradesman might have undertaken an apprenticeship and there may be records of that. Any tradesman may have tools and equipment, even property if he was successful, to leave to sons and other family, and all of this will lead to sources that will help prove relationships.

Another important point to note about occupations is that those occupations that required travel – sailors, bargemen, traders, customs and excise officers, army and so on – might very well have meant a whole family moving from place to place with children born, baptized or buried in different towns, ports or countries. On the other side of the same coin, if you have already found a family that has obviously moved around a great deal, and you are unsure of the paternal occupation, then you should consider what occupations might have caused them to move in just such a pattern, and then investigate from that angle.

Sometimes occupations can be problematical pieces of evidence if information about them conflicts. For example, is a gun-maker also the general labourer found thirty years later? Has the hairdresser become a grocer? In each case, the evidence has to be examined for the individual, although in general, while one does often find people sliding down the social scale as well as climbing up it, it is rarer to find individuals who totally cross class barriers.

The artisan or tradesman who works with his hands very rarely becomes a bank clerk, although his son might.

The same rules for identification apply to religious groups. Religious groups stick together in order to worship together. They tend to settle in the same areas as other members of their community and, in the case of Jewish families in the nineteenth century, often with people from the same original village. If you are looking for Jewish ancestry in areas where there was no synagogue, then you might need to reconsider the search. In other words, look first for the communities. It is known that religious groups such as the Huguenots tended to worship only in their own churches, until such time as the old links gave way and they assimilated and spread into the wider population. However, that took many years. If you are searching for Huguenots from a period in time near to their exclusion from France in the late seventeenth century and early eighteenth century, then you need to be concentrating on the known Huguenot communities before looking anywhere else. If your family is not found in one of these communities, then it is possible that they were not, after all, Huguenot.

You may be able to use records relating to siblings of an ancestor to get round problems. For example, if your ancestor was too old to be recorded in the civil registers of births which start for England and Wales in July 1837, he or she may have a younger sibling who was recorded, and a birth certificate for them will answer the question of the mother's maiden name. Or, you may be unable to find a birth place for your ancestor, but he or she may have had a sibling who worked in a place where birth place was recorded – for example, in the civil service, or the military. That birth place can then be used to get information about parentage.

Sometimes you need to spend money to find what you need. I am always amazed at the number of people who will spend hours and hours of their own time and then pay out for professional research when all they actually needed to do was to buy a few certificates. When working with civil registration indexes sometimes it can be necessary to collect index entries, even the certificates, of all events for all people of the surname in an entire district or sub-district. Addresses, occupations and names of witnesses can help you reconstruct families and to eliminate those who do not belong.

If you are sure of your place and time period and cannot find a birth entry, try looking under the mother's maiden name. The birth could be illegitimate or simply recorded incorrectly. Bear in mind when dealing with marriages that the bride may have been a widow and therefore married under her previous married name, and not a maiden name. Sometimes you will need to search according to the name of the groom only.

Has your ancestor fallen into a gap? It is a rare series of records that has no missing parts at all, and working out where the gaps lie is an essential tool for the genealogist. The gaps that are most commonly encountered by English genealogists are those of known parts of the census that are missing or damaged: deficient parish registers, and indexing gaps in the coverage of the IGI, and other indexes available at Family Search. You must make it your job to find out whether any of these gaps is affecting your research. One of the most useful pieces of advice I ever had early on was to work out systematically which parishes were covered by the IGI, which ones were not, and then to make my searches within the ones that were not. Often this will involve making a table with all the possible parishes listed down the left-hand side, and the IGI or other index coverage down the right-hand side.

As the price of DNA testing comes down, more and more people are turning to DNA evidence to test not only paternity events, but also historical relationships. However, those who are experienced with research that combines DNA testing as well as documentary genealogical research warn that the approach must be a dual one. DNA might settle a problem of ancestral identification – for example, are all of us with this particular surname descended from the same man? However, it does not provide you with all the links in between; the genealogy research still needs to take place.

In Chapters 1 and 6, I introduced the subject of historical interpretation, pointing out that making sure you properly understand the historical context is normally very helpful. Background reading on the history of the area, as well as social history to understand more about the period of time when you are stuck with a problem, will help. You might even want to include some background reading in your research plan.

Back to the Beresfords

Finally, I am returning to analyse my Beresford plan again in the light of all the above and to tell you what happened next. We left the story with my plan pointing to a more focused search of just Paris Street on the census. This sort of area search used to be very common when we searched the census on microfilm; but now the census surname indexes tend to mean that we only do surname searches. findmypast has census street indexes, but you can also search page by page at Ancestry.co.uk within the correct area until you get to the right street. I used the street index on findmypast.

My next discovery was that Caroline senior was on the 1851 census at 19 Paris Street, indexed and enumerated as **Carolin Beresford**, widow, aged 60, born St Martin Ludgate. In the house she had two lodgers and a live-in servant. This quickly led to her discovery on the 1841 census, but not before I had again to use the street index to find her, since she had actually been indexed and enumerated as **Carlione Bersford**. That particular combination of names I should probably never have discovered on my own and it is a very neat example of why you may need to try several different ways to get to information.

The fact that Caroline was alive in 1851 prompted further searches in the census returns, and then a search in the National Probate Calendar, and she was found in the following entry:

7 March 1883, The will with a codicil of Caroline Beresford, formerly of 71 Westminster Bridge Road, Surrey, but late of Taunton Road, Lee, Kent, Widow, who died 27 December 1882 at 45 Taunton Road, proved at the Principal Registry by George Beresford Nye, 1 Sansom Rd, Leytonstone, Grandson

The grandson's name is the best piece of evidence that this is the correct Caroline. A double check with the GRO death indexes shows an entry for the correct quarter, December 1882, for Caroline Beresford, aged 95. This gives Caroline a possible date of birth of around 1787.

Now my quest is to discover why those three girls were baptized as 'adults' in 1832, whether Caroline was ever married to a Benjamin or in Ireland and, if so, when, to purchase a copy of the will (although I doubt Harriet is mentioned since she herself died in 1876), and to make further efforts to discover more about the family in the round. My problem is not entirely solved, but it has become a great deal clearer why I had the problem in the first place (no baptism when and where expected) and I have gained plenty of new information.

8

Recording Information and Citing Sources

You may remember that I said in the previous chapters that documenting your searches is important. This chapter aims to set out why and how genealogists should record their findings and keep a record of the sources consulted. Unfortunately, providing good documentation for the growing family tree is a habit or skill almost no genealogist has right from the start. It needs an effort of will and it is all too easy to put it off and procrastinate even when we have become convinced that it would be useful and we can see why it is necessary. Of course, we are all doing *some* recording of information. We would not get very far at all if we did not record something about what we find. But it is the way we record what we find that marks out the true professional. Almost all of us have records of some kind; original documents like certificates, copies of census returns, other items taken from the internet, notebooks, perhaps charts we have drawn, family stories we have attempted to write about or have discovered, computer records of some kind, perhaps even audio recordings if a relative has been interviewed. Part of being well organized is that you know where to search for the documents and records you have collected and filed away. Equally important is making sure that you keep a precise record of all your sources, which should be recorded with both your paper collection and records you have on computer. This simply means keeping information about where you found something linked to the fact you found.

Sounds OK so far, doesn't it? But hang on, it gets a little bit more complex and this is mainly due to the relative value of our evidence and the huge range of sources that we use: primary, secondary, derivative, online, printed, transcribed, index and so on. Keeping a note of sources and making sure that each event in the life of everybody in your tree has an attached source is known as documentation. Good documentation will not only save you time when you need to revisit your own research again, but will also ensure that others who follow after you can recreate your steps quickly and easily. Most important of all, it helps you to justify your conclusions.

It was not until I joined the Society of Genealogists that I came across the pedigree chart, which the Society refers to as a 'birth brief'. Before I became a member, I had exclusively used the drop line chart or familiar tree chart, and mainly on a huge bit of wallpaper lining roll. This was before computer packages were widely available for genealogy. In fact, I was so green that I had not really given any particular thought to recording people systematically, generation by generation. The pedigree chart or birth brief blank form given out by the Society to new members is meant to be filled in by the budding genealogist and submitted back to the Society when completed; it is then bound and kept as an on-going record of a member's interests. The information needed starts with you, includes parents, grandparents, great-grandparents and great-great-grandparents, and it forces you to fill in all the relevant dates – birth or baptism, marriage and death or burial (where relevant) – for everyone. I was immediately struck by the usefulness of the chart in forcing the researcher to take one step at a time and to record accurately the dates of birth and marriage for everyone. For the first time, I was tasked with searching for and buying the certificates in order to get those dates, and I also began to realize how proceeding blithely with research that was based on vague or incomplete knowledge wasted research time and, more importantly, money.

I was, however, already familiar with sources and how they are used within historical research. I just needed to tie together my newly accurately recorded information with my sources. A source is very simply a person, book, document or perhaps an artefact that supplies information. It is *wherever you get your information from*, but it will mainly be from a record or document. A source could be a birth certificate, a baptism entry from a parish register, a bit of text on a website, or even an oral tradition passed down in your family. Sources can be held on many different media; original documents in their original formats and located in an archive, surrogates on microfilm and held digitally, books, journals, magazine articles, Wikipedia and other online information sources, indexes, transcriptions. We have seen in previous chapters how we can divide sources into primary and secondary, and how some sources like transcriptions and indexes are derived from others. A citation is just the full textual reference to the source and is required when you need to refer to the source in a piece of writing on a chart, on a tree, or within a family tree database. So, to recap, documentation consists of accurate recording of findings, in a systematic way, with a place to cite sources.

There have long been citation standards for work required at university level and within academic publishing, but the sources that most academics use and quote from are often books and journals, and these are quite easily understood and used. Genealogists have had to devise their own way of citation because of the very varied nature of our sources, and because of the many prints, copies, surrogates and derivatives that can be used – as well, of course, as the growing number of sources that can be found on the internet.

There is not very much information for British genealogists on anything much to do with standards in genealogy – whether/how to cite sources, produce transcriptions, or produce an error-free tree – whereas the situation has evolved differently in North America, with standards and rules being advocated by American writers. I believe there is one main reason for this and it is not because the British do not care for high scholarly standards, but because there have traditionally been some big differences between the sources routinely consulted. In the USA there is a vast amount of uncritical, unscholarly work deposited in the big genealogical libraries that has found its way into many family trees. With so many Americans being descended from relatively few early migrants, those trees have multiplied and been copied many times until the wrong information has been reproduced everywhere. The situation only got worse with the internet, making trees even easier to copy and disseminate. Some American genealogists decided they had to declare a kind of war on all this mistaken information and to try to go back to basics.

The lineage societies also wished to improve their standards. Added to this, researchers in Canada and the USA find original sources more difficult to access. In contrast, in England, being a relatively small country, it has been far easier to get to see the original documents and hence we do not rely on published work by other genealogists to anything like the same degree. We are therefore one step closer to the source almost all the time. But this does not mean that we shouldn't cite our sources.

Consistent recording of where we found our information is a big part of good organization, and good organization saves you time. As I have shown with my examples, genealogy research is a complex process and it is all too easy to forget where you found something. Cast your mind back to the Beresford searches and how much more difficult I could have made it for myself if I had not recorded my findings and used my plan as I went along. Some might argue that if you are doing your family history as a hobby, then recording and citing sources accurately and to a high scholarly standard is not necessary because it is only you who needs to know. I would counter this by pointing out that you can waste a great deal of time tracking down the reason *why* you think something is true, if you get into a muddle, but have not recorded where you found that something. Also, you never know if the next generation might want to pick up your research later on. Another reason is that if research is worth doing at all, then it is worth doing it well. The best guarantee of quality research is that others are able to examine in detail the arguments used to make any proof case by repeating the steps using citations. A well-documented tree with full source citations means that others can weigh up the reliability of your sources, and the likelihood that you have reached the correct conclusions.

There has always been a sharp divide between those who defend their right not to record their sources to any kind of standard and those who understand and see the need for a very rigorous standard indeed. It is true that any kind of information giving names, dates and places will provide clues for further genealogy research regardless of whether it comes complete with full citations or not, and that it is probably an impossible dream to expect hundreds of thousands of hobby genealogists to stick to complicated academic standards.

However, there are very good reasons for at least attempting to apply standards to your own work, while at the same time recognizing that it is impossible to be perfect all of the time. Everybody makes mistakes, even good genealogists, and bad ones make a lot of mistakes; following some documentation rules helps to prevent this. We saw in previous chapters how getting to the facts and cutting out supposition and assumption helps with solving a research problem. Being disciplined about recording source information is a vital part of this. 'How do I know this is true?' is actually a question we should ask ourselves all the time as we fit people and events into our trees. When we document our sources, it ties in the people and events to the evidence much like a buttress will support a wall.

I think that, in the main, we all can see that recording where we found information is useful. What is not so evident to the beginner is that it is also extremely useful to make a record of searches that have proved negative as well as to record positive findings. At a yet more sophisticated level the great genealogist will also be recording whether a complete search in the record series was made or whether it was partial; allied to this is noting whether the record source itself had missing or damaged parts, or was from a transcription or index rather than the original record. How many times have you had to go back to something with the question 'I wonder if I searched all of that really thoroughly, or did I miss something?'?

When and how do we record both our sources and our searches? The answer is as we go along. If you start recording at the beginning of your research, it becomes a habit. However, if you have not been doing this then it is not too late to start right away. The process is made easier if your family tree software prompts you for source information when you add in vital events to your tree. When family tree software had only just come on the market, I chose Legacy Family Tree because at that time this was the only genealogy software package that allowed detailed writing of sources. The source writer within this particular program is based on established citation standards. More and more programs help with the process now, but not all of them have the same standard of holding citations and references and this is an important consideration.

There are three interrelated issues:

1 What you should aim to record about the research process as you go along.
2 The facts you will need to try to find out and their correct documentation.
3 How to display the sources within the text or on charts.

Recording the research process

The first principles of any research should be that you do not need to repeat the search as a result of your own carelessness, and that you have recorded your results accurately and acknowledged the source of the information correctly.

If you never take notes when you research, you will live to regret it. At the very least you need to make sure you keep a record of the documents you look at, together with the date that you looked at them and where you were looking. This advice used to be much more obvious when all genealogy research, like any kind of historical research, was done in the record office – either looking slowly through microfilm, or looking at original documents. Not that long ago, even getting photocopies of documents was difficult and handwritten notes were all that one could take away from the record office. However, since much is now online, more and more people are referring to websites as sources of information, rather than the actual records that the websites hold or display. The emphasis has changed from 'I found this in the parish registers of X which I had to travel to Y to look at' to 'I found this on Ancestry.co.uk'. Along with other genealogy data websites, Ancestry.co.uk is a publisher, so saying that you found something on Ancestry.co.uk is akin to saying that you found it in the local library; it doesn't answer the question of exactly where, or tell us about the source of the source, because Ancestry.co.uk databases cover many hundreds of different sources.

Your notebook need not be the old-fashioned kind, but could be any note-taking or word processing program you have on your computer, or in the research log section of your family tree software. Try to get into the habit of recording your searches as you go along.

Obviously, your notes need to be legible and you need to be able to understand what it all means in ten years' time when you revisit this particular notebook or digital page. It will turn into a useful log of what you have done. Keep your research log in the same place as the rest of the information about the branch of the family being researched. When you have problems or hit a dead end, your research log will be one of the first places you look as you work out your plan. I give below some simple rules to try to follow. I don't set these out from any sort of desire to make your research more difficult and less fun, but simply because I have committed each and every one of these note-taking sins myself, so can speak from experience that they have tripped me up further down the line.

The first thing to record is the date you made the search. This is important not only in a record office, but also when researching online because websites are constantly being updated with new information and a search at different dates will more than likely have different results.

The second thing to record is where you are. This might seem overly obvious, but it will either be the physical record office, or archive, or a website. It is very easy to forget to input this step, but it can cause problems later on if you forget.

Then note down the record series you are looking at. Is it the 1851 census, birth indexes from Kentucky, the IGI, or are you at TNA looking at CUST 116, or are you doing a blanket search of all the databases held on a website to see what happens?

When you perform the search, points to note might be any different spellings tried, and what combinations of spelling, place and date were tried.

All your results should be recorded, whether positive or negative. This will help to prevent you doing the same search again and wasting time.

As you record results, make sure you distinguish between searching within original documents, transcriptions, or just index entries. If you cannot immediately work out from the website you are using what exactly it is an index to, or a transcription of, then note that down and make sure you find out. Do not add the results into your tree until you have confirmed the ultimate source and can acknowledge what it is.

Ensure that you collect all names, places and dates accurately. If you cannot read them, then do not guess; simply put a bracket around an unreadable letter or word or put your guess into brackets, as in this example:

John, son of [.]tofer and Ara[bella?] his wife

If you use abbreviations, then be consistent. Pay particular attention to the use of the letter 'b' for born, baptized or buried, and get into the habit of using 'b' for born only, 'bp' (or 'c') for baptized, and 'bur' for buried.

If you use documents that have unreadable or missing parts, record the unreadable parts. It might be very helpful to know that many pages of a baptism register are badly water damaged, or that the legal document you are taking notes from has a page torn in half.

When searching through a large index – for example, the GRO indexes – record whether you stopped at the first match, or whether you went on to make a complete search of the whole index, or made a complete search within a date range. Similarly, if searching any index that can be divided by geographic area, and you only searched Lancashire when you could have searched the whole of the UK, then you also need to note that it was a partial search based on the criteria you chose.

Make sure that when you go back to re-read your notes later on, you can see the difference between a fact that you have taken from a record and your own notes on that fact. If you start off by transcribing a line or two from a document, make sure you mark clearly where the original words end and your own notes begin. If you need to transcribe a complete chunk of text, then do so using all the original words and their spelling. If you are not making a transcription, then make it clear that you are paraphrasing or putting something into your own words. A good rule to abide by is that if you start transcribing, then make sure you finish it off! A partly transcribed document may look later on as if it contains all the original text, but if you stopped before the end due to boredom, or being distracted, what you are left with might be very misleading.

If you take photocopies, print out images from the internet or take digital photographs of documents, you should aim to put the full document reference on the front of the copy you produce. This helps prevent the image and its source being separated from each other should it be reproduced again. This is even more important if you are only able to take an image of part of a document or part of a page within a document. You should do this immediately you have taken the copy to prevent forgetfulness later on.

Finally, beware of any website that encourages digital capture of information without also digitally assigning the correct sources and reference to it.

To show how easy it is to produce misleading notes while also appearing to write things down accurately, here is an example from some handwritten notes I made which, if not corrected, would later cause me to go back and check it all again, unnecessarily:

St Dunstan in the West,
Catherine dau. of Thomas and Ann Beresford, Bp 16 June 1782, born May 23 in Fetter Lane

St Martin Ludgate,
Frances, dau. of Thomas and Ann Beresford, April 5, 1792, born March 10, 1792

[married St Mary, Islington Thomas Hibble Esq of Hornsey Bach. With the consent of Ann Beresford, Widow 15 July 1811]

It looks OK, doesn't it? While it remained fresh in my mind, I knew exactly how I found these results, but in a few months' time I have forgotten; I will also have forgotten whether that entry in brackets refers to Frances or to someone else, and it will send me back to search for it again. I may very probably have to go and look again to see whether there is any information I missed, whether I have actually transcribed it word for word, and I will have forgotten how I searched and whether there could have been any other entries that would be useful. In other words, it shows what I found, but it does not record the full research process.

Here is a better recorded version:

Date of research: 26 September 2011
London Metropolitan Archives parishes on Ancestry.co.uk;
online indexes used, searched for any Beresford baptism and
marriage with parents Thomas and Ann. Original page images
looked at.

St Dunstan in the West, Baptism Register, 1782
Catherine, dau. of Thomas and Ann Beresford, 16 June 1782,
born May 23 in Fetter Lane

St Martin Ludgate, Baptism Register, 1792
Frances, dau. of Thomas and Ann Beresford, April 5, 1792,
born March 10, 1792

[More baptisms were found, also children of Thomas and
Ann, but I didn't note them]

St Mary Islington, Marriage Register, 1811
15 July 1811, Frances Beresford of this parish and Thomas
Hibble Esq of Hornsey, Bach. with the consent of Ann
Beresford, Widow

Extra important information has been added to the second set of
notes: the date the search was carried out; the online database used;
a note that the search results are incomplete; and the marriage has
now been correctly noted to show both parties and to take away
any ambiguity about the notes made. These notes, however,
although they give a very good idea of the sources, still do not meet
the very highest standards of source citation.

Making your own transcriptions

The making of transcriptions from records seems to be a dying
art because so many people nowadays either acquire a photo-
copy or a digital image of any document they need for their geneal-

ogy. Sometimes it is necessary to have a transcription done if the handwriting is very difficult, but I also find the disciplined act of writing out exactly what is on a document is a very useful habit for letting the mind think about what is being said and the evidence it contains. You just do not get this pause for reflection time if you are quickly scanning a document and taking a few notes. Writing things down also helps you to remember and to fix details in your mind.

An accurate (or attempt at accurate) transcription is also vital when analysing older documents that may be faded or damaged or difficult to read because of the palaeography. A painstaking reconstruction, letter by letter and word by word, may be necessary to make any sense of it at all. I often find that palaeographic skills I have learned come in useful with the scrawl of Victorian handwriting, which can be very difficult to decipher. In other words, sometimes transcriptions are necessary simply to read a document properly.

The basic rules of transcription are simple; each and every letter should be reproduced as faithfully as possible. The discipline required to do this is immense, and if you are typing beware the spell checker that automatically alters the 'misspelt' words as you go along. Normally what happens when we read is that the eye and brain skip letters and scan along a line, guessing at what is there. This approach will not provide accuracy, and meaning will be lost if attempts are made to read documents without a letter-by-letter approach. When reading legal documents such as wills or deeds, particularly those from the nineteenth century forwards, there is often a great deal of repetition and legal terminology that seem designed to obfuscate the meaning of the document to the non-legal brain. In these cases as well, if you truly wish to get under the skin of the document, a transcription of it all, including all the lengthy boring clauses, does help immensely.

There are several different standard rules for transcriptions, the first of which is to be consistent in any approach you choose. If you are transcribing for a publication or a report that others will see, and not just for your own benefit, then you must tell your reader about the rules you are following. For example, you may choose to keep, or at least show, the original line breaks as I did in the examples of the two wills in Chapter 6. Are you going to keep the original punctuation, or would you modernize it? Will you modernize dates? There are many aspects to consider, just as any editor of a modern text has to consider options for format, punctuation, the use of capital letters and so on. It is very important not to guess letters as this could alter the meaning. If you really cannot read them, then leave a blank or put one letter above another. Even experts have to do this and there is no shame in it.

The style you choose might be one of the following:

- Faithful reproduction of everything, including all the original abbreviations, contractions and punctuation, with the only difference being that it is put into a modern hand or typed.
- Faithful reproduction of all letters, but expanding contractions and abbreviations by placing them into brackets or using other symbols to indicate that you have done this.
- Modernizing the text in part, perhaps adding modern punctuation and expanding the abbreviations and contractions without showing that you have done so.
- A greater amount of modernization, including converting the spelling into modern spelling, using modern capitals, or lower case letters where appropriate, but keeping the order of the words. This approach needs a lot of editorial skill and a deep understanding of the sense of the original text.

You can read more about transcription rules and practise your palaeography by taking an online tutorial at The National Archives website. There are also a number of good publications that will help you improve your palaeography skills, although the only way to really learn it is to practise and practise. The most common mistakes are to modernize spellings and forget to provide a document reference.

Recording sources and document references

As mentioned previously, because of the vast number of potential sources of information, genealogists have had to come up with some very precise ways of referring to sources and a standard or style guide has been developed, based on the *Chicago Manual of Style* for the humanities. This is called the Mills system, after the author Elizabeth Shown Mills, who has written extensively about citing and documenting sources. Her work has revised the *Chicago Manual of Style* to make it more relevant to genealogists.[44]

In theory, style guides like Mills's are not really necessary if you are using genealogy software that prompts you to provide the correct information in a series of forms and where the written or published work will be created using this software. Sometimes you might be submitting an article to a family history journal which has to be composed outside of the dedicated family tree software, or when you are using software that does not have a good citation system built in; in these cases you may need to know how to cite sources correctly and consult a style guide.

Citation standards appear very complex, pernickety even, and this has proved a double-edged sword for their supporters. Complexity puts people off, and they simply reject the whole idea of citation standards unless they can be persuaded of the underlying principles.

Different types of sources have different ways of citation. A document or manuscript from an archive will have a special reference, usually made up of an alphanumeric code. We met these in the chapters on records. You will also need to record the repository holding the document, and the title of the record series or class. It may also be necessary to quote the page or folio number. This ensures that anyone following in your footsteps can close in on the information and get right to the same page without having to search again.

If I had looked at the marriage register for St Mary Islington at the London Metropolitan Archive, then the reference for that particular register would be the following:

London Metropolitan Archives, Saint Mary, Islington, Register of marriages, P83/MRY

---

44 Elizabeth Shown Mills, *Evidence! Citation and Analysis for the Family Historian* (Baltimore: Genealogical Publishing Company, 1997).
Elizabeth Shown Mills, *Evidence Explained: Citing History Sources from Artifacts to Cyberspace* (Baltimore: Genealogical Publishing Company, 2007).

You might also add in the year range, although if the date is apparent in the entry, then that might be superfluous. Because, in this case, I looked at the images of the register online on Ancestry.co.uk, then I must also add in that information to give an even more complete picture of what I was doing. This shows that I have used a surrogate source and should also include when and where I accessed it.

If I had taken information from a book, then I would cite the author's name, the title of the book, the publisher and the date of publication.

Transferring information from notes into the tree – what should I aim to collect about each person?

At the very minimum, for each direct line ancestor on your tree you should aim to collect:

- Birth or baptism dates, preferably both where possible, together with locations as precise as possible.
- Marriage date, place and details of spouse, together with witnesses (if shown).
- Death or burial, preferably both; exact dates and place.

Collecting all these pieces of information, and not skipping any of them, helps you to collect enough evidence to prove your connections. This is a subject that we shall come back to in the next chapter. It goes without saying that you should aim for a very high standard of accuracy. Here is an example of a precise record, which doesn't yet have any sources added:

Ellinor Jane Beale
Born [date unknown]: Location [assumed to be Manchester, Lancashire]

Christened: 24 May 1809: Location: St Ann's, Manchester,
    Lancashire
Married: 14 May 1839, to Isaac Sutton: Location:
    Manchester Cathedral, Manchester, Lancashire
Died: 15 October 1892, Location: Westbourne House,
    Barbourne, Worcestershire
Buried: [unknown place and date]

The same information recorded in a great hurry, and in an inaccurate and deficient manner, could well look like the example below and be very misleading. See how many discrepancies you can spot:

Eleanor Beal, b. May 1809 in Manchester, married Mr Sutton, died in Brabourne age about 90.

This sloppily recorded information would not stop someone finding Ellinor, but it would slow them down and waste time, particularly the little spelling error in the place of death which would lead to a search of Brabourne in Kent and not Barbourne in Worcestershire. If it were used by someone who did not think to look at different spellings of both Beal(e) and Eleanor/Ellinor/Elinor, then it could bring the research to a halt. There are nine copying mistakes in just one short set of life events.

As well as being accurate about the basic facts for Ellinor, the sources for each event should be recorded; therefore for her date of christening I would need to add the information that this comes from the IGI, that the marriage date comes from a GRO marriage certificate, and that the place and date of death come from the National Probate Calendar. This allows me to weigh up the evidence from each of these sources and to work out whether they need to be corroborated with anything else, or followed up elsewhere. This is how the same information looks with the sources added:

Ellinor Jane Beale
Born [date unknown]: Location [assumed to be Manchester,
    Lancashire]

Christened: 24 May 1809: Location: St Ann's, Manchester,
   Lancashire [**source: IGI**]
Married: 14 May 1839, to Isaac Sutton: Location:
   Manchester Cathedral, Manchester, Lancashire [**source:
   GRO marriage certificate**]
Died: 15 October 1892, Location: Westbourne House,
   Barbourne, Worcestershire [**source: National Probate
   Calendar**]
Buried: [unknown place and date]

An example from further back in the past makes the reason for
source recording more obvious when sources that definitely need
further corroboration are made clear:

Martha Manaton
Born: date not known, she was said to be of Kilworthy,
   Devon [source: handwritten family tree]
Married: 1773, to Cornthwaite Ommany [date calculated
   from birth of youngest child] Location: Not known
Died: 1813 [source: handwritten family tree] Location: Not
   known

Here I have noted that the information comes from a handwritten
tree. I could improve the source information by giving this tree a
file location, so that I know where exactly I have placed this particular tree and where to find it again. This file location could be
either a reference to a computer file or a folder in my filing
cabinet, or it could be 'from a tree in the possession of my cousin,
X, seen by me on [date]'. In any case, the vagueness of the information is a warning bell to me to corroborate the sparse
information from the handwritten family tree with better evidence, preferably from original documents. A further point to
note is that where you have guessed dates or speculated them
from events in someone's life, it is important to make a note of
the fact that this is a guess. This means that when I come back to
search for the marriage, I will know to expand the search for

some years either side of 1773. In fact, Martha was not born in Kilworthy, but in London, although the tree was right about the year of her death as her burial is recorded at St John's, Westminster, on 18 March 1813.

The above examples show the beginnings of a system of documentation. It is a system that is adequate for genealogists interested just in building their own trees to their own satisfaction, and wanting to record information that is helpful and that will provide clues as to where to continue the search. However, it doesn't yet reach the highest possible standards as advocated by Mills.

Examples of depth of documentation

I now give three examples of family group information; the first is an undocumented version for some of my Beresford information, the second is a documented version, and the third version I have called a 'hyper-documented version', with full citation standards adhered to. In these examples I am using the evidence and sources found up to the point when I had discovered baptisms for the three girls, but before I had completed searches for the mother, Caroline.

The first family group record below for the Beresfords is correct as far as it goes, and absolutely typical of many of the family trees found on Ancestry.co.uk or GenesReunited and other places where people can publicly place family information. Here, the information has not been filled in with the exact dates and places and shows inconsistencies. For example, all three girls were baptized on the same day and at the same place, yet this is not shown. No sources are shown for any of the information. Anyone who was given the record as it stands, even though much of it is accurate, would have to seek to verify almost all the information again, and without clues as to where the information came from in the first place; undocumented trees can waste huge amounts of time.

Beresford family group – undocumented example

Husband: Benjamin Beresford, Gent
    Born: Ireland
  Christened:
    Died: 1819–1832?
  Buried:
  Marriage: Place:
==
Wife: Caroline
==
    Born:
  Christened:
    Died:
    Buried:
==
Children
==
1. Caroline Beresford
    Born: Abt 1814 – Shoreditch
  Christened:
    Died:
    Buried:
    Spouse: George Frederick Nye
----

2. Catherine Ann Beresford
    Born: May 1814
  Christened:
    Died:
    Buried: 7 March 1835
    Spouse:
  Marr. Date:
----

3. Harriet Beresford
    Born: Cal 1819 – Judd Street, Holborn, London
  Christened: 1832
    Died: 16 July 1876
  Cause of Death: Pneumonia, age 56
    Buried:
    Spouse: Richard Stephens Taylor (1808–1882)
  Marr. Date: 13 October 1840

The next example is better recorded and documented with notes on sources for all events, although the source citations do not comply with the Mills standard.

Beresford family group – documented example

Husband: Benjamin Beresford
    Born: Ireland[45]
Christened:
        Died: 1819–1832?[46]
    Buried:
    Marriage: Place:
==

    Wife: Caroline[47]
==

        Born:
    Christened:
        Died: 1832?[48]
    Buried:
Living at, 1832? – Paris Street, West Lambeth[49]
==
Children
==
1. Caroline Beresford
        Born: Abt 1814 – Shoreditch[50]
    Christened: 1832 – St Mary, Lambeth
        Died:
        Buried:
        Spouse: George Frederick Nye (–   )
    Marr. Date: 31 May 1840 – St Mary, Lambeth, Surrey[51]

Catherine Ann Beresford
        Born: May 1814

---

45 Family story.
46 Speculation; death date not known.
47 Name from Baptism Register of St Mary, Lambeth; 1832 entry for daughters Caroline, Catherine and Harriet.
48 Speculation; death date not known.
49 The Paris Street address occurs in several sources for the children, and for Caroline in the Baptism Register of St Mary, Lambeth; 1832.
50 Census, 1851.
51 Marriage Register, St Mary, Lambeth.

Christened: 1832 – St Mary, Lambeth
    Died:
    Buried: 7 March 1835 – St Mary, Paddington Green, London[52]
    Spouse:
Marr. Date:

Harriet Beresford
    Born: Cal 1819 – Judd Street, Holborn, London[53]
    Christened: 1832 – St Mary, Lambeth, Surrey[54]
    Died: 16 July 1876 – 3 Field Court, Grays Inn, London[55]
Cause of Death: Pneumonia, age 56
    Buried:
    Spouse: Richard Stephens Taylor (1808–1882)
    Marr. Date: 13 October 1840 – St Mary, Lambeth, Surrey[56]

This type of partly documented information, albeit with a little inconsistency of source citation, is a great deal better than nothing at all. If you can do similar with everybody in your family history programme and in your note-taking, then you are to be commended.

In the final example I show what I am calling a 'hyper-documented' family group. I have also updated the information to reflect the most recent findings. The fullness of the documentation here is to a higher and more complete standard. Whereas the source information in the documented example would enable any researcher to follow the trail and to start to weigh up the evidence as presented, in the hyper-documented case the extra step of citation according to style rules has been applied. If you were considering publication for your work, then attempting to meet these standards would be a good idea.

---

52 Burial Register, St Mary, Paddington Green.
53 Census, 1851, birth year varies from 1819 to 1821 according to source.
54 Baptism, St Mary, Lambeth.
55 GRO death certificate.
56 GRO marriage certificate.

Beresford family group – hyper-documented example

Husband: Benjamin Beresford
    Born: Ireland[57]
Christened:
    Died: 1819–1832?[58]
Buried:
Marriage: Place:
===
============
Wife: Caroline[59]
===
============
    Born:
Christened:
    Died: 27 December 1888[60]
Buried:
Lived at, 1851 – 19 Paris Street, West Lambeth[61]
===
============
Children
===
============
1. Caroline Beresford
        Born: Abt 1814 – Shoreditch[62]
    Christened: 17 October, 1832 – St Mary, Lambeth[63]

57 Family story, from handwritten notes in the possession of Helen Osborn [address could be added here].
58 Speculation; death date not known.
59 Name evidence from baptism of daughters Caroline, Catherine and Harriet, 17 October 1832, London Metropolitan Archives, Saint Mary At Lambeth, Register of baptisms, P85/MRY1, Item 358, online Ancestry, http://ancestry.co.uk, accessed 5 October 2011. [No direct evidence of marriage between Caroline and Benjamin.]
60 National Probate Calendar, England and Wales, online Ancestry, http://ancestry.co.uk, accessed 5 October 2011.
61 1851 Census, England and Wales, Ref: TNA; PRO: Class: HO107; Piece: 1571; Folio: 430; page: 22, online Ancestry, http://ancestry.co.uk, accessed 10 October 2011.
62 1851 Census, England and Wales, Ref: TNA; PRO: Class: HO107; Piece: 1513; Folio: 514; page: 23.
63 London Metropolitan Archives, Saint Mary At Lambeth, Register of

---

Died:
Buried:
Spouse: George Frederick Nye (–   )
Marr. Date: 31 May 1840 – St Mary, Lambeth, Surrey[64]

---

2. Catherine Ann Beresford
    Born: May 1814
    Christened: 17 October 1832 – St Mary, Lambeth[65]
    Died:
    Buried: 7 March 1835 – St Mary, Paddington Green, London[66]
    Spouse:
Marr. Date:

---

3. Harriet Beresford
    Born: Cal 1819 – Judd Street, Holborn, London[67]
    Christened: 17 October 1832 – St Mary, Lambeth, Surrey[68]
    Died: 16 July 1876 – 3 Field Court, Grays Inn, London[69]
Cause of Death: Pneumonia, age 56[70]
    Buried:
    Spouse: Richard Stephens Taylor (1808–1882)
Marr. Date: 13 October 1840 – St Mary, Lambeth, Surrey[71]

---

baptisms, P85/MRY1, Item 358, online Ancestry, http://ancestry.co.uk, accessed 5 October 2011.

64 London Metropolitan Archives, Saint Mary At Lambeth, Register of marriages, P85/MRY1, Item 415, online Ancestry, http://ancestry.co.uk, accessed 1 October 2011.

65 London Metropolitan Archives, Saint Mary At Lambeth, Register of baptisms, P85/MRY1, Item 358, online.

66 London Metropolitan Archives, Saint Mary, Paddington Green, Register of burials, P87/MRY, Item 064, online Ancestry, http://ancestry.co.uk, accessed 5 October 2011.

67 1851 Census, birth year varies from 1819 to 1821 according to source.

68 London Metropolitan Archives, Saint Mary At Lambeth, Register of baptisms, P85/MRY1, Item 358, online.

69 General Register Office, England and Wales, death certificate, September 1876, Holborn 1b, 406.

70 Ibid.

71 General Register Office, England and Wales, marriage certificate, December 1840, Lambeth 4, 291.

When do I use footnotes or endnotes?

Footnotes and endnotes are used when you publish your family tree information as a piece of text – for example, as a written family history. If you are never going to publish any of your family history or send it to anyone else, or place it on any website as a chunk of text, then you can skip this section. Sources are usually displayed in two places in the text, when the fact is first presented, and again at the end in a bibliography or separate list of sources. A footnote is a system using numbers, or sometimes special characters, to draw the attention of the reader to a note at the bottom of the page. You can use either footnotes or endnotes – the latter come at the end of your text. Although footnotes on each page are a great deal easier for the reader to follow if they wish to follow up your sources immediately, many people prefer not to have their reading broken up. The following needs to be decided:

a) How you mark the source in the text.
b) How you arrange the references or source list at the end.

You need to decide whether to use a number within the text and then footnotes/endnotes, or whether to put the full reference within the text. It does not matter which you choose as long as you are consistent.

In a system of footnotes, each fact in the text is keyed to a consecutively numbered footnote which carries the source citation. Source citations are not just for pieces of prose, but should be used for charts, trees and family group sheets – in fact, all pieces of information you compile about a family. The more explicit they are, the better. Clarity is extremely important; in fact, in the Mills system clarity is placed even more highly than consistency. It is obvious from the above examples how attention to detail is paramount. All stated facts in your tree need a source. If you give a birth date or place, it needs a source. If you quote from a document, it needs a source.

Referring to books and journals

If you find details and facts about your family in a printed book, then you also need to know specifically how to reference the book. There are several different styles or systems for referring to books and articles. I show two of them here. The Short Title system gives the full reference to start with – e.g.:

Colin D. Rogers, *The surname detective; Investigating surname distribution in England, 1086–present day* (Manchester University Press, 1995), p. 82.

Then, whether footnotes or endnotes, all later references to this work are shown as:

Rogers, *Surname detective*, p. 82.

Or you can use the system known as Author-date, which is largely used in sciences and social sciences; this is very similar to the Short Title system. Again, the full reference is given to start with:

Colin D. Rogers, *The surname detective; Investigating surname distribution in England, 1086–present day* (Manchester University Press, 1995), p. 82.

And subsequent mentions look like this:

Rogers (1995), p. 82.

You can see examples of a system used for scholarly history papers found online by visiting the online version of the Victoria County History of the Counties of England at www.british-history.ac.uk, where they have a facility to show you different types of citation style for the work you are looking at.

Complications are added when citing a work that is both printed and online and, of course, nowadays some works that would previously have been printed are only available online. There are many online journals, blogs and sites where you might find information you want to cite which can need more specialized treatment than just citing website and author.

It is now best practice to cite a web page *with the date accessed*; this is because websites are continually changing.

Referring to manuscripts and documents

If you are referencing primary sources, then you use whatever form of reference is used by the repository or owner of the manuscript. For example, a full 1881 census page reference is written like this:

The National Archives: PRO: RG11/1200/54 p.24

And within the references at the end of the paper, you would include a word definition of the series code (RG 11), which in this case is:

RG 11, Registrar General, 1881 Census.

There are a full set of instructions for quoting primary sources from TNA, 'How to Cite Documents in The National Archives', on their website (www.nationalarchives.gov.uk/catalogue/RdLeaflet. asp?sLeafletID=333&j=1).

Other institutions have their own referencing systems, but almost all archive repositories follow the same broad pattern of alphanumeric series code followed by numbered piece information.

When citing your sources in a tree you have compiled, or family history you have written, it is not necessary to repeat the full citation each time. The second time the source is cited you can use an abbreviation; likewise, you don't have to repeat information about the repository over and over again. However, don't do this before you actually publish a final version, because when you are working on a document the page order changes as you work. The use of the same source for a number of different facts signals that you have really used the source to the full and helps the reader feel confident.

In my example of the hyper-document Beresford family group one of the sources is the parish registers of St Mary, Lambeth, and my second and subsequent citation of the same source could have been abbreviated. However, if you are never going to publish, this bit of advice can be safely ignored.

How do I construct a source list and bibliography?

A source list occurs at the end of your text. Again, if you are never going to publish, you can ignore it. However, if you are, then the source list should include all the items cited in the text and no others.

As well as your source list you can also include a *Bibliography*, and this may contain either more or fewer references. The layout of the references should be clear and consistent. Book titles can either be in italics or underlined (publishers normally use italic rather than underlining), but do not mix the two. References should be arranged in alphabetical order by author.

Citation software has been around for a number of years, and if your family tree software does not already come with a good source recorder and writer, then you might want to consider using something extra to help. Mendeley (www.mendeley.com/) allows you to share research, and also to collect (free) bibliographical references from PDFs and from a variety of websites. It is easy to work with, although aimed at the academic community. There is also an optional citation tool (www.mendeley.com/citation-generator-maker/). Citation Machine (http://citationmachine.net/) and End Note (www.endnote.com/) are also well known.

Further information about citing sources

You must never cite a source you have not used personally, even though it is sometimes tempting to repeat the notes made by another author. In these cases you can only cite the other author.

This helps prevent the repetition of errors since the other author may have made a mistake with his or her sources. And, by the way, you should get into the habit of checking other people's sources to make sure they have got them right. Because source citations are fiddly, it is easy for authors and publishers to muddle up citations, give wrong page numbers, and so on. This is extremely frustrating when you try, as a reader, to follow up on a source.

Documents seen on microfilms and microfiche often need special citation treatment, as do other surrogate or derivative sources like transcriptions and indexes. Use your common sense; in most cases they may be good surrogates, but it is still prudent to quote the film number, rather than the reference to the original document. If you have used a transcription of a parish register, then quote the author of the transcription as the first part of the citation.

If you do use a style guide, you will probably find that you have an example of a source that does not seem to fit into any category that is covered. In these cases it is useful to have fully understood the underlying principles, so that you can follow your nose.

Once you have understood the reasoning behind documentation and citation standards and principles, it becomes much easier to acquire the habit of implementing them and to make sure your work is the best it could be. Much will depend on whether you are looking at original primary sources, secondary or derived sources, or published books. A major rule of British genealogy has always been to seek to confirm all your secondary sources with the primary source. This is not always possible in the short term, but in the meantime we should cite the sources that we do have, even if they are not primary. With over 2,000 people in my family tree, and more being added every now and again, I realize that it is becoming increasingly unlikely that I shall ever get the time to double-check all my secondary source information against original documents, yet that does not mean that I can't cite the IGI as a source where I have used it. If someone else picks up my work after I am dead and gone, then at least they will know which parts of the tree need the most confirmation work done.

This chapter has had to cover some quite technical issues and it may not all have been your cup of tea. The most important point to take away is that you will find it very helpful when you get stuck if you have made a clear and consistent record of your sources that include the type of record, its correct title and its covering dates, rather than just the website where you came across an entry. If you only record the web address, in a few years' time this will have changed and your source citation will no longer be of any use. If you do manage to cite your sources to the very highest standards by comprehensively following Mills, then your research will stand the test of time and be worthy of passing on to the next generation of researchers who might follow you.

9

Organize, Store and Pass On

All researchers have to organize themselves and their records, whether the records they hold are paper based, or held electronically on their computer. What actually matters are principles, rather than the exact medium of storage. Unfortunately, filing is not a very exciting subject and it is all too easy to put off confronting the mountain of documents we collect, whether they are paper or digital. Good genealogists tend to be naturally methodical and systematic people with good organizational skills; but not all of us can be all of these things all of the time. Anybody who has a slightly scatty side will know of the struggle they endure just to get their desk organized, let alone all their family records. Yet organize you must. We are not all blessed with ample office space and unlimited bookshelves on which to store our reference works, magazines and papers, and most of us have to make do with very little. Lack of space, both physical and even electronic, forces us to make choices about what we keep and how we store it for the long term, and the need to find things quickly and efficiently will dictate how it is stored. Allied to this is the question, however far away it might seem now, of what happens to all your hard work when you are no longer around to look after it. And, of course, many people want also to produce something, charts or a book of family history, for all the family to share. The subjects of organization, storage and display of information are all interlinked, as indeed they are with the other themes of recording and documentation.

Most modern genealogists will have a dual system of paper-held records and digitally held ones, and there is now plenty of computer software on the market to help you organize your basic pedigree or tree, and to keep track of your sources. Organization of your growing pile of family facts is an on-going process and it is something that most of us struggle with. Only the most hyperactive on the document organization front will have the problem of proper organization licked. Therefore if you feel that your record-keeping could be improved, you are certainly not alone.

There are two important points to consider:

1 Paper copies of documents are normally collected in some quantity by the genealogist. We have to buy certificates, we print off copies of census entries, we make copies of parish register entries, we buy copies of wills, we collect and make hand-drawn trees, we take notebooks into the archives.

2 Much research is now done via the internet and using digital media and it is becoming increasingly possible to store everything digitally. However, it is not just a case of putting it into your computer and not thinking about organization again. There are still good organizational practices to follow.

Physical storage is not really the issue – or not the whole issue. The issue is how you retrieve the information you need, when you need it. And also how to work with the unique complexities of keeping records relating to several interrelated families discrete from one another and yet easily cross-referenced, so that marriages into a family and collateral branches are kept neat and tidy.

I have experimented with a number of differing methods, including an old-fashioned index card system, and, even given the huge advantages of a computer-based system, I do not feel that it is at all easy to abandon my original paper-based system. I will go on to discuss specific issues relating to long-term storage later on.

The exact arrangement and organization of records will greatly depend on the kind of pedigree building you are attempting. If you are like me, then you will be researching outwards in ever-increasing rings each of your 2 x grandparents, 3 x grandparents, 4 x grandparents and so on, while at the same time expanding particular parts backwards more rapidly as new sources of information are found and assimilated. A complicating factor arises from the fact that you will be both *collecting* records and *creating* records. On the one hand, you are acting as a library of source materials for the pedigrees you are working on, but you are also creating those pedigrees in the first place, with trees, notes, research logs, lists, and so on. I am going to start by describing some systems for paper-based systems because, however much you work with computers, understanding file arrangement is easier if you can visualize physical files in a filing cabinet.

Dealing with paper

A simple system to start with and a very useful tip comes from the Family History Library at Salt Lake City, from the American genealogist Mary Hill. This system is known by some as the Mary Hill colour-coding system. It is this: divide your paper files into a colour-coded system. For each of your 4 grandparents, use 4 colours:

My paternal grandfather's family is coded blue (shown here in roman text) – GARDNER

My paternal grandmother's family is coded green (shown here in bold italics) – *BLYTH*

My maternal grandfather's family is coded red (shown here in italics) – *BEACHCROFT*

My maternal grandmother's family is coded yellow (shown here in bold) – **TAYLOR**

All the files related to these families carry the correct colour coding. You can either buy coloured files, or mark them with sticky coloured tape or dots, easily purchased from stationers.

Further subdivisions have to be made when the file gets too unwieldy. For myself, I decided to divide files at the 2 x grandparent stage, which makes for 16 surname subject files. They each have a document wallet-type folder and take up about half a filing cabinet drawer:

Gardner
Rankin
Cussons
Strickland
Blyth
Ness
Bilton
Eden
Beachcroft –
    subdivided into 4 files, divided by *time period* reflecting
my particular interest in this family
Bayly
Cooke
    Subdivision – *Leigh*
Clowes
Taylor
Humbert
Bentley
Sutton

Each file here not only represents a family line, but of course it also represents a married couple. The Gardner/Rankin line represents William Gardner, who married Jane Rankin. Information about Jane has to be split into two parts. Her life before her marriage to William Gardner is contained in the Rankin file. Her life after her marriage to William is in the Gardner file, as are the details of their descendants and also William's family going backwards.

There are then two options: one is simply to open up a new file for each family found going backwards, although this would quickly mean 32, and then 64 files, and you would soon need a filing cabinet just for the file covers, most of which would remain empty or with only a scrap of paper in them. The alternative is to keep details of all females and their own lines going backwards with their husbands, until the physical file gets too fat for one file and a series of new files has to be created.

Additional files may be added outside the colour system for charts and general information that relates to the whole ancestry. If you keep a lot of correspondence with family member(s) about family history matters, you may need to make a subdivision specifically for them within the coded system.

When you have a very big family tree that goes back many generations on plenty of lines, you will need to create further subdivisions. Because I have some lines going back many, many generations, most of them collected from other family members, and from published sources, and all of this information needs to be checked against original sources, I found it helpful to also create a letter-coded system to quickly identify family groups. This meant that I could keep a paper-based lever arch file containing sheets for all my direct ancestors filed alphabetically.

I created a system whereby each person in this paper system was coded based on the first 3 letters of surnames of the 16 people above. This is an extension of a card catalogue, and for every direct ancestor in my tree I have one side of A4 which contains a quick reference to everything known about them. It is written in pencil, so that mistakes can easily be corrected and new information added in. I file them in alphabetical order of surname, and within surname by the relationship to myself, thus my grandfather is on the page before my great-grandfather and the page after that is my 2 x great-grandfather. I can remove the sheets from the ring binder and take them with me to the record office if I wish, or have them to hand by the computer screen. These pieces of paper are placed in the lever arch file alphabetically by surname, and their code helps me to quickly identify which part of the family they are from.

The first person in this record system is my 5 x great-grandmother Milcah ABRAM (code CUS), who married John Cussons on 23 March 1761 at Old Byland in Yorkshire, and the last person is my 9 x great-grandfather Robert YEVELY (code CLO), and the only thing I know about him (and that is not for certain) is that he lived at Langley near Macclesfield and was the father to Catherine who was baptized in 1621. The code CLO shows me that he is a line coming into the CLOWES family.

Each sheet sets out:

Relationship to me and their code

Title
Name
Born
Baptized
Place
School/Apprenticeship
University
Occupation
Married to whom
Date
Lived at
Other details (such as children)
Date of death
Age at death
Where
Buried at
Will proved

You would be free to alter these details. I used them because they made sense to me at the time, and reflected specific details I was interested in. My own handwritten system is labour intensive, yet it suits me as I often get new inspiration for research when physically writing something out in pen or pencil.

Father's lineage codes are therefore:

GAR for Gardner
RAN for Rankin
CUS for Cussons (and so on)
STR
BLY
BIL
NES
EDE

Mother's lineage codes are:

BEA
BAY
COO
CLO
TAY
HUM
BEN
SUT

At their great-great-grandparents, these files and their codes are further subdivided (a potential subdivision of 16 x 16 = 196) so that COO becomes

COO/LEI
COO/BRY
COO/BEE

The more subdivisions a code has, the more the relationship is concerned with female lines. My 10 x great-grandfather GARDNER, the direct ancestor of my father, should I ever find him, is always going to have the code GAR.

I settled on these sheets before I had a computer and before I came across the family group record sheet used by many other genealogists and available to print out from most family tree software programs. The family group sheet shows information organized by husband, wife and children. Group sheets are very handy as they keep all information about a family together; however, in a paper system they do require some duplicate information to be entered because of course everybody has dual roles: as a child, as a spouse, and as a parent. Complications occur if you have multiple marriage partners who in turn also have multiple partners. They work best with a small nuclear family. My coding system and individual sheets reflect my desire to go backwards on all ancestral lines: 2, 4, 8, 16, 32, 64 and so on. The drawback of my system for people who wish to pursue many collateral lines where you research and build up trees with a much flatter structure by follow-up on siblings and cousins, and not expanding backwards, is how to keep a coherent system using just one surname. In this case, different branches of a family could be coded according to where they break from the main trunk, or by location if, for example, you have a Yorkshire branch and a Lancashire branch. In these cases you may prefer to use the family group sheet idea to keep information based around marriages and the children produced from them in discrete files. Again, some sort of colour coding will be useful. If your files become extremely voluminous, then you will need to have some kind of key or mini catalogue to help you navigate easily through all the marriage files.

An example of a family group record sheet is given below. You will notice that it is the same format as I used to illustrate the Beresford citations back in Chapter 7.

Family group record for Samuel Beachcroft

```
================================================
Husband: Samuel Beachcroft
================================================
       Born: 1673
  Christened: 13 Aug 1673 – Lavenham, Suffolk
     Died: Nov 1733 – Wandsworth, Surrey, London
   Buried: 29 Nov 1733 – St Michael Bassishaw, London
   Father: Rev Samuel Beachcroft (Abt 1647–1686)
   Mother: Susanna Gurnall (Abt 1650–1685)
   Marriage: 30 Oct 1701          Place: St Giles, Cripplegate,
                                         London
================================================
  Wife: Mary Mathews
================================================
       Born:
  Christened: 16 Oct 1680 – St Michael Bassishaw, London
     Died: 3 Mar 1732 – Wandsworth, Surrey, London
Cause of Death: Apoplectic Fit
     Buried: – St Michael Bassishaw, London
   Father: Richard Mathews (Abt 1640–1706)
   Mother: Martha Stanlake (1651–1706)
================================================
Children
================================================
1  M  Matthews Beachcroft
       Born: 1707
```

Christened:
    Died: 17 Jul 1759 – Wanstead, Essex
    Buried: Jul 1759 – St Michael Bassishaw, London
    Spouse: Elizabeth Porten (1703–1767)
Marr. Date: Apr 1729
    Spouse:
Marr. Date:

----

2 M Rev Robert Beachcroft
        Born: 1708 – <All Hallows, Barking>
Christened:
        Died: 13 Dec 1775 – Walthamstow, Essex
        Buried: – St Swithin's, London Stone, London
        Spouse: Susanna Hudson (Cal 1696–1770)
Marr. Date: 5 Apr 1738 – City of London, London, England
    Spouse:
Marr. Date:

----

3 F Mary Beachcroft
        Born: 1714
Christened:
        Died: 23 Dec 1761
        Buried:
        Spouse: Joseph Beachcroft Esq (1678–1757)
Marr. Date: Between 1729 and 1731
    Spouse: Osborne Fuller (–   )
Marr. Date: 10 Apr 1760 – Tottenham, Essex
    Spouse:
Marr. Date:

==

Medical Notes: Wife –

==

11 March 1732 'On Friday last the Lady of Samuel Beachcroft of Wandsworth Esq one of the Nephews and Heirs of the late Sir Robert Beachcroft was taken ill a little after dinner of an Apoplectick fit of which she dy'd.'

A note in the possession of Mary Beachcroft

Last Modified: 2 Nov 2011

I have not added in the sources.

There is a very big temptation to physically file some documents by the *type* of record – for example, to keep all copies of wills together regardless of who they refer to, or to keep all birth certificates in the same folder. This should be resisted, unless you are going to go to the trouble of making a key or index at the front of the wills folder, or birth certificate folder, and then cross-reference them to other information elsewhere about that person. It is far better to keep the documents that relate to one family together in their own family folder. Then when you suddenly need to answer a question – for example, 'Did I ever find and get the will for Joe Smith?' – you will only need to go to the family file to find out. You will also see at a glance how few or how many facts and sources you have collected for a family, depending on how fat the files are. Similarly, do not file copies of documents by repository or where the information was found. This will inevitably lead you to amass a great deal of information that you cannot find again.

Computer systems

Now in case you have dismissed me as a complete Luddite, I of course recognize that for the majority of people most of their family information is going to be stored digitally on a computer, whether that is a PC, a laptop, or even a mobile phone, and it will be accessed via the specialist software that is used to hold the information. The family tree software will use a database and this means that there is a huge advantage over any paper system because of the ability to sort information electronically and ask questions, such as how many people in my tree were born in Cheshire?

Ultimately, however, the medium should not be mistaken for the message. In the main what you need to be concerned about is whether you can retrieve what you need, when you need it, and how you are going to keep the information secure and accessible for the next generation without it degrading so that it cannot be read.

All family tree computer databases assign an individual key or number to each person and the sorting and storing of information takes place out of sight. This does not mean that you can totally ignore it, as what you can eventually do with all your data in this database will depend on how consistently you enter the data into the system.

The software on offer differs quite considerably, although at first glance they all seem more or less the same. Currently Family Tree Maker and Legacy are two of the most comprehensive packages, coming top in best buy tables, but you will want to check that any software you choose includes the following:

- An ability to assign sources and to write source citations to the best standards; also an ability to assign sources to media and not just data. A rating system for sources is also a good idea, allowing you to put together numerical values for your evidence.
- Flexible screen views allow you to easily understand the relationships you see on screen. There should be options for multiple relationships (adoption etc.) and a relationship calculator to allow you to see how you are related to the person on the screen. It is useful to be able to see an individual view, a family view and a pedigree view.
- Flexible data entry, which also ideally prompts you to be consistent when entering place names and other names. Sources should be easy to assign consistently. A drop-down menu for county selection can be a good idea.
- Dates should be treated so that there is an automatic date format, but which can also be overridden. Check that old style/ new style dates can be accommodated for dates prior to 1752.
- Notes and facts or events pages should be available to enter extra information about a person's life. There may also be options for an automatic age display on charts and print outs.
- The import export function should allow you to import and export your data as a Gedcom file.
- A powerful search or query tool that allows you to quickly and easily search for individuals or marriages, and also be able to sort all of the data by event, place or date. This will allow the most flexible use of all your data and help you to make some interesting connections. For example, I find it very useful to be able to see who in my family tree was baptized or married in any particular county; this reminds me what person

to search for extra information about when making a visit in person to a record office. The query or search tool is definitely an important consideration. Also very useful is an automatic problem spotter that lets you know when you have people in the tree who are over 100 or who marry at age 10, or mothers who are linked to births over the age of 55.

- Multimedia support will allow you to add photos and audio files and scanned documents into the database as attachments to people and events.
- An ability to import data direct from online sources can be useful, but make sure proper source citation is available for the process.
- Support for different languages might be important to you if you have ancestors from outside the English-speaking world.
- Open more than one database file at a time.
- Making and printing reports and charts will probably be extremely important for you, so make sure you can produce charts in different formats, such as ancestor and descendant charts, as well as compile narrative reports to provide the basis for a full family history. Other helpful functions are the facility to produce:

> To-do lists
> Timeline files
> Place reports (people and events)
> Web pages
> Printed books (without an additional program required)
> Printed wall charts (without an additional program required)

Some extras, like a Soundex Calculator, or the ability to store DNA results and track medical conditions, might also be important for you, as will the help and support available for the program.

It is possible, using a scanner, to input all your bits of paper into your computer for storage and to aid retrieval as well. In this case, you will definitely need to have some kind of system for linking the right document to the right person and cross-referring it to others who might be mentioned in it. For example, a birth certificate commonly tells us about three people, the child and two parents; a marriage certificate normally contains information about four people, with the witness signatures of another two as well. A will may contain information about dozens of people. You could consider using folders on the computer that mirror the physical folders you would have held the paper documents in, or you might want to store digital documents with an index system linking them into your family tree database. Using your source lists can also help you do this. For example, if I have assigned a copy will as the source of information about many people in the family tree, then using the source citation as a key piece of descriptive data within my scanned files will enable a link between the two to be made – for example, TNA: PRO PROB 11/1249 f.24. This is because each document has a unique key already built into its citation. In this situation, where a key for a document is easily used to find the document again, you can store the digital copies in a folder called 'wills'.

Your family tree software program may allow you to do some of this. In the program Legacy Family Tree, for example, you can add a picture or a scanned document and attach it to any person. Although the facility to add documents and photographs is very useful, personally I think it is simpler and less time-consuming to keep copies of paper documents separate and only to consider digitizing if space is really at a premium for you. For me, two paper documents on the table will always win out for ease of use, against two documents side by side on the screen; and a whole file of paper relating to one family spread over the table enables me to feel somehow that I am more tangibly in touch with the family concerned.

Even if you do scan in all your source documents, you still have the problem of what to do with the paper. Should it be discarded, or kept in the loft until you die and your children have to decide what to do with it? There are no easy answers to that one.

Collecting information about people who may or may not be related

It might be that you are collecting all instances of a surname, or doing a community reconstruction, or you just need a holding area before you have checked connections and you can transfer information into a family tree database. I have just cleared out a huge pile of paper that was in a physical 'dumping ground', waiting for entry into the computer, by deciding to file it within the relevant family folder. And this is another very relevant point; sometimes we simply collect paper or digital copies of information that we intend to add into the family tree, but it gets put to one side and it then builds up. Where do we store it while it is in 'pending' and once we have entered it into our system? Does it always go into the relevant file? Do the files contain a mix of unchecked and checked information? One way around this dilemma is to have a separate plastic wallet inside your files for un-entered information. Then you can see at a glance which paper documents have had their information entered into the computer and which ones still have to be dealt with.

If you have lots of people who are unconnected and you are waiting and hoping to connect them into your tree, a sensible way of storing their information would be to enter the details into a computer spreadsheet (or if you prefer paper, make an index card for them). In this case, you will need to be very careful to set up fields that are meaningful and to keep your data entered in a very consistent way. One means of keeping tabs on all these people who are *not* linked into families is by assigning them a unique code – again, one that is based on place of birth or other geographical event will work well.

Sorting your information

As well as being able to retrieve information about people quickly, the one other thing that an electronic system can do more easily than a paper system is *sort* the information so as to provide the basis for more analysis and greater insight into your family. The timeline or chronology that I suggested in Chapter 7 is easy to produce when you already hold the information in a database or even a simple spreadsheet. As mentioned above, it is now a feature of many family tree packages. You may also be able to retrieve all the people born in a certain parish or other place, all the people who are buried in a particular cemetery, or even all the men who have more than one marriage. Age at marriage and age at death are also interesting facts to squirrel out along a whole ancestral line. There are many interesting permutations that you can play with once you have enough people in the tree. I love the extra insights that this can bring to a search, or where I realize that two unrelated parts of the family were living in the same place at the same time and might have known each other.

Use of geocoding for locations

Geographical Information Systems – GIS for short – have sprung up all over the internet and are fast becoming a useful tool for genealogists. Google Earth and Google Maps are both GIS systems. A relatively new and exciting way of visually sorting and displaying information is to show events such as birth, marriage and death on an electronic map using geocoding. This works by assigning a longitude latitude map reference to your information – for example, for a birth place – and translating it into computer code. It has become a feature of the latest developments within family tree software, as well as on some websites.

These kinds of tools have many advantages for genealogists because they can visually display vital events for many generations, allowing you to easily plot migrations and help you to understand the geography of events. However, such systems are simply another way of sorting your information – in this case by location – and then allowing you to see it in a new way. In some cases, older maps, such as those produced by the Ordnance Survey, can also be used as a layer over the modern map, so that not only can you see your ancestor's birth place on an electronic map, but you can also see the features of the landscape from a contemporary or near-contemporary map.

Consistency in recording method

Whatever system you use for recording information – pen and paper or software and keyboard – keeping a consistent system for what is recorded and how it is recorded is very important. Actually, this advice is probably more important for electronic systems than paper ones. The reason for this is that when you do come to sort your data, whether by name or by location or by date, an electronic system will only understand what is entered. Thus a county that is entered as Herts, and a county that is entered as Hertfordshire, will be sorted into two separate places because of the spellings. When you have only a few counties and a few people to deal with, such discrepancies do not seem very significant; however, as your research grows and the tree expands, it becomes more and more important to set and work to consistent standards. You will also have to deal with the problem of whether to enter modern place names or historical place names. For example, I have fifty-five people in my tree who were born in 'London', because I entered this as a modern term. However, from the point of view of keeping my further research neat and tidy, it would be better to have entered the old county: London or Middlesex or Surrey because the current county of Greater London was not set up until 1888. There are many other problems with choosing terms for places in the past and making sure that consistency is applied.

The same problem occurs with dates – is it to be 11, March, 1800 or 11th March 1800, or March 11th 1800? There are actually many more permutations of the simple date than you might have thought of. You will also need to know how to deal with the old date versus new dating styles, so whether you choose 1 January 1600, 1 January 1601 or 1 January 1600/01 does not matter as long as you make a note of your choice and are then consistent.

Dealing with photos and other family records

You may have inherited a large number of photos and family letters, or wish to add your own family photos into the genealogical record. You should try to be pragmatic about these. If they are few in number or you have a great deal of space, then you might be content to keep them all, but more often than not you will have photo albums full of unidentified Victorian people – many of them babies and children, and you will have no clue as to who they are.

Should you keep the album they are in, even though it is bulky and probably damaged? Should you scan the photos and store them in an electronic system? For long-term storage it will probably be better for the photos to be removed from the albums and stored using acid-free mounts and in acid-free boxes. The albums themselves normally have no intrinsic value, although if you do have a particularly beautiful album you will want to consider keeping it and its collection together. If you take photos out of an album, then make sure you keep them together as a discrete collection because there is evidential value in the fact that all the photos were together and probably all belonged to one person or family. This may help you identify them in the future. You may find that there is identification information on the reverse, or at least the name and place of the photographer is noted, and this also gives a good clue as to who they originally belonged to and who the people may be.

The advantage of scanning photos digitally and holding them on a computer system is that you can very easily share them with people around the world via the internet; you can also link them to the people in your family tree so that charts will print together with the photos. It also provides a way of ensuring that duplicates exist should the originals become damaged.

If you are going to scan any documents or photos you still need to a) do something with the original, and b) migrate the electronic scans on to newer and newer technology as it appears. However, if you truly cannot identify all those baby shots, and there is no knowing who took the photo or other identifying marks and you have duplicate photos of other people who are identified, then I see no shame in throwing them out.

Whatever you do, do not scan and burn them on to DVD and then forget about them. In ten years' time we will probably not be using DVDs or CDs because technology will have moved on to something else.

Collections of family letters and papers can also cause a great deal of angst for those who inherit them. They can be bulky to store and they are unlikely to have much appeal to a local archive unless the people mentioned in them were prominent, the letters unusually interesting, or they come with a large donation of money to help keep them. Careful appraisal is the key. Two love letters from Grandpa to Granny can be delightful to preserve, but probably not all the letters she was ever sent on any subject. If you do inherit such a collection, then sorting them by addressee and then chronologically is one very good way to organize them and take stock of what you have. Often envelopes have been kept along with contents, and keeping them in the envelopes makes sorting by addressee very simple. If you have both letters and photos of one person, then you might like to keep them together – for example, in archival standard clear polyester pockets in a ring binder. Do not use cheap plastic film or pockets because over time they will damage the contents. Make sure that fragile paper and photos are kept in stable atmospheric conditions to help lengthen their life; not anywhere near a radiator, and definitely not somewhere damp.

If you also have old title deeds, then they should be organized by each property's address. These may be of more interest to an archive in the location where the property is located so, having extracted the information from them you need, perhaps by transcription, consider donating them to a place where other people can make use of them.

Long-term storage

The 'elephant in the room', and one that is rarely discussed in family history circles, is that electronic storage is not inherently stable. Whereas paper files kept in a cupboard securely protected from fire, damp, dust and insect attacks will be expected to last many generations, the same is not true of computer files. Not only does the technology currently move very fast so that the operating systems needed to read back files constantly change (our first home computer purchased in 1991 ran from DOS and we then successively upgraded to Windows 3.1, Windows 95, Windows XP, Windows Vista, and now Windows 7, and that is at quite a frugal rate of turnover), but computer storage is basically storage by magnetism and even the best-maintained systems might be expected to last only around twenty-five years, unless migrated on to new media. Migrating your files means continually buying new computers and making sure that all of your records can be read by your new computer. It sounds simple, but what about the CD of Word files you saved five years ago? I have a floppy disk of transcriptions from wills that I did not get around to saving on to a new computer and now I cannot read them using my current equipment. It will not be long before computers do not come with CD or DVD drives, and a Word file that was readable in the majority of computers five years ago might not be readable in five years' time – or at least not without specialist help and software that might be expensive. Are you really going to expect that your children and grandchildren are going to faithfully keep up with all this work of migrating files? Not only might this be costly, but with a large number of files it is time-consuming as well.

Worse, the problem is not just for the actual data files; the software to read them is important as well, particularly if it is software designed for one operating system – for example, Windows XP. If the company goes bust or it just doesn't keep up the upgrades, you won't be able to use the software on operating systems in the future. CDs are not inherently stable either. Despite manufacturers' claims that they last for long periods of time, I have found significant failures among disks that are only a couple of years old, and it is now generally acknowledged that they are not a good solution for more than a few years.

Just recently a new development in the world of data storage has occurred that does offer a glimmer of hope. This is the Millenniata disc, which is far more stable than any other electronic storage device yet found. This technology is very new, so it may be some time before it becomes mainstream. If it does, and we can only hope it does, then it could finally offer us a proper long-term solution, although there is still the problem of maintaining operating systems. In the meantime, we are stuck with continuous migration of data.

Pass on your work

You are the expert on your own research and the history of your family – nobody else. Wouldn't it be wonderful if you could easily convert that expertise into something of lasting value? After all, there has to be some purpose to all this relentless collection of information.

The genealogy community is in desperate need of written and pub-lished work that is coherent, consistent, correctly documented, and based on high-quality research. More and more people are gathering information about their families; all of it is unique since every family is unique, but there it stops. No other use is being made of the infor-mation. Your information could be of interest not only to other family members, but to local historians and other genealogists. You may feel there is little point in collecting dead ancestors unless you can let others know about it. If you practise genealogy to the highest stand-ards, then your work not only is more than capable of being passed on to future generations, you are positively under an obligation to do so. The potential value for them is immense. Even if you just want to pass your research on to family members and not be concerned with wider publication in any shape or form, you need to start thinking now about how you can achieve that, whether you wish to write a family history, create a personal website to share among the whole family, or simply preserve your records for others to interpret.

We need more work on the strengths and weaknesses of any number of commonly used sources, particularly comparative studies and statistical analysis. What are the error rates, what are the main difficulties or pitfalls with interpretation?

'The growing popularity of the subject means that an increasing number of people amass information but unfortunately make no creative use of it.'[72] This statement was written about local history thirty years ago, but is just as true of genealogy. In fact, the big argument against genealogists from the academic historians has always been that it was entirely selfish and did not accomplish any-thing of note because without an academic structure it could not be trusted, and in any case it was not published. This might have been true in a pre-internet age when the only recourse to the genealogist was vanity publishing, which was expensive, or depositing one's research with any library or organization happy to accept it. However, it is now possible to publish both online and using print for only a small cost and, in the case of online publication such as

---

72 David Dymond, *Writing Local History* (British Association for Local History, Phillimore, 1988 edn), p. 2.

the use of a dedicated website, there is no longer much excuse for putting it off. Your research could help other people.

If you want to publish something about your family history, you don't have to put everything you know into writing. Articles just on one person or one part of the family can be equally interesting and of value to others. The traditional approach, which is to write about a family starting at the earliest known ancestor and working forwards, does not have to be copied. Why not write just about the family in the seventeenth century, or just about a branch that had an unusual occupation, or just about the life of an ancestor where you have been able to find a lot of biographical material. Can you see themes in your family history?

In previous chapters I have stressed how important it is that you record and cite your sources and do so consistently if you refer to any published or unpublished work, or perhaps to any primary sources. The main purpose of this is not to trip you up, or to show off how much reading you have done, but so that your reader can easily recreate your steps, evaluate what you have done, and if you are referring to other books or published works, follow them up as well. When I read an article I often find the footnotes of most interest, yet you can look in vain in most British family history magazines and genealogy journals for any footnotes, or any list of references. Sometimes what should be a bibliography is disguised as 'further reading', so as not to frighten the general reader. Other people's notes, however, can often provide excellent clues for your own research and you will enhance your own work if you attempt the same approach.

Display of information

Family relationships are complicated, and once you have more than about three generations with collateral lines as well, it becomes very difficult to hold all the information in your head or to represent it visually, other than by some tried and trusted methods of representation. The most common ways of arranging pedigrees are in drop-down charts or descendant charts, pedigree charts or ancestor charts, family group sheets, and fan charts. There are also bowtie charts and hourglass charts, and charts specific to DNA projects. As far as prose is concerned, the most common way of arranging ancestral lines in a very formal style is that adopted by the peerage books, such as Burke's *Peerage*, using an indented style with numbers.

The newcomer may be a little bewildered by the large number of ways that exist to record information in trees and charts and it is true that the genealogy world has never come close to standardizing what sort of charts should be used, although once again the Americans have proposed some standards or formats for compiling pedigrees, such as the Sosa-Stradonitz System and specific formats for applying to the lineage societies.[73] In general, you should use whatever style is useful to you. There are, however, pre-existing standards for abbreviations and nomenclature on hand-drawn charts, some of which have not been picked up by the computer software companies for use in computer-drawn charts. Nevertheless, the visual representation of your information in a way that other people can understand is important if you wish to engage other family members in your results and pass on something all the family can benefit from.

The descendant chart or drop-down line chart

The drop-down line chart is the one I was most familiar with when I started out and is still the way I jot down relationships on paper to try to make sense of my findings. This type of chart starts with the earliest known ancestor and, keeping each generation on its own horizontal line, moves down the page, generation by generation. The drawback with these charts is that room rapidly runs out, and if you hand-draw them there is nothing forcing you to record all the information you may have about someone. They are most useful when they show the male line only and when each generation does not have too many children.

A drop-down line chart looks like this and can be displayed with or without the boxes:

---

73 *The BCG Genealogical Standards Manual* (Washington DC, 2000, Board for Certification of Genealogists).

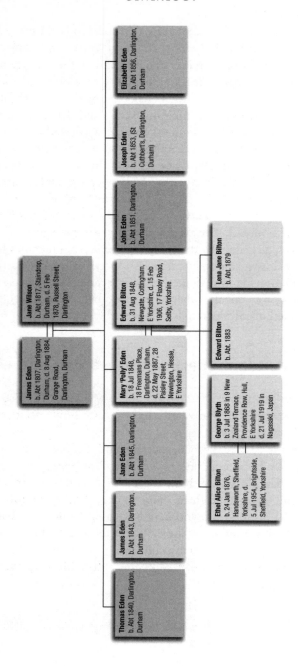

Thomas Eden
b. Abt 1840, Darlington, Durham

James Eden
b. Abt 1843, Darlington, Durham

Jane Eden
b. Abt 1845, Darlington, Durham

James Eden
b. Abt 1807, Darlington, Durham. d. 8 Aug 1884, Grange Road, Darlington, Durham

Jane Wilson
b. Abt 1817, Staindrop, Durham. d. 5 Feb 1878, Russell Street, Darlington

John Eden
b. Abt 1851, Darlington, Durham

Joseph Eden
b. Abt 1853, (St Cuthbert's, Darlington, Durham)

Elizabeth Eden
b. Abt 1856, Darlington, Durham

Mary 'Polly' Eden
b. 18 Jul 1848, 18 Freemans Place, Darlington, Durham, d. 22 May 1887, 28 Paisley Street, Newington, Hessle, E Yorkshire

Edward Bitton
b. 31 Aug 1848, Newgate, Cottingham, E Yorkshire, d. 15 Feb 1906, 17 Flaxley Road, Selby, Yorkshire

Ethel Alice Bitton
b. 24 Jan 1876, Handsworth, Sheffield, Yorkshire, d. 5 Jul 1954, Brightside, Sheffield, Yorkshire

George Blyth
b. 3 Jul 1868 in 9 New Zealand Terrace, Providence Row, Hull, E Yorkshire d. 21 Jul 1919 in Nagasaki, Japan

Edward Bitton
b. Abt 1883

Lena Jane Bitton
b. Abt 1879

Drop-down charts are a very good way of showing up to three generations on one page, together with all the birth, marriage and death information. I find that drawing up these charts helps my thinking process and I am immediately able to spot gaps or places where extra information needs to be found. They are particularly useful for showing gaps where there might be other children in a family, or presenting you with two children who could not be in the same family due to birth dates being too close. I would always aim to include not only the full name, but also the exact date and place born, and/or the exact date or place baptized, the date and place of death or burial, making sure there was a distinction between the two, and any known marriage dates and partners, again with exact places and dates. When people are added into the tree without baptism or other supporting dates, then it is a good idea to add where the information that connects them to this tree comes from. For example, a child may be mentioned in a parent's will, but a baptism might never be found for that child, and in that case the source for them should start 'mentioned in father's will' followed by the citation.

If your collection of information is only with hand-drawn trees, then you will definitely have come across a situation where you have added extra information and lines have crossed and the whole thing has become a muddle, causing you to have to redraw the tree. This is where a computer software package is invaluable in saving you the time in continually redrawing the tree. As you gain information, you may be surprised at just how many events in some ancestors' lives you have collected. You might have birth date, baptism date, school attended, university attended, more than one marriage, details of work, and so on. How do you consistently represent what is needed on a chart? They cannot all fit on, and so another kind of recording system will be needed. Again, computer programs will help with this aspect by keeping the basic vital data in a format separate from other events.

The main problem with drop-down charts is that for most families they will extend horizontally for a long way and are often difficult to print and very hard to display. In these cases, if you are particularly keen on having charts to hang on the wall, then you will have to make a careful decision about whether you can break the tree up into separate charts for separate branches. You can get a calligrapher to draw up a tree for you, but this tends to be expensive because a well-drawn tree takes a good deal of care and time to produce. There are some printers who can print on very large-size paper and a few who advertise on the internet or in family history magazines who will be able to take a Gedcom file and produce a tree from it on your behalf.

Conventions of line-drawn charts

If you do want to produce drop-down charts as gifts for family members, there are certain conventions that should be used. The more people who abide by standards and conventions, the easier it is to swap information and understand other people's trees and charts. However, this is an area that has proved fraught with difficulty in the past. Nevertheless, some standards need to be encouraged.

Ancestral lines that are proved are drawn as a line; ancestral links that are not proven, or where there is conjecture, use a dotted line. A married couple should be shown with a double line, as in Thomas Harris = Julia Brown. The use of a question mark denotes that the information immediately before the question mark is subject to question. Use 'b' for born, 'bur' for buried and 'c' or 'bp' for christened or baptized. A single person or spinster should have 'sp' against them or 'died u/m' for died unmarried. A full list of useful symbols can be found on page 11 of Patrick Palgrave-Moore's *How to Record Your Family Tree*.[74]

Birth brief or pedigree chart

These types of charts are probably of most use to you in order to see ancestral lines quickly when you are working on your own research. However, the Society of Genealogists adopted them for all members to fill and deposit with the Society as a permanent record, and once you are used to looking at them, they make a very handy visual reference. They do not display siblings, and some people find

---

74 Patrick Palgrave-Moore, *How to Record Your Family Tree* (Elvery Dowers Publications, 6th edn 1994).

them confusing, so if you do use them to show your work to other people, you may need to provide some explanation.

Here is an example from Legacy Family Tree of a pedigree chart:

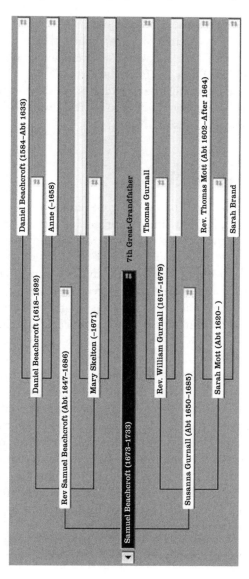

I have a paper pre-printed 12-generation pedigree chart which I am slowly filling in with pencil. It is about three-feet square and comes with pre-punched holes for a variety of binders so that you can fold it down and keep it neat, and it is printed with the generational lines, numbers and event symbols.

There are a whole range of other charts that can be produced either using family tree software, or pre-printed, which you can purchase and then fill in carefully with a pen.

You may see bowtie charts, circular or concentric charts, heraldic charts, and drawings of actual trees festooned with names and portraits or photographs of ancestors.

Narrative pedigrees

A narrative pedigree takes the same information as in a drop-down chart, but presents it in prose. It normally starts with the earliest known ancestor on one ancestral line and then gives details of all the children proceeding down to the present day. Everybody is numbered in order of their birth within the family. This style was used by Burke's and other early reference works. Again, it can be confusing for those who are unused to seeing information presented like this. There are different types of numbering system that can be used in conjunction with a narrative pedigree, and you will often also see the children indented down the page.

Opposite is an example of the narrative pedigree, from the excellent Peerage.com[75] site. Note the full source citations.

Because the narrative pedigree can become very confusing on the printed page when there are lots of children and each child has marriages and other children also to record, the editor of the above website has given the children live html links, so that children can be followed though as necessary, or not. On the printed page, however, an indented style used by Burke's is very confusing, and for this reason it can be better to display a long pedigree using numbers to identify people and generations.

---

75 www.thepeerage.com/p46744.htm#i467437, accessed 1 May 2012.

Charles Reeve[1,2,3,4,5]

M, #467435, b. 31 May 1821, d. 3 August 1893

Last Edited=20 Feb 2012

Charles **Reeve** was born on 31 May 1821 at Leighton Buzzard, Bedfordshire, England.[6] He was the son of Samuel **Reeve** and Mary **Turner.** He was baptised on 21 July 1847 at Eggington, Bedfordshire, England.[6] He married Frances Mary **Deverell,** daughter of Edward **Deverell** and Frances Mary **Sadler,** in 1847 at Leighton Buzzard, Bedfordshire, England. He married Frances Mary **Deverell,** daughter of Edward **Deverell** and Frances Mary **Sadler,** on 19 August 1847 at Leighton Buzzard, Bedfordshire, England.[6]

He died on 3 August 1893 at age 72 at Leighton Buzzard, Bedfordshire, England.

He was Brewer.[6] He lived in 1841 at Leighton Buzzard, Bedfordshire, England.[5] He lived in 1851 at Leighton Buzzard, Bedfordshire, England.[1] He lived in 1861 at Leighton Buzzard, Bedfordshire, England.[2] He lived in 1871 at Luton, Bedfordshire, England.[3] He lived in 1881 at St Mary's, Buckinghamshire, England.[4]

Children of Charles Reeve and Frances Mary **Deverell**

1. Mary Louisa **Reeve** b. 13 Jul 1848, d. 1938
2. Agnes Caroline **Reeve** b. 4 Oct 1850, d. 1923
3. Samuel Charles **Reeve** b. 5 Sep 1851, d. 1875
4. Edith Fanny **Reeve** b. 1852, d. 1877
5. Alfred Edward **Reeve**+ b. 4 Feb 1854, d. 10 Feb 1947
6. Alfred Edward **Reeve**+ b. 4 Feb 1854, d. 10 Feb 1947
7. Amy **Reeve**+ b. May 1855, d. 26 Dec 1936
8. Frank Hamilton **Reeve**+ b. 28 Oct 1857, d. 14 Apr 1937
9. Charles Frederick **Reeve**+ b. 7 Apr 1859, d. 7 Mar 1941
10. Arthur Henry **Reeve**+ b. Apr 1861, d. 8 Aug 1946

Citations

1. [S4718] Ancestry.com, *1851 England Census* (n.p.: Online publication - Provo, UT, USA: Ancestry.com Operations Inc, 2005.Original data - Census Returns of England and Wales, 1851. Kew, Surrey, England: The National Archives of the UK (TNA): Public Record Office (PRO), 185). Data imaged from the National A, unknown publish date), Class: HO107; Piece: 1756; Folio: 78; Page: 14; GSU roll: 87685-87686.

2. [S4728] Ancestry.com, *1861 England Census* (n.p.: Online publication - Provo, UT, USA: Ancestry.com Operations Inc, 2005.Original data - Census Returns of England and Wales, 1861. Kew, Surrey, England: The National Archives of the UK (TNA): Public Record Office (PRO), 186). Data imaged from the National A, unknown publish date), Class: RG9; Piece: 1005; Folio: 63; Page: 11; GSU roll: 542735.

3. [S4715] Ancestry.com, *1871 England Census* (n.p.: Online publication - Provo, UT, USA: Ancestry.com Operations Inc, 2004.Original data - Census Returns of England and Wales, 1871. Kew, Surrey, England: The National Archives of the UK (TNA): Public Record Office (PRO), 187). Data imaged from the National A, unknown publish date), Class: RG10; Piece: 1572; Folio: 31; Page: 11; GSU roll: 829800.

4. [S4714] Ancestry.com and The Church of Jesus Christ of Latter-day Saints, *1881 England Census* (n.p.: Online publication - Provo, UT, USA: Ancestry.com Operations Inc, 2004, 1881 British Isles Census Index provided by The Church of Jesus Christ of Latter-day Saints © Copyright 1999 Intellectual Reserve, Inc. All rights reserved. All use is subject to the l, unknown publish date), Class: RG11; Piece: 1477; Folio: 6; Page: 6; GSU roll: 1341358.

5. [S4719] Ancestry.com, *1841 England Census* (n.p.: Online publication - Provo, UT, USA: Ancestry.com Operations Inc, 2006.Original data - Census Returns of England and Wales, 1841. Kew, Surrey, England: The National Archives of the UK (TNA): Public Record Office (PRO), 184). Data imaged from the National A, unknown publish date), Class: HO107; Piece 5; Book: 21; Civil Parish: Leighton Buzzard; County: Bedfordshire; Enumeration District: 4; Folio: 19; Page: 31; Line: 14; GSU roll: 241193-

[S5909] Compiler: Mary Jane Hooker Mary-Jane Hooker, *gedcom: Mary-Jane Hooker* (n.p.: 19 February 2012, unknown publish date).

You may find that your family history software has the facility to produce an Ahnentafel report. This is a narrative pedigree that begins with a specific person and moves back through the person's ancestors for a given number of generations. This system gives each person a unique Ahnentafel number. The starting individual is number one. From then on, an individual's father has a number that is twice the number of the individual. The mother has a number that is twice the individual's, plus 1. If you are number one, your father is 2, your mother is 3, your father's father and mother are 4 and 5, and your mother's father and mother are 6 and 7, and so on. If a person is missing, their number is skipped. The child of any person always has a number that is one-half the number of the father. This system goes hand in hand with the pedigree chart as it does not give numbers to siblings, except as i, ii, iii, iv, v, etc. within the narrative. An example, without editing in any way, is the following:

1. **Samuel Beachcroft**, son of **Thomas Seward Beachcroft** [2] and **Charlotta Lewis** [3], was christened on 12 Nov 1801 in St Michael, Queenhithe, London, died on 10 Nov 1861 in Richmond Road, Putney, London aged 59, and was buried in Barnes Cemetery, London (St Mary, Putney). The cause of his death was Pneumonia, age 60.

> General Notes: Samuel was an Architect and District Surveyor for Chelsea, but his career does not appear to have been particularly distinguished.

Samuel married **Elizabeth Acworth Ommaney**, daughter of **Sir Francis Molyneux Ommaney** and **Georgiana Frances Hawkes**, on 21 Jul 1840 in Mortlake Church, Surrey, England.

Children from this marriage were:

i. **Frank Porten Beachcroft** was born on 7 May 1841 in Cadogan Place, Chelsea, London and died on 10 Feb 1912 in Worthing, Sussex aged 70. The cause of his death was Unknown, age 70.

ii. **Samuel Beachcroft** was born on 17 Jun 1842 in Chelsea, London and died on 23 Aug 1843 in Chelsea, London aged 1.

iii. **Elizabeth Beachcroft** was born on 7 Sep 1843 in
   Chelsea, London.
iv. **Helen Beachcroft** was born on 12 May 1845 in Chelsea,
   London, died on 4 Aug 1846 in Chelsea, London aged 1,
   and was buried in St Luke's, Chelsea.
v. **Mary Beachcroft** was born on 16 Apr 1847 in
   Tavistock, Devonshire, England, was christened on 2
   Jun 1847 in Holy Trinity, Chelsea, and died after 1901.
vi. **Thomas Seward Beachcroft** was born on 9 Sep 1849 in
   Cadogan Place, Chelsea, London and died in 1912 in
   Hastings, Sussex aged 63.

It is when you use a computer-generated report like this that you
fully understand the need for consistency in citations, recording of
places and other information. The entry above shows a number of
places where editing is needed. Considering that your report may
run to dozens of pages and I have seen them when they run into
hundreds of pages, this is a task that must be thought about before
you enter any information into the computer, or you risk having to
go back and revise your entries.

Writing a family history

Many people are interested in writing a family history in a free
style without recourse to computer-generated reports; or sup-
plementing the computer-generated report with much additional
information and explanation about family events. This can be a
formidable task, but of huge value to others if also used with plenty
of charts and ways of illustrating relationships, and of course using
proper source citations.

A very early book on writing family history – Phillimore's *How
to Write the History of a Family*[76] – suggested the following for each
family member:

---

76 William P. W. Phillimore, *How to Write the History of a Family: A Guide
for the Genealogist* (London, 1896) p. 39–40.

1 Name, date and place of birth.
2 Occupation and residence.
3 Age at marriage.
4 Age of husband or wife. Number of children living or deceased and their ages.
5 Mode of life so far as affecting growth and health.
6 Was early life laborious? Why and how?
7 Adult height, colour of hair when adult, colour of eyes.
8 General appearance.
9 Bodily strength and energy, if much above or below the average.
10 Keenness of imperfection of sight or other sense.
11 Mental powers and energy, if much above or below average.
12 Character and temperament.
13 Favourite pursuits and interests; artistic attitudes.
14 Minor ailments to which there was special liability in youth, in middle age.
15 Other illnesses in youth, in middle age.
16 Cause and date of death, and age at death.
17 General remarks.

Just imagine if one of your ancestors had decided to make such a chart for all his relatives and that it had survived – how happy would you, the family history researcher, be? This list of criteria, with some of it altered or omitted, is still used today as the basis of the individual group sheet, which is a subset of the family group record sheet. Naturally some of these categories reflect a Victorian interest in physical appearance, but you can adapt the questions to suit yourself and to get you thinking about what sort of information you might like to provide about yourself and your own immediate family. In our family we have the written account of the early life of an ancestor. It is very interesting, but for some reason he has totally omitted to put any names of people or dates or even exact places. It could not be more frustrating to read and just leaves us wanting so much more. If you do decide to embark on a family history, then please make sure you write about yourself and your parents and provide precise information!

Start wherever you like. As long as you get something down on paper or on the computer screen, then progress is being made. The process of writing has been so vastly improved by word processing software that I can hardly imagine having to go back to writing out facts by hand and then typing up a draft. Paragraphs and words can be rearranged at the click of a mouse so that drafting and redrafting have been made so much easier. It does not matter if your first attempts are not perfect. Give yourself plenty of time to redraft, think again, and redraft. The first step is to be sure how you are going to write – pen and paper, software and PC, laptop or note-book on the dining room table, in an office, in the garden. It does not matter as long as there are no distractions.

The next step is to focus upon your subject. Some of that will be easy, since you are writing about your family history, all the knowledge of which is in your head and in your records.

Here are some points to consider:

- Who is the audience? Make sure you are addressing them.
- Present your information in a logical order.
- Add in relevant historical context; not just names and dates, but occupations and places as well as background.
- Make it readable and interesting.
- Visual interest – what illustrations could you use?
- Be concise; something that is written sparingly is easier to read than something that suffers from great verbosity.
- Check your facts.
- Cite your genealogical sources, and acknowledge anybody's else's work if you have used it.

Before you start, consider how you are going to balance and structure the work. How will it be introduced? Do you want to run from earliest known ancestor back down to yourself, or would you like to follow a journey backwards?

The title will be important since it grabs the reader and sets the scene, but you don't have to decide on that before you make a start on the writing. A title will suggest itself to you as you proceed. At school when you wrote an essay you had to stick to what you were given, but now you are free to choose your own title, subject matter and emphasis. This is freedom, but it can cause anxiety and uncertainty as you wonder whether your work will be interesting enough. Try writing down your aims. If suitable, this can form the basis for an introduction. Don't be afraid to write a tentative introduction and then go back and revise it later on to make it more attention grabbing.

The process of writing is hard. It takes effort. You must expect that, and at the same time be prepared to face the challenge. In order to fight that urge to leave it until tomorrow, it is a good idea to try to make at least a start on something right away, however minor. This can be as little as writing out a working title, drafting a couple of ideas, and then saving it as a new file. Psychology plays a huge part in this. Once you have something underway, you can put it aside and then come back to it every day and write a bit more. Before you know where you are, you will have nearly finished. If you have enthusiasm for your subject and it deeply interests you, then you are halfway to writing about it in an interesting way. If the writer is bored, then that shows through in the text.

If you are writing using a computer, you may find that you do not read a computer screen as thoroughly as the printed page. I find it very helpful once I have reached the final draft stage to print the text out and then make my final edits in pen, sitting somewhere comfortable. The act of sitting somewhere different than at your desk, and reading and editing using a different method than a computer screen, forces the brain to reconsider the text. If you leave yourself enough time, this will also give your brain a rest and may spark some new insight or better arrangement. In other words, take time to stand back from the text and let it 'mature' before making your final edits.

There are now more places than ever to get the results of your researches published or publicized. Here are some suggestions:

Self-publishing

Self-publishing, also known as 'vanity' publishing, has been given a huge boost by the internet. No longer is it prohibitively expensive to produce a bound book. From quick and easy downloads for e-readers to traditional hardback and soft-bound formats, you can choose to go it alone and produce something wonderful that can be turned into great long-lasting gifts. Companies such as lulu.com provide a basic service or a more deluxe one (www.lulu.com/publish/books/?cid=uk_tphp2_1millionauthors_041310).

Wordclay offers something similar (www.wordclay.com/Default.aspx) with a free basic service, although you pay for each edition that you have to buy. Using 'print on demand' means that books can be more cost-effective and it is no longer necessary to have a print run of 1,000 unsellable books taking up space in the loft. For downloads to e-readers, try Smashwords (www.smashwords.com/).

Family history magazines and journals

Family history magazines will often publish articles. However, you need to make sure that you are not treading the same path as everybody else. You must have an unusual angle or a very cleverly constructed story. There is nothing to lose by emailing the editors of the magazines to find out whether they might be interested. If your article is published, you should also be paid a fee.

If you have greater ambitions and wish to publish in a more academic journal, then you must read the instructions for authors. There will probably be specific instructions for citations and you should expect that any peer-reviewed system will mean that comments on your work will be made and that you will be expected to improve your article or take on board any suggestions made. The expectation will be that your article is unique and based on new research, not a re-hash of something published elsewhere.

Your own website or blog

Why not create your own family history website. This is not as scary as it sounds and may even be a way of contacting other people researching the same ancestral lines and working together. There is so much information available on the internet about setting up a website that I hesitate to point you in any particular direction.

However, three things *are* important, regardless of whether you choose to design and set it up yourself, or whether you pay someone to do it for you:

1 HTML coding (the technical bit).
2 Design – layout, colours and illustrations used.
3 Text – the writing, but also the keywords used so that your site is found in the search engines.

You will need the following if you go it alone. I found this list on the BBC guide to websites:

- A computer.
- A modem.
- Internet access via an ISP.
- Your own domain name (optional, but if you want 'www. YOURNAME.me.uk', you need to register and pay for it).
- Web space (often this comes with your ISP package).
- Web authoring or HTML editing software.
- FTP software to upload to the internet.
- Plenty of time!
- Some good advice.

I cannot give you particular advice on coding, nor on design, except to say that you should choose a simple colour scheme and stick to it for all the web pages on the site. Stick to one font and aim for a clean visual style, stay away from anything that revolves or moves, and keep it simple.

If you cannot be bothered with any of that, then an excellent way round it is to set up a blog. A blog is a website with a pre-defined format that you do not have to design; you just provide the content. They are mainly used for newsletters and by people who are writing in a personal diary style, but there is no reason why you have to use the space like that. It is a way of keeping together a collection of articles in a dedicated web space. You can find free blog software on the internet.

People read a website in a different way from the printed page.

They expect to be able to skim read quickly. What they don't do (usually) is carefully read all of the text. They glance at each new page, read a bit of the text, and then click on the nearest link that seems to satisfy their inner question – or looks likely to. One of the gurus on writing specifically for the web, and web usability, is Jakob Nielson (www.useit.com/jakob/); if you are contemplating your own website, then it might be useful to browse through some of his work.

The BBC has some basic guides to the internet, including how to set up your own website (www.bbc.co.uk/webwise/askbruce/articles/browse/buildwebsite_1.shtml).

10

Prove Your Research and Meet Your Challenges

History is but a pack of tricks we play on the dead

Voltaire

How do you build up a family tree that is neither based on fantasy, nor prematurely pollarded by the need for absolute truth? How can you accept family connections that are less than certain? These are such common questions, yet there is no clear-cut or easy answer unless you are able to use DNA evidence for specific paternity problems. Even DNA is not infallible. The simple answer is 'because I have collected enough evidence to be convinced'; but you may be over-keen on your own theories and collect only evidence that seems to support them. You might be convinced, but are other people? And what do you do if the evidence is conflicting? Ignore some of it? This chapter sets out how to take the utmost care to ensure you don't play tricks on the dead.

There is not very much advice in British family history literature about the knotty question of proof, and I think there may be some specific reasons for this. It involves the perceived differences between the scientific study of lineage (genealogy) and what is more generally termed family history. If you have previously not taken time to think about whether there could be a difference between genealogy and family history, I would certainly not blame you for being surprised that there *is* a difference, because the words are used so commonly and interchangeably without anybody bothering to define them, and the concepts overlap. There is certainly very little attempt by either genealogists or family historians to define what it is they actually do.

Some dictionary definitions of genealogy are: the use of documentary sources to prove pedigree or lineage; an account of a person's descent from an ancestor or ancestors by enumeration of the intermediate ancestors; the investigation of pedigrees as a branch of study or knowledge. I see genealogy as both a technique or an historical method, and also the action of studying ancestry so as to produce pedigrees. On the other hand, family history is an overarching term for investigation into the lives of our ancestors – the history of our family, with all that implies for social history as applied to our family. There is an argument for saying that genealogy is a term for the technique by which we build evidence for the relationships between people, whereas family history is far broader. So far, so good. Now it just so happens that family history has become a more fashionable term than genealogy. It is more appealing and sounds much less like something scientific or difficult, or disciplined. It is true that genealogy has a more forensic or scientific side to it because it revolves around proving lineage, showing relationships with charts, and not (unless needed for proof arguments) taking into account the totality of the lives of the people it connects. The term family history, on the other hand, is a warmer, more fuzzy term, less closely defined and more open to interpretation.

In the recent past, genealogy suffered from a snobbish appeal, and a reaction against this then led to the rise of the more democratic term family history, which seeks to show us that any family can be traced backwards in time and that all family history is equal. I believe that the democratization and popular appeal of family history has led to a decline in the number of people writing and lecturing on the more scholarly aspects of what Wagner called scientific genealogy, which people like Dugdale, with his new system of references or citations, and Round, with his critical analysis, had worked so hard to emphasize. A general encouragement by the British media to step right in and have a go at tracing your family history has obscured the fact that there are disciplines that have to be learned, and even standards by which to do things. In an attempt to popularize, any aspect of scholarliness has been ditched. This is why I often meet people who are interested in 'proving' their research, but have no idea whether this is possible or how to go about it. This is where the techniques of genealogy are used: techniques of documentation, source citation, effective searching and document analysis, which have never been learned by many British family historians. Once learned, these techniques will help to meet the challenges outlined at the beginning of this book.

I have shown how a lack of trust in the research process inevitably means that searches are repeated, thought processes go round in circles, and brick walls are built up. An effective search is objective, even scientific; and it does not rely on hearsay evidence, or indeed evidence only collected from indexes or derivative sources. Additionally, we build trust into our research process by demonstrating good documentation and also by learning to correctly interpret and examine documents for all relevant content. How we build further trust into the research process to build up a good proof case is the theme we return to here. In this chapter I want to try to pull together some of the scholarly methods and standards for proving connections that belong to genealogy, and that we have seen also in the chapters on analysis and documentation. In doing so I will show that family history and genealogy require each other and that everything taken together will help you to meet those seven challenges I talked about at the start of this book.

You may feel that research can never be proved because you are seeking some kind of absolute truth. People with scientific backgrounds sometimes struggle with the problem of there being no absolutes in genealogical and historical evidence. Unfortunately, if you do want to find the absolute truth, then you may need to come to terms with its non-existence and learn to get used to probability. Also, there is a lack of university-funded research into many aspects of the work of genealogists. Our work is most often carried out by professionals and amateurs alike, on their own, without reference to one another and without collaborative effort to examine either method or source materials. This means that there are unanswered questions about technique and standards, not least about the quantitative measurement of the reliability of our most commonly used sources. For example, nobody has investigated the percentage of birth certificates with errors.

One fact that we all have to come to terms with is that paternity can never be proven except by DNA testing – think about this for a moment in connection with all the fathers who people your family tree! It might be a depressing thought, however confident you might be, to realize that paternity was unlikely to have been questioned at the time. But there comes a point when all genealogists have to accept the *most probable* solution to a problem. This has been termed the 'preponderance of evidence'. We have to learn to deal with uncertainty. However, this does not mean we cannot prove ancestral connections.

Why do we need to prove connections and why should the number one genealogy rule be to start with what is known and well documented? Obviously, a major reason is so that you do not add people into your tree who should not be there. If the name you are searching for is a rare one, you may feel certain about identifying an ancestor or family connection quite quickly, with not very many facts. But those of you looking for people with common names face a far greater challenge. That challenge increases if you do not know exactly where people lived, or lack specific dates of vital events in their lives. If you find several people of the same name, of roughly the same age and living in a region that seems logical, based on what you know, then you must find out more about all these individuals. Only as additional identifying evidence emerges can you be sure to put a finger on 'your' people. David Hey, in his book *Journeys in Family History*,[77] says 'we must proceed as carefully as if we were proving a case before a court of law. It is not enough to find a baptism with the right name in about the right place at the right time and assume we have found our ancestor.' Thus a document might include a person of the same name as the ancestor you are looking for, but it does not follow that the document relates to your ancestor. If both name and age are given in the document and they correspond with the name and age of our ancestor, then there is a greater prob-ability that they are one and the same, but it is *only a probability*. For more convincing 'proof' we would need extra factors, as well as the knowledge that our research has been systematic and covered all the possible sources so as to eliminate other candidates.

---

77 David Hey, *Journeys in Family History* (PRO Publications, 2003). P.7

The process of getting to the most probable solution, and therefore proof, has not been discussed at length by British genealogists. The Society of Genealogists has put principles and proof together in this statement:[78]

The Society has established the following principles to be essential in the conduct of acceptable genealogical research:

- Accuracy and honesty of all personal research and of work published, promoted or distributed to others.
- Provision of clear evidence from primary sources to support all conclusions and statements of fact.
- Use of original sources and records (or filmed images of originals) to gather key information.
- Citation and recording of sources used so that others may also evaluate the evidence.
- Logical and reasoned development of family links with each step proved from valid evidence before further deductions are made.
- Investigation and analysis of all possible solutions and of contradictory evidence with each alternative hypothesis examined and tested.
- Qualification of less certain conclusions as probable or possible so that others are not misled.
- Acceptance of the possibility that a solution may not be found and acknowledgement of circumstances in which this occurs.
- Awareness of gaps in the availability of, and information from, sources at all levels.
- Receptiveness to new information and to informed comment which may challenge earlier conclusions.
- Acknowledgement and attribution of research done by others and use of such work as a secondary source only.
- Evidence only becomes proof through a reasoned and logical analysis and argument capable of convincing others that the conclusion is valid.

---

78 www.sog.org.uk/education/standards.shtml.Date accessed: 1 November 2011.

Notice that we have come across many of these principles in this book. I have pointed out the problems of using secondary sources. I have argued for citations and proper recording of sources, and I have exhorted you to find out where the gaps in any records lie. I have also given examples where willingness to accept new information, or to think in new ways, has provided a means to make a breakthrough when a search has got stuck.

With these principles the Society seems to be saying that evidence changes into proof via an argument which can convince others, and that this argument should be based on clear evidence from primary sources and that the original sources should always be sought out. But this might be difficult to apply to individual bits of research, however much you agree with the basic idea. What happens if you cannot get access to the original sources, and what exactly should you do about original sources that provide conflicting information? What if your argument starts from a position of ignorance because you haven't yet found all the sources or know about a conflict in the first place? I am not convinced that this 'principles and proof statement' quite covers all the bases.

The proof of the pudding also lies with the *efforts* of the researcher. This is a very important point which I cannot stress too strongly. This book has shown how analysis of documents, and knowledge about the record-making and record-keeping process, is so important. It has also shown how we need to guard against those little voices in our heads that urge us to stop a search prematurely, or to choose the easy path. These are the challenges of historical interpretation, technique and of effective searching that we need to put so much effort into. The overall effectiveness of the researcher also has a bearing upon proof.

The Genealogical Proof Standard

American genealogists have been more active than British ones in establishing standards of evidence and proof, partly because the study of genealogy in the USA has evolved from the requirements of the lineage societies' rules for admittance and proof of lineage from an immigrant ancestor. In earlier times these societies had suffered from a number of fraudulent pedigrees being submitted and this, as well as the growing number of professional genealogists practising in the USA and the development of an academic tradition from the universities, prompted the development of a set of standards for genealogical proof. There is no exact counterpart (as yet) in the UK, and perhaps we do not need to add anything further, but simply to adopt the work of the Americans on this important subject.

Whether we do or don't make our own refinements, all British genealogists should be aware that such standards exist. This has become known as the Genealogical Proof Standard and it evolved from a previous system known as the 'preponderance of evidence' based upon what would be needed to prove a case in a court of law. It just so happens that the preponderance of evidence and proving a case in law have a direct parallel with the 'argument capable of convincing others' part of what the Society of Genealogists has stated. However, I would argue that the 'argument capable of convincing others' has some flaws. Surely if we rely on a convincing argument, then the person being convinced plays a part in the question of proof. Any jury can have the wool pulled over its eyes by a clever advocate. It was because of questions like this that the Americans thought it would be a better idea to turn a preponderance of evidence or convincing argument into something more rigorous.

The Genealogical Proof Standard poses this:

- The research has been reasonably exhaustive.
- Analysis and correlation of the collected information.
- Conflicting evidence is resolved.
- Complete and accurate citation of sources.
- A soundly reasoned and coherently written conclusion .[79]

I admire the simplicity of this approach, and it puts the onus squarely on the efforts of the genealogist.

---

79 Board for Certification of Genealogists, online at www.bcgcertification.org/resources/standard.html. Date accessed: 14 April 2012.

All five elements are necessary to properly establish proof, so what does that mean to our research? Let's examine each point in turn.

The research has been reasonably exhaustive – the point of this is to ensure that you have examined a wide range of high-quality sources in an organized way and that you have minimized the probability that undiscovered evidence will overturn a conclusion that was made too quickly. Does this mean that you have to locate and interpret every single record or source available for your ancestor? Not necessarily. You need to have examined original sources wherever possible – certificates, census, parish registers and so on, which relate to your specific genealogical question (identity, event, relationship, etc.). You should, however, bear in mind that as long as one source remains out there still unexplored, there may be a potential time bomb waiting to destroy your theory.

The reason for insisting upon original sources as far as possible is because there are so many mistakes in secondary or derivative sources – for example, other people's family histories, transcriptions and indexes. Any mistake in date or name in such sources could have caused you to go astray, and reliance on these sources might have led you to come to the wrong conclusions and is therefore not sufficient proof. However, this does not mean that you have to be dogged about collecting every single possible source if you have no conflicting evidence, and there is a very high likelihood that one or two sources are perfectly correct. In the UK, when we apply to the passport office for a passport for the first time, we have to supply a birth certificate. We do not also have to supply a baptism certificate or anything else to prove our age. Of course it may be that a baptism certificate or entry in the register has some extra information that might be of use genealogically, and there might even be an extra or different baptized first name, but where you are otherwise quite sure of a person's existence and parentage from a birth certificate and have also located him or her on all possible census returns and there are no particular conflicts, then pursuing more information may not be necessary.

Genealogists sometimes speak of a rule of three – that there must be at least three pieces of evidence in order for it to become a genealogical 'fact'. This rule is helpful as a guideline, but we do not have to be rigid about it. For example, three pieces of information about one person's birth can come from the census and from their birth certificate and marriage certificate. Does this 'rule' mean that a birth certificate cannot stand on its own? Of course not! Neither can the rule of three settle the question of proof for us where there is conflicting evidence or lack of evidence. But neither should we feel obliged to repeat a process that quite reasonably is proof. For example, I might know that my grandmother's birthday was on 27 February because not only do I remember her and we always picked snowdrops for her birthday, but I also have evidence from my mother who knew her for a great deal longer than I did, and I also have my grandmother's birth certificate which proves it. I do not need any further documentary evidence for my grandmother's birthday, nor any other evidence for her age. Where I might need to consider the rule of three, which could of course be the rule of four or five, is if I had no personal knowledge of her birth date and month, where her birthday was equally unknown to other family members, and where her marriage and death certificate gave conflicting evidence. Then the question of 'have I got the right information?' would occur. The further back in time you go in search of ancestry, the more this question will arise.

The exhaustive search also takes note of where events are not found as well as where they are. If you need to look for proof that person A in Wales in 1841 is the same as person B in England in 1851, then you must have examined all the sources and places where you might otherwise have expected person A to turn up.

Analysis and correlation of the collected information means that each source is interpreted and that the conclusion takes account of all of the evidence. In other words that the evidence is reliable and correctly interpreted – any of our sources can be wrong; that is why we need to analyse and evaluate our evidence. We also have to be fully informed about our sources within their historical context. It is not always cut and dried, however. While original, primary sources, like a birth certificate, may seem the most conclusive, the individuals who created that record may have made mistakes in their statements or recording, lied about certain details, or omitted information. On the other hand, a faithful transcript of a parish register entry may not be an original record, but it could be more reliable as evidence than a birth certificate with mistakes on it. The goal here is to apply sound interpretation of the data contributed by each source based on its own merits. Interpreting sources correctly is not a skill that genealogists acquire overnight; it takes quite a bit of familiarity with the records. We looked at this in the chapter on document analysis.

Contradictory evidence is resolved – where two pieces of evidence clash, in order to reach the standard of proof you must make every effort to resolve the contradictions you find. On top of this, you need to re-evaluate each piece of evidence in the light of the conflict, and ask yourself which is more likely to be correct. Objectivity is the key. If the census suggests the person was born in 1851 and the marriage certificate suggests 1856 and you cannot resolve this by recourse to a birth certificate or baptism, then the age is not proved until you have found further sources. Think back to my search for the birth of Harriet Beresford. I do not currently have good proof of her year of birth, although the balance of probability on what I have found so far is that she was born in the second half of 1819 or the first half of 1820. Then there is the problem of the 'adult' baptisms. This could be contradictory evidence unless the vicar was not being entirely accurate, and in fact Harriet was really only a teenager, not an adult. What if Harriet really were over 21 in 1832? Play devil's advocate over all your pieces of evidence and challenge your own theories to see if they can be rebutted. If you still have conflicting evidence that cannot be rebutted, then you do not have proof.

Each statement of fact is completely and accurately cited – you must cite your sources; this not only enables other researchers to repeat your work, but it is a standard for any historical discipline. If you don't know where a piece of evidence came from, how can you evaluate it? For this reason and as we saw in the previous chapter, it is very important to document all sources as you find them. It is also very important to record all the sources that you have examined, whether or not they provided any new facts for your family tree. These facts, which seem useless now, may provide new connections in the future when combined with other sources. Being scrupulous about the process has to be a given, and this is particularly important when working more with derivative sources than with primary sources.

Conclusions and deductions are clearly reasoned and coherently written – deductive reasoning means setting out your arguments for the case in a clear and logical manner and explaining how the evidence leads to your conclusions. Because I have evidence of three girls all with the mother Caroline, and all baptized in the same place at the same time, then they are sisters. Because two of these girls mention a father called Benjamin on their marriage certificates, then their father was called Benjamin. In practice, I would suggest you physically write out your arguments and conclusions. If you try to do this whenever you have a question of proof or question of identity, then you may well find that new avenues to research suggest themselves to you.

Logic and evidence

We have seen how there are different types of evidence. There is evidence that answers the questions directly – a birth certificate, for example, is direct evidence of the birth. There is indirect evidence or circumstantial evidence; this does not stand on its own and needs another piece of evidence to back it up. The order of children's names in a will is indirect evidence of their order by age. Finally, there is both absence of evidence and evidence of absence. Absence of evidence does not make a proof for something – it just means that you have not found any evidence for it. Evidence of absence is completely different, and only comes when an exhaustive search has been made within complete records. For example, a search of a particular street on the census shows that a family who were living there in 1861 are no longer there in 1871, or a search within a burial register shows that no one with your ancestor's name was buried there between the dates searched.

What you must guard against is any kind of argument from ignorance. This is an argument made in the absence of evidence because the research has not been systematic or effective enough. An argument from ignorance would lead me to state at the start of my Beresford search that both Harriet Beresford's parents were dead by 1840 because I could not find a suitable set of parents on the 1841 census.

Let's turn to another example of a common situation in genealogy – that where you have a clue (or several clues) to an ancestor's place of birth, but you cannot find him/her with his/her parents on the census. Plus, your other evidence that might show a father – for example, the father's place on his marriage certificate – is just taken up with 'deceased', and therefore you cannot be certain of even one of his/her parents' names. Let's say that the parish of birth is Shoreditch in London and you can find a possible baptism of a child of the right sort of age, with the right name in Shoreditch. How can you prove that this baptized child is the same child that grows up to be your ancestor?

First, the search must be exhaustive for all other ways of determining the parents. In many cases this means that family reconstruction has to take place. If siblings are known, then their baptisms might be sought. Other pieces of evidence for both birth place and birth date must be searched for and carefully assembled together. If you have a lot of differing ages, it may be that the ones nearest birth are the most accurate, although I have also come across cases where the age given on the death certificate was a great deal more accurate than in a census taken in childhood. Widen the birth search in the parish registers of Shoreditch to see if any other candidates pop up. The searches for both Henrietta Hobbs and Harriet Beresford show that adult baptisms may have to be sought, and these may not be in the parish of birth, so keep widening your searches until all possible years and all possible places have been covered. As well as positive searching for your ancestor, try to eliminate candidates that are found. Any other candidates with the same name and age should be sought out and traced backwards and forwards until they have been eliminated. In general, it is always necessary to kill off any candidates. In particular, when using parish registers, burial registers need to be searched for the child dying in infancy.

While it is common folklore that 'you cannot prove a negative', actually philosophers and logicians can show that it is possible to prove a negative.[80] You might think it impossible to prove a specific sort of negative – for example, that children for any particular couple do not exist. But you can use this formula (which can be applied to other types of search):

1 If children had existed, then there will be evidence in civil registration.
2 There is no evidence for any children in civil registration, *following an exhaustive search by an effective researcher.*
3 Therefore, children did not exist.

This is an inductive argument: we have looked thoroughly at all birth registrations in civil registration, found absolutely no evidence, therefore they do not exist. The problem is that negative results from inductive arguments do not give us certainty about anything. It just gives us a probable conclusion. However, it is not correct logic to dismiss inductive arguments just because there is no certainty. Yes, inductive reasoning is not infallible, but the logicians argue that we cannot dismiss this type of reasoning as that would leave us only with our own perceptions.

You may not be able to show that a couple did not have any children, or that any one person had no children, just as it may be impossible to show, using evidence from just parish registers or civil registration, that a couple did not have more children than you have found. Probate genealogists who have to take cases before a court of law to show exactly how many relatives there are living in cases of intestacy are asked to provide evidence of exhaustive searches in all major sources, but even then the absolute truth cannot be discovered – only what is most likely, and this is accepted by the courts, because otherwise they would not be able to accept anything. In other words, the court system accepts the inductive argument following exhaustive searches, and genealogists should as

---

80 Steven D. Hales, 'Thinking Tools: You *Can* Prove a Negative', *Think* (vol. 4, issue 10, Summer 2005), pp. 109–12.

well. In fact, showing that something did *not* happen is very often an important part of building up a proof case in genealogy and is a valid part of any research strategy.

Evaluating your evidence

Genealogy has to be based upon a close and informed examination of the records – our sources – in order to work out what might be 'facts'. Genealogical facts can be established by the same basic principles of source criticism, which are also used by historians. The historian asks each document or record a set of questions:

1 Is the record authentic; is it what it seems?
2 Where did the record come from and where was it found?
3 When exactly was it produced? What is its date? How close is the date of the record to the date of the events to which it relates?
4 What type of record is it?
5 Who produced it and who was it intended for?
6 How exactly was it understood by contemporaries?

However, we have also seen that genealogists often have to make their sources work even harder than historians do because we are interested in the personal and specific, rather than drawing conclusions about whole communities or populations, and because we also have the situation of searching among many transcribed documents and indexes as well (our derivative sources). There are therefore some further refinements to the six questions above to think about when we weigh up our evidence.

Evidence can be seen on a scale of reliability, from the most reliable direct evidence of an event (for example, the marriage certificate is reliable evidence that marriage took place) to the least reliable indirect or inferred evidence (for example, the witness to the marriage with the same surname as the bride must be her biological father).

Factors that provide a greater reliability of evidence, although not absolute certainty:

- The informant is in a position to know.
- The record was made close to the time of the event it describes.
- The record was made under oath or with other formality or ceremony.
- The record series shows care with its creation and maintenance.

Factors that warn of a lesser reliability of evidence are:

- A potential bias or self-interest on the part of the informant.
- The original or its image is altered.
- The source is derivative.
- The record has been created or maintained in a haphazard manner (therefore there are gaps).
- The information has been recorded some time after the event.

And, even taking all of the above into account, this still does not account for the question of simple errors within the original record. Because the historian is working on a larger scale than the genealogist, it is not so important for him or her to think too much about errors in primary documents that affect the information about just one person. Genealogists, on the other hand, often have to deal with conflicting evidence where one document will say one thing and another document will tell a slightly different story. Just think how often you have information from the census returns that doesn't quite tally from one year to the next, or seems to contradict information from vital records such as marriage certificates. In these cases, you must find as much evidence as possible from all possible sources and then weigh them up against one another.

In Chapter 6, I discussed what questions you need to ask of documents, and how to get every bit of information out of them. But we did not really look at how errors get on to documents commonly used for genealogy, and how to deal with them when they do by keeping an open mind. In my remarks here, I am only going to consider civil registration certificates, although it would be possible also to collect reasons for errors from all kinds of records by considering the record-creation and record-keeping process.

I have seen thousands of birth, marriage and death certificates from the General Register Office in England and Wales, and there is a significant rate of error and mistake on all three types, with marriages probably being the documents that contain the largest amount of 'non-truths'. Discrepancies between census and certificates cause much worry for inexperienced genealogists, because the expectation is that official documents like a birth certificate must be right. Yet again, as I have argued before, it is necessary to understand exactly how the documents came into being, the law at the time, and the process. Then we can understand how the illiterate mother might get flustered in front of the registrar and give the wrong information, and then not be able to read what had been written down. And we will know that the law before 1874 was not strong enough to prevent the unmarried mother turning up before the registrar and registering a child in her 'husband's' name.

Here are just a few of the reasons why evidence from certificates, as a result of error, needs to be evaluated on a case-by-case basis:

- The date of birth or mother's maiden name may be incorrect because the mother or informant got muddled and could not read what was written down.
- A late registered child may have had his/her birthday brought forward to avoid a fine.
- The name on the birth certificate does not have to be the same as a baptismal name, and it may not be the name commonly used later in life.
- The name of the informant is important on both birth and death certificates because it will help you determine how accurate their information was likely to be. The more remote the relationship, the more inaccurate the information could be.
- A signature on a certificate does not guarantee that the informant could read – only that they had learnt to sign their name.
- Names on a marriage certificate can differ from what you expect. No documentary proof of name was required.
- Age on a marriage certificate is only as accurate as the bride or groom wished it to be. I have seen many cases where there is a discrepancy in ages and the groom or the bride have

'narrowed the gap' on the marriage certificate. I have plenty of examples from my own family.
- Likewise, the ages on death certificates can be misleading as a result of the informant not having the correct information.

There is a wealth of difference between the evidence that is found in our sources and proof of events. Whereas evidence is found in the records, proof is something that ultimately happens in the mind of the genealogist and hopefully gets documented for others to follow. The genealogist who has offered a clear proof has researched soundly, understood the evidence, questioned the sources, and evaluated the whole in a disciplined, logical and critical manner. It is not a quick and easy process and it does take time and effort. It is, however, the only way.

Finally, I come back to the question of trust in our research. We have to learn not to trust to luck that we will find what we need, but that our methods and techniques will produce answers. As we gain experience and learn to apply our knowledge, fewer mistakes are made and more and more trust is built into the process. Sometimes our own trust that we have made the right connections will ultimately rest not only on the fully documented and systematically and effectively researched work, but also on a kind of instinct that comes from long practice. We cannot produce this instinct as evidence, but it does exist. Meet the challenge of overcoming belief, the challenge of technique, practise documentation, research planning, learn to analyse documents and cite your sources, and your own trust in yourself and your research will soar.

How about my own family and the potential tricks on the dead I might have been guilty of playing on Harriet Beresford? Just as I was finishing the writing of this book, the post brought me a copy of the will made by Caroline Beresford and proved at the Principal Registry in London in 1883. My speculations about this family, and particularly about Caroline, had ranged widely: among them had been thoughts such as she died in Ireland, she died before 1841, she had not been married, she had no money, and the will would tell me nothing because it was made after Harriet had died. I successfully fought off all these 'tricks' and persevered in a pursuit of documents.

I had certainly not expected the will to contain the ultimate proof of relationship and meet my aim to finding Harriet's parents. However, I was to be pleasantly surprised. Although it was proved in 1883, the will had originally been drawn up prior to Harriet's death and did prove that my Harriet was definitely the daughter of Caroline Beresford since she was mentioned by married name as 'my daughter'. It also showed that Caroline was the leaseholder of three houses in Lambeth and gave evidence of the relationship to the Nye family, which tied all the findings in the parish registers neatly together. I still have not found good evidence for Benjamin, but there is plenty of time for that. I look forward to the challenges that will come my way as I continue to place the pieces of this particular jigsaw puzzle into their rightful places.

Recommended Short Reading List

Amanda Bevan, *Tracing Your Ancestors in The National Archives, The Website and Beyond* (The National Archives, 7th edn, 2006)

Peter Christian, *The Genealogist's Internet* (The National Archives, 2009)

Peter Christian and David Annal, *Census: The Expert Guide* (The National Archives, 2008)

Mark D. Herber, *Ancestral Trails* (The History Press, 2nd rev. edn 2004)

David Hey, *Family History and Local History in England* (Longman, 1987)

Cecil R. Humphery-Smith (ed.), *The Phillimore Atlas and Index of Parish Registers* (Phillimore & Co., Institute of Heraldic and Genealogical Studies, 3rd edn, 2003)

W.E. Tate, *The Parish Chest: A Study of the Records of Parochial Administration in England* (Phillimore, 3rd edn, 1983)

Andrew Todd, *Nuts and Bolts: Family History Problem Solving through Family Reconstitution Techniques* (Allen & Todd, 2nd edn, 2000)

Bibliography

Tom Arkell, Nesta Evans and Nigel Goose (eds.), *When Death Do Us Part: Understanding and Interpreting the Probate Records of Early Modern England* (Local Population Studies, University of Hertfordshire, Leopard's Head Press, 2000)

G.B. Barrow, *The Genealogist's Guide: An Index to Printed British Pedigrees and Family Histories, 1950–1975* (London, 1977)

Amanda Bevan, *Tracing Your Ancestors in The National Archives, The Website and Beyond* (The National Archives, 7th edn 2006)

Board for Certification of Genealogists, *The BCG Genealogical Standards Manual, Millennium Edition* (Ancestry Publishing, 2000)

Brian de Breffny, *Bibliography of Irish Family History and Genealogy* (Golden Eagle Books, 1974)

Sir Egerton Brydges, *Collins's Peerage of England*, 9 volumes (London, 1812)

Burke, John and Bernard, *Burke's Genealogical and Heraldic History of the Landed Gentry* (various publishers, since 1826)

Burke, John and Bernard, *Burke's Genealogical and Heraldic History of Peerage, Baronetage and Knightage* (various publishers, since 1826)

Judith Butcher, Caroline Drake and Maureen Leach, *Butcher's Copy-editing: The Cambridge Handbook for Editors, Copy-editors and Proofreaders* (Cambridge University Press, 4th edn, 2006)

L.J. Butler and A. Gorst, *Modern British History: A Guide to Study and Research* (IB Tauris, 1997)

C.R. Cheney (ed.), *Handbook of Dates for Students of English History* (Cambridge University Press, 1995)

Peter Christian, *The Genealogist's Internet* (5th edn, The National Archives, 2012)

Peter Christian and David Annal, *Census: The Expert Guide* (The National Archives, 2008)

George E. Cockayne, *The Complete Peerage of England, Scotland, Ireland, Great Britain, and the United Kingdom Extant, Extinct, or Dormant* (1st edn, 8 volumes 1887–1898; 2nd edn revised by the Hon. Vicary Gibbs et al., 1910–1959 and continuing)

Sir William Dugdale, *The Baronage of England (1675)* (Georg Olms, 1977, reprint)

David Dymond, *Writing Local History* (British Association for Local History, Phillimore, 1988 edn)

Joan P.S. Ferguson, *Scottish Family Histories Held in Scottish Libraries* (National Library of Scotland, 2nd edn, 1986)

Michael Whitfield Foster, *A Comedy of Errors or The Marriage Records of England and Wales 1837–1899* (published privately, 1998; ISBN: 0-473-05581-3)

Jeremy Gibson and Else Churchill, *Probate Jurisdictions: Where to Look for Wills* (Federation of Family History Societies, 5th edn, 2002)

Jeremy Gibson and Frederic A. Youngs Jr, *Poor Law Union Records: 4. Gazetteer of England and Wales* (Federation of Family History Societies, 1993)

Steven D. Hales, 'Thinking Tools: You *Can* Prove a Negative', *Think* (vol. 4, issue 10, Summer 2005)

Mark D. Herber, *Ancestral Trails* (The History Press, 2nd rev. edn, 2004)

David Hey, *Journeys in Family History: Exploring Your Past, Finding Your Ancestors* (PRO Publications, 2003)

Tim Hitchcock and John Black (eds), *Chelsea Settlement and Bastardy Examinations, 1733–1766* (London Record Society, vol. 33, 1999)

Cecil R. Humphery-Smith (ed.), *The Phillimore Atlas and Index of Parish Registers* (Phillimore & Co., Institute of Heraldic and Genealogical Studies, 3rd edn, 2003)

Cecil R. Humphrey-Smith, *Armigerous Ancestors, Heralds' Visitations: A Catalogue and Index of Genealogical Resources in the Visitations of the Heralds and Related Documents* (Family History Books, 1997)

Thomas W. Jones, 'What is the Standard of Proof in Genealogy?', *National Genealogical Society News Magazine*, vol. 33 No. 2, April – June 2007 (USA)

Samuel Lewis, *Topographical Dictionary of England* (London, 1831, 4 volumes)

Samuel Lewis, *Topographical Dictionary of Wales* (London, 1833, 2 volumes)

Pauline Litton, *Pitfalls and Possibilities in Family History Research* (Swansong Publications, 2010)

London Topographical Society, *London Parish Map: A Map of the Ecclesiastical Divisions within the County of London, 1903* (London Topographical Society, pub. no. 155, 1999)

London Topographical Society, *A–Z of Victorian London* (London Topographical Society, pub. no. 136, 1987)

Susan Lumas, *Making Use of the Census* (PRO Publications, 3rd edn, 1997)

Edward MacLysaght, *Bibliography of Irish Family History* (Irish Academic Press, 2nd edn, 1982)

George W. Marshall, *The Genealogist's Guide* (privately printed by Billing and Sons, 4th edn, 1903)

The Marquis of Ruvigny and Raineval, Melville Henry Massue, *The Plantagenet Roll of the Blood Royal Being A Complete Table of All the Descendants Now Living of Edward III, King of England* (London, England: T. C. & E. C. Jack, 1905–1911).

Elizabeth Shown Mills, *Evidence! Citation and Analysis for the Family Historian* (Genealogical Publishing Company, 1997)

Elizabeth Shown Mills, *Evidence Explained: Citing History Sources from Artifacts to Cyberspace* (Genealogical Publishing Company, 2007)

Elizabeth Shown Mills (ed.), *Professional Genealogy* (Genealogical Publishing Company, 2001)

C.T. Onions et al. (comp.), *Shorter Oxford English Dictionary* (Oxford University Press, rev. edn, 1956)

Stephen Oppenheimer, *Out of Eden, The Peopling of the World* (Constable & Robinson, rev. edn, 2004)

George Ormerod, *The History of the County Palatine and City of Chester* (Lackington, Hughes, Harding, Mavor and Jones, 1819)

Patrick Palgrave-Moore, *How to Record Your Family Tree* (Elvery Dowers Publications, 6th edn, 1994)

William P.W. Phillimore, *How to Write the History of a Family: A Guide for the Genealogist* (E. Stock, 1896)

Francis Pryor, *Britain in the Middle Ages, An Archaeological History* (Harper Perennial, 2007)

Stuart A. Raymond, *Netting Your Ancestors: Tracing Family History on the Internet* (The Family History Partnership, 2007)

Alex Shoumatoff, *The Mountain of Names: A History of the Human Family* (Simon & Schuster, 1985)

Eugene A. Stratton, *Applied Genealogy* (Ancestry, 1988)

Margaret Stuart and Sir James Balfour Paul, *Scottish Family History* (Oliver & Boyd, 1930)

T.R. Thomson, *A Catalogue of British Family Histories* (Research

Publishing Co., 3rd edn with addenda, 1980)

Andrew Todd, *Nuts and Bolts: Family History Problem Solving through Family Reconstitution Techniques* (Allen & Todd, 2nd edn, 2000)

Anthony Wagner, *English Ancestry* (Oxford University Press, 1961)

Cliff Webb (gen. ed.), *National Index of Parish Registers: Volume 9, Part 5 London and Middlesex* (Society of Genealogists Enterprises Ltd, 2nd rev. edn, 2002)

J.B. Whitmore, *A Genealogical Guide: An Index to British Pedigrees in Continuation of Marshall's Genealogist's Guide, 1903* (Walford Bros, 1953)

Other Sources

Web Pages

findmypast, 'Knowledge base, 1841–1901 censuses, Known issues'
www.findmypast.co.uk/helpadvice/knowledge-base/census/index.jsp

Elizabeth Shown Mills, 'Building a Case When No Record
"Proves" a Point', 1 March 1998
http://learn.ancestry.com/LearnMore/Article.aspx?id=803

National Genealogical Society Quarterly, 'Guidelines for Writers'
www.ngsgenealogy.org/galleries/Pubs_files/3.1.1_Guidelines_for_
NGSQ_Writers.pdf

Jakob Nielson, 'How Users Read on the Web', **Alertbox, 1
October 1997**
www.useit.com/alertbox/9710a.html

W.R. Powell (ed.), 'East Ham: Manors and estates', A History of
the County of Essex: Volume 6, British History Online
www.british-history.ac.uk/report.
aspx?compid=42741&strquery=east ham

Society of Authors, 'Vanity Publishing', 2002 www.societyofau-
thors.org/sites/default/files/Vanity%20Publishing%20Paper.pdf

Society of Genealogists, 'Standards'
www.sog.org.uk/education/standards.shtml

The National Archives, 'How to Cite Documents in the National
Archives', General Information Leaflet 25
www.nationalarchives.gov.uk/catalogue/RdLeaflet.
asp?sLeafletID=333&j=1

Websites referred to

Access 2 Archives
www.nationalarchives.gov.uk/a2a

Ancestry (UK)
www.ancestry.co.uk

Archer software
www.archersoftware.co.uk

Archives Wales
www.archiveswales.org.uk

ARCHON
www.nationalarchives.gov.uk/archon

BBC guidelines for building a website www.bbc.co.uk/webwise/
askbruce/articles/browse/buildwebsite_1.shtml

Booth maps of London poverty
www.booth.lse.ac.uk

British History Online
www.british-history.ac.uk

British Isles Genweb Project
www.britishislesgenweb.org

Citation Machine
http://citationmachine.net

Cyndis List
www.cyndislist.com

End Note
www.endnote.com

Families in British India Society
www.new.fibis.org

Family Relatives
www.familyrelatives.com

Family Search
www.familysearch.org

Family Search Jurisdictions and Maps
http://maps.familysearch.org

Family Search Library Holdings www.familysearch.org/Eng/
Library/FHLC/frameset_fhlc.asp

Family Tree DNA
www.familytreedna.com/projects.aspx

Federation of Family History Societies
www.ffhs.org.uk
findmypast
www.findmypast.co.uk

FreeBMD
www.freebmd.org.uk

FreeCEN
www.freecen.org.uk

Genes Reunited
www.genesreunited.co.uk

GENUKI
www.genuki.org.uk

Guild of One-Name Studies
www.one-name.org

Hugh Wallis IGI Batch Numbers http://freepages.genealogy.
rootsweb.ancestry.com/~hughwallis

Jakob Nielson
www.useit.com/jakob

Lost Cousins
www.lostcousins.co.uk

Lulu.com
www.lulu.com/uk/publish/index.php?cid=en_tab_publish

Mendeley
www.mendeley.com

Millard's Probate Information
www.dur.ac.uk/a.r.millard/genealogy/probate.php

National Register of Archives
www.nationalarchives.gov.uk/nra/default.asp

Online Historical Population Reports
www.histpop.org

Online Parish Clerks
www.onlineparishclerks.org.uk
Origins Network
www.origins.net

Public Profiler Name Mapping
http://gbnames.publicprofiler.org

Scottish Archives Network
www.scan.org.uk

Smashwords
www.smashwords.com

Society of Genealogists
www.sog.org.uk

The National Archives
www.nationalarchives.gov.uk

The Peerage.com
www.thepeerage.com

Wordclay
www.wordclay.com/Default.aspx

Manuscript sources

1851 census, Midhurst, Sussex: The National Archives: PRO: HO
107/1654/104 pp. 4–5

Ancestry.co.uk, 'Slave Registers of Former British Colonial Dependencies', The National Archives T71

London Metropolitan Archives, Saint Barnabas, Homerton, Register of marriages, P79/BAN1, Item 014 online at www. ancestry.co.uk

London Metropolitan Archives, Saint John At Hackney, Hackney, Register of marriages, P79/JN1, Item 086 online at www.ancestry. co.uk

Will of Sarah Bayly, Wiltshire and Swindon History Centre, Ref: Archdeaconry of Salisbury, P2/B/1133

Will of Thomas Hoare, Centre for Buckinghamshire Studies, Ref: D/A/WF/26/229
RG 11/304/71 p38
RG 10/326/86 p.24
RG 9/295/148 p.26
HO 107/1553/841 p.20

Index

abbreviations, use of in genealogy, 181, 185, 198, 223
Abram, Milcah, 206
Access 2 Archives, 84, 85, 163
administration
  county, 33, 64
  local, 17, 59, 62, 67
  parish, 24, 65
  town and borough, 67
administrative systems, 17, 61, 62–73
analysis, 15, 41, 52, 122–148, 150–154, 215, 240, 242, 244, 246
Ancestral File, 119
Ancestry.com, 97, 107, 168
Ancestry.co.uk, 43, 55, 65, 95, 101, 118, 140 passim, 167, 172, 179
Antigua (St George Parish slave register), 141–143
antiquarians, 109, 162
appraisal, 60, 107, 219
archdeaconry, 23, 65, 71
archives, 31–32, 59, 60, 73, 76, 79, 81, 92
  business, 83, 85
  catalogues, 61, 90–91, 93
  county record offices, 32, 66, 71, 83, 85, 86, 92, 93, 113
  keeping systems, 82–83, 90
  local, 83
  national, 82
  private, 83, 85
  terms used by, 87
  See also the National Archives, Access 2 Archives
ARCHON, 84

baptism, 26, 52, 62, 66, 98, 102, 116, 118, 146, 164, 165, 175, 187, 225, 241, 245, 247, 253
Bayly, Sarah, 1687 will of, 132–135
Bayly, William G. and household in 1851 census return, 136–140
Beachcroft
  Elizabeth, 231
  Frank Porten, 230
  Helen, 231
  Joseph, 210
  Mary, 210, 231
  Matthews, 209
  Robert, 210
  Samuel, 209, 210, 230
  Thomas Seward, 230, 231
Beale, Ellinor Jane, 187
Bengal European Fusiliers, 51
Beresford
  Ann, 182, 183
  Benjamin, 151 passim, 173, 190 passim
  Caroline, 101–102, 150 passim, 172–173, 190 passim, 254, 255
  Catherine, 153 passim, 182, 183, 191 passim
  Frances, 182, 183
  Harriet, 99–102, 150–154, 190 passim, 254, 255
  Thomas, 182, 183
Beresford family
  and analysis, 150–154
  documentation examples, 190–195
  research planning, 154–158
  search examples, 99–104
Bevan, Amanda, 36
bibliographies, 196, 199, 222
  published genealogy, 112–113

Bishops' Transcripts, 62, 72, 100
boundary changes, 63, 64, 70, 85
brick walls, 11, 21, 35 *passim*, 240
British Library, 82, 99, 113
Burke's *Peerage*, 108, 109, 116, 223, 228

calendar, 87
Cambridge (missing census returns), 33
catalogues, 61, 76, 78, 86, 87, 92, 206
  Family History Library, 94, 113
  hierarchy of arrangement, 82, 92, 113
  National Archives, the, 89 *passim*, 92, 140, 141, 142
  online, 31, 84, 163
  organizing your research and, 206, 209
  Society of Genealogist's Library, 94, 96, 113
census, 62, 71, 74, 78, 80, 95, 103, 117, 120, 122, 145
  analysis of an entry in 1851, 136–140
  problem solving, 160, 164, 167, 171, 172, 248, 249
charts, 175, 202, 223, 222, 239
  citations and, 176, 196
  conventions of, 226
  descendant, 223
  drop-down line, 153, 175, 223 *passim*
  pedigree, 29, 175, 226, 230
  software and, 212, 213, 218
chirograph, *See* indenture
Christian, Peter, 84, 145
Church of England, 69, 146
  administration of, 63
  courts, 71, 130
  jurisdictions, 71–72
  records of, 62, 66, 77
citations 117, 177, 176, 213, 214, 231
  proof and, 177, 240, 244, 247
  styles and standards, 176, 178, 183, 186, 190–201, 212, 228
  See also Dugdale, Sir William; Mills, Elizabeth Shown

civil registration, 36, 69–70, 72, 160, 164, 170
  certificates, errors on, 252–254
class and social structure, 16, 107, 108, 110, 147, 169
Cockayne, G.E., 108
Collins, Arthur, 109
consistory court, 71
copyhold, 68, 69, 130
counties
  administration, 62, 63, 64
  Genuki indexes and sources, 97
  Heralds' Visitations, 108
  See also boundary changes, archives, Victoria County History
cousins
  cousinship, 107, 111, 112, 164
  finding and sharing research, 118–120
  pedigree collapse, 111
Cussons, John, 206
Cyndi's List, 97

Darlington, Durham (example of search), 98
Data Protection Act, 121
dates and dating
  analysis and, 122, 125
  census dates, 136
  charts and, 225
  other people's research and, 116, 117, 118
  recording, 175, 180, 181, 185, 187, 189, 201, 212, 217
  in searches, 55, 57, 58, 160, 167
Daughters of the American Revolution, 114
Devon (loss of records), 33, 53
dialects, 148
diocese, 63, 71, 72
DNA, 20, 22, 28, 106, 110, 112, 115, 171, 213, 238, 241
documents, 17, 19, 59–62, 74, 76, 79
  analysis and working with, 122–148; checklist, 126
  catalogues and, 89 *passim*
  common form, 124, 125
  document references, 117, 185–186, 198

documentation, 31, 41, 53, 149, 174–184, 190–195, 200, *See also* source citation
See also surrogates
Dorset (missing census returns), 33
Dugdale, Sir William, 108, 239

East Ham, 65, 68, 69
East India Company, 50, 51, 140
elimination of candidates, 38, 43, 45, 167, 241, 249
endnotes, 196–198
Essex (missing census returns), 33
evidence, 29, 60, 108, 239
  conflicts in, 246, 247
  documentation and, 178, 187 *passim*, 212
  evaluation of, 59, 73–74, 117, 122–123, 126, 174, 184, 246–247, 251–255
  hearsay, 41, 240
  indirect or inferred, 143
  logic and, 248–250
  preponderance of, 241
  probability versus possibility, 42, 57, 240, 241, 245
  problem solving with, 149, 150, 167, 169
  proof, 238, 241 *passim*
  trust in, 254
  See also sources
Exeter (loss of records), 33
extracts, 25, 31, 37 *passim*, 43, 44, 165

false belief, 28, 29
Family Group Record Sheet, 190, 191, 196, 208, 209, 222, 232
family history
  difference to genealogy, 239
  societies, 27, 96–97, 106
  writing and publishing, 231–237
Family History Library, 94, 98, 113, 204
Family Search, 26, 54, 72, 171
  Map of English Jurisdictions 1851, 72
family stories, 27–28, 42

Family Tree magazine, 14
family tree software, 120, 168, 178, 179, 186, 202, 208, 212–213, 214, 216, 225, 228, 230
family trees, published and existing, 105 *passim*
  pitfalls with, 116–118
  See also charts
Federation of Family History Societies, 27, 96, 97
fictitious actions, 124
filing, *See* storing your records
finding aid, 87
findmypast, 43, 95, 167, 172
footnotes, *See* endnotes
Foster, Michael Whitfield, 39
France, administration and records, 61
Fuller, Osborne, 210

gavelkind, 69
gazetteers, use of, 23, 64, 67
Gedcom files, 120, 212, 226
Genealogical Proof Standard, *See* proof
genealogies
  bibliographies of, 112–113
  finding published and existing, 112–116
  See also family trees
genealogy
  definition, 107–108, 239
  history of, 239
General Register Office, 253
  use of the indexes, 37 *passim*, 70, 166
Genes Reunited, 119, 120, 190
gentlemen, 19
Genuki, 64, 86, 97
Geographical Information Systems (GIS), 216
geography, 17, 62 *passim*, 76, 78, 98, 103, 160
government records, *See* records
Guild of One-Name Studies, 20, 115, 116, 118, 119, 166

handwriting, 39, 168, 184, 185
Harleian Society, 25

Hawkes, Georgiana Frances, 230
Hearth Tax, 18, 79, 122
heralds, 107–108,
  visitations, 108, 112
Herber, Mark D., 78
Hertzell, Frederick, 50 *passim*
Hey, David, 20, 241
Hibble, Thomas, 182, 183
Hill, Mary, colour coding system, 204
historical context, 17, 79, 126, 130,
  164, 171, 233, 246
historical interpretation, 15, 144–148
Hitchcock, Tim, 145
Hoare, Thomas, 1627 will of, 126–
  132
Hobbs
  Alice, 47 *passim*
  Arthur, 46 *passim*
  Eleanor, 47, 49
  Frederick, 49
  Henrietta, 45 *passim*
  Mary Ann, 47 *passim*
  William, 46 *passim*
  William Frederick, 47 *passim*
Hobbs family, research example, 45–
  53
Hudson, Susanna, 210
Hugh Wallis and the IGI, 100
Huguenots, 170
hundreds, 62
Huntingdon Library, California, 86

identity and names, 20–22
indenture, 124
indexes, 24 *passim*, 92, 171
  partial, 26–27, 17
International Genealogical Index
  (IGI), 26, 27, 100, 102, 114, 117,
  171, 188, 200
internet
  discussion groups, 106
  as a research tool, 76, 78, 79, 81,
  83–86, 106, 113

jurisdictions, 23, 24, 62, 63, 65, 72,
  76, 130, 162
  ecclesiastical jurisdictions, 23, 66,
  71–72, 129, 160, 161

Kensington (missing census returns),
  33
Kent, 97

land holdings, 17, 62, 67–69, 124
land records (in problem solving),
  162, 166
Latter-day Saints, Church of, 26, 94,
  95, 96, 98, 107, 113, 119
law, 17, 18, 19, 21, 69, 77, 124, 130,
  253
  accepted practice in, 20, 144, 145
  Courts of Law, records of, 82, 89,
  125
  legal framework, 12, 17, 18, 23, 42,
  77, 78
  legal language, 148, 184
  names and, 52
  See also fictitious actions,
    jurisdictions, land holdings,
    Married Women's Property Act
Lay, Mary Ann, 47
Legacy Family Tree, 178, 214, 227
Lewis, Charlotta, 230
libraries, 82, 83, 86, 104, 176,
  using, 81, 93–94, 108, 113–114
lists, 18, 45, 77, 84, 87, 89, 92, 97
Litton, Pauline, 14
London, 64, 83, 85, 217
  examples of research in, *See*
    Beresford family and Hobbs family
London Livery Companies, 85
London Record Society, 145
Lost Cousins website, 120

Manaton, Martha, 189
Manchester (missing census returns),
  33
manors, 67–68
  Manorial Documents Register, 68
  manorial and estate records, 68,
  131, 162, 165, 166
  manorial system, 63, 67–69, 130
Married Woman's Property Act, 147
Mathews, Mary and Richard, 209
memory, 28–29
Middlesex (missing census returns), 33
Midhurst, Sussex, 136

migration, 24, 27, 28, 106, 162, 169, 216
Millard, Andrew, 23
Mills, Elizabeth Shown, 186, 190, 192, 196, 201

names,
changes of, 20, 21, 36
common names, 16, 21, 22, 55, 115, 166, 241
first name searches, 45, 55, 57
naming patterns, 168
spelling, 20, 41, 180
surnames, 20–22
too many candidates, 38
uncommon names, pitfalls with, 26
See also one-name studies, Soundex
National Archives, the, 62, 72, 78, 82, 89–91, 185, 198
National Burial Index, 27, 97
National Index of Parish Registers, 66, 100
National Library of Wales, 71, 82
National Probate Calendar, 23, 45
National Register of Archives, 84–85
negative results, 57–58, 250
note-taking, 179–183, 187–195
Nye,
George Beresford, 172
George Frederick, 152

occupations, as identification tools, 77, 169, 170
use of in Hobbs example, 46, 47, 49
Omman(e)y,
Cornthwaite, 189
Elizabeth Acworth, 230
Sir Francis M., 230
one-name studies, 20, 115, 116, 119, 165, 166, 168
organization of research results, 202–219
See also storing your records
Ormerod, George, 109

Paddington (missing census returns), 33
palaeography, See handwriting

parish administration, 24, 62, 63, 65–67, 70, 72
parish records, 161
parish registers, 25, 26, 32, 62, 66, 69, 86, 94, 95, 96, 116, 171
pedigrees, 112, 113, 115, 203, 212, 222–223
collapse, 111
narrative, 228–231
See also charts, family trees
peerage, 108, 109, 112, 116, 223, 228
Periodical Source Index (PERSI) 114, 116
Phillimore's Atlas and Index of Parish Registers, 66
phonetic matching, 55, 56
place names, 23, 70, 85, 212, 217
Poor Law Examinations, Chelsea, 145–146
Poor Law Unions, 69, 70, 72
Porten, Elizabeth, 210
poverty, 148, 150
presentation of results, 222–237
Price, Edward (example of death search), 37–40
probate, 102, 128 passim, 134, 147, 166, 250
problems and problem solving, 149–164
checklist of record sources, 159–163
proof in genealogy, 238–255
Proof Standards, 242–248
See also citations

Rainbow, Susan, 46
Raymond, Stuart, 84
recording results, 174–196
need for consistency, 216–217
records, 59–62
classes or series, 61, 87, 90
copies, 62, 123
creation, 17, 59
definition and life cycle, 60–61
difference between countries, 80–81
finding, 76–81
gaps, 33, 53, 100, 154, 171
government, 32, 59, 60, 62, 72, 89
See also the National Archives

record offices, *See* archives
record sources, a checklist for
    finding, 159–163
survival, 16, 17, 31–33
types used by genealogists, 79–80
See also surrogate sources
Redmonds, George, 20
registration districts, 69–71
religious groups, use in identification,
    170
research guide, 87
research log, 154, 179, 180
research planning, 154–158
results, display of, *See* presentation
Righy, Maria Julia, 21
Roehampton University, 79
Round, J. Horace, 108, 109, 110
rule of three, 245–246

scanning, 218
Scattergood family, 112
Scottish Archives Network, 85
Search engines, 54–57, 76, 77, 78,
    83–84
searching, effective, 41–42
slave register, example of, *See* Antigua
social class, *See* class structure
social rules, 147
Society of Genealogists, 66, 175, 242,
    244
    Birth Brief, 175, 226
    document collection, 112
    Library of, 94, 96, 103, 113
Soundex, 55–56, 213
source combining, 46
source criticism, *See* evidence
source discounting, 45
sources
    definition, 73
    derivative, 74–75, 245, 248, 251,
        252
    original, 29, 41, 53, 73 *passim*, 79
    primary, 150, 198, 246, 252
    primary and secondary sources
        definitions, examples, 73–75
    printed or published, 74

proof and, 243 *passim*
surrogates, 53, 67, 77, 94–96, 98,
    140, 141, 143, 176
    citation of, 187, 200
    See also, citations, documentation
spreadsheets, 215
standards in genealogy, 176–178, 184,
    185–186, 216, 223, 226, 240–248
storing your records, 202–220
    family tree software, 211–124
    paper, 204–211
Suffolk (missing census returns), 33
surname studies, *See* one-name studies
surnames, *See* names
Sutton, Isaac, 188, 189

terrier, 62
textbooks, genealogy, 78, 144
timeline, use of, 151, 152, 166, 215
Todd, Andrew, 165
transcriptions, 95, 96, 97, 183–185
trust, in results, 39, 41, 43, 57, 58, 79,
    240, 254
    in work of others, 107, 109, 116–
    118

USA, example of records in, 80, 86

Victoria County History, 67, 68, 197

Wagner, Sir Anthony, 15–16, 20, 35,
    109
Wales
    Archives Wales, 85
    diocesan records, 71
    missing census returns, 33
    place-names, 23
Warminster, Wiltshire, *See* Bayly,
    Sarah
West Ham, 68
whole community reconstruction, 166
whole family reconstruction, 46, 53,
    164
wills, *See* probate

Yveley, Catherine and Robert, 206